W9-ASC-547

Slavery in Early Christianity

Dorja —
One of the few things (almost)
as happy as seeing one's own
name listed as author is seeing
a colleague's name stamped
on the page. Looking forward
to celebrating your first book
JENNIFER A. GLANCY with you.

Jennifer

OXFORD
UNIVERSITY PRESS

2002

OXFORD
UNIVERSITY PRESS

Oxford   New York
Athens   Auckland   Bangkok   Bogotá   Buenos Aires   Cape Town
Chennai   Dar es Salaam   Delhi   Florence   Hong Kong   Istanbul   Karachi
Kolkata   Kuala Lumpur   Madrid   Melbourne   Mexico City   Mumbai   Nairobi
Paris   São Paulo   Shanghai   Singapore   Taipei   Tokyo   Toronto   Warsaw

and associated companies in
Berlin   Ibadan

Copyright © 2002 by Jennifer A. Glancy

Published by Oxford University Press, Inc.
198 Madison Avenue, New York, New York 10016

Oxford is a registered trademark of Oxford University Press

All rights reserved. No part of this publication may be reproduced,
stored in a retrieval system, or transmitted, in any form or by any means,
electronic, mechanical, photocopying, recording, or otherwise,
without the prior permission of Oxford University Press.

Chapter two incorporates a revised version of "Obstacles to Slaves' Participation in
the Corinthian Church," which first appeared in the *Journal of Biblical Literature* 117, no. 3 (1998).
Chapter two also includes revised material from "Family Plots: Burying Slaves Deep in Historical Ground,"
which first appeared in *Biblical Interpretation* 10, no. 1 (2002). Chapter four incorporates a revised version of
"Slave and Slavery in the Matthean Parables," which first appeared in the *Journal of Biblical Literature* 119, no. 1
(2000). I am grateful to the editors of those journals for granting permission to reprint this material.

Library of Congress Cataloging-in-Publication Data
Glancy, Jennifer A.
Slavery in early Christianity / Jennifer A. Glancy.
p. cm.
Includes bibliographical references.
ISBN 0-19-513609-8
1. Slavery and the church—History.   2. Church and social problems—History.
I. Title.
HT913.G53   2002
261.8'34567'093—dc21   2001036368

3 5 7 9 8 6 4 2

Printed in the United States of America
on acid-free paper

For David

Shining above his head with a thousand rays brighter than those of the sun and moon put together is a placard in Roman letters proclaiming him king of the Jews, surrounded by a wounding crown of thorns like that worn, without their even knowing and with no visible sign of blood, by all who are not allowed to be sovereigns of their own bodies.

—José Saramago, *The Gospel according to Jesus Christ*

Everybody knew what she was called, but nobody anywhere knew her name. Disremembered and unaccounted for, she cannot be lost because no one is looking for her, and even if they were, how can they call her if they don't know her name?

—Toni Morrison, *Beloved*

Acknowledgments

Thanks, first, to my editor, Cynthia Read, for her enthusiasm for this project, as well as for her keen editorial insights. Other members of the Oxford University Press editorial team, including Theodore Calderara and Stacey Hamilton, have also been unfailingly helpful. I am grateful to Merryl Sloane for her meticulous and intelligent copyediting.

I am indebted to Stephen Moore and Elizabeth Castelli for offering encouragement and, still better, insightful and constructive criticism at an early stage of this book.

When I began to write about the impact of slaves and slaveholders on the early churches, I realized that I would have to explore simultaneously the culture of slavery in the Roman Empire. The present volume would have been inconceivable without ground-breaking studies of slavery in the Roman world by (among others) Keith Bradley, Sandra Joshel, Orlando Patterson, Richard Saller, and the late Moses I. Finley. In the summer of 1999, I participated in a seminar sponsored by the National Endowment for the Humanities on Society and Culture in Roman Egypt. The seminar greatly enriched my thinking about material aspects of slavery in the Roman world. I am grateful to the NEH, to Columbia University, and especially to the seminar's erudite director, Roger Bagnall. Although the names of these scholars appear in the notes, the impact of their scholarship on my thinking extends even beyond this documentation. Nancy Thompson, assistant museum educator at the Metropolitan Museum of Art, was kind enough to confer with me about possible cover images. Those with ears to hear and eyes to see may discern the influence of my teachers, J. Louis Martyn and the late Raymond E. Brown. The usual caveat that the author is responsible for all errors applies, perhaps more strongly than usual.

I am appreciative of criticisms, questions, and encouragement from audiences who heard portions of this work at meetings of the Bible and Cultural Studies Section of the Society of Biblical Literature, the International SBL, the Mid-Atlantic AAR/SBL, the Eastern Great Lakes Bible Society, and the International Centre for the History of Slavery at the University of Nottingham (England). I am deeply grateful for access to the collections of the E. S. Bird Library, Syracuse University; the Ambrose Swasey Library, Colgate Rochester Divinity School; Butler Library, Columbia University; and the Burke Library, Union Theological Seminary (NYC).

Closer to home, my debts multiply. For the collegial atmosphere in which I work, I thank all my colleagues in the Religious Studies Department at Le Moyne College, especially Nancy Ring, Mary MacDonald (who read and commented on the manuscript), Kathleen Nash (who performed radical surgery on the first chapter), and Fred Glennon. The women of the Tuesday lunch crowd, including Lynne Arnault, Susan Behuniak, Maria DiTullio, and Karmen MacKendrick, have accompanied me through some difficult times. Dale Wilson went well beyond legitimate demands of duty to prepare the manuscript. I am especially pleased to acknowledge the contributions made by students in my spring 2000 seminar on Christianity and Slavery. They read early drafts of several chapters and pointed out to me, in no uncertain terms, places where I relied on jargon or failed to persuade them. At Le Moyne's Noreen Reale Falcone Library, both the interlibrary loan department and Gretchen Pearson, public services librarian, have been tireless in helping me obtain sources. Finally, my colleagues at Le Moyne College have repeatedly recognized my work with financial grants and gifts of time. In support of this project, the Faculty Senate Committee on Research and Development awarded me sabbatical leave, a course-load reduction, and a subsidy for research expenses. I thank the colleagues who recommended my appointment as the Joseph C. Georg Endowed Professor. Finally, I gratefully acknowledge the late Joseph C. Georg, who so generously endowed the professorship that bears his name.

Elizabeth Salzer (whose precise criticisms of the manuscript were exactly on-target) and Joanna Shulman turned their apartment into a kennel for Lucifer, my dog, one summer, thus enabling me to pursue critical research. Because of Ginger and Bill Andrews, I had a cabin in the woods where I could retreat and think. Alice Bach encouraged this project from the outset and later offered generous comments on the manuscript. More important, when I didn't feel like writing, Alice told me to write anyway.

I would have loved to share this book with my parents, Kathleen and James Glancy. They died too soon. In more ways than they may realize, Meghan Glancy, Erin Johnson, Amy Glancy (who read and commented on portions of the manuscript), Jim Glancy, and Bridget Short, my siblings, made it possible for me to persevere with this work.

From my survey of the genre of acknowledgments, I infer that I should thank my spouse, David Rogers Andrews, for the many ways that he daily makes my life easier. The list is long: David tends the computers, walks Lucifer (the dog) on icy Syracuse mornings, empties mousetraps, and keeps us supplied with homemade pesto. I prefer to emphasize, however, his greatest contribution to this project, his congenital intolerance for bad arguments. David and I first discussed over dinner many of the claims I advance in this book, and he later read multiple drafts of the manuscript. His impatience with intellectual sloppiness has greatly improved the book you have before you. Finally, his commitment to social justice inspires me. This book is for him.

Contents

Abbreviations

Dates: B.C.E. (Before the Common Era) is the equivalent of B.C., and C.E. (Common Era) is the equivalent of A.D.

Abbreviations for papyrological sources appear in J. F. Oates et al., *Checklist of Editions of Greek and Latin Papyri, Ostraca and Tablets*, 4th ed. (*Bulletin of the American Society of Papyrologists* Supplement 7, 1992).

Where abbreviations are listed for both the name of an author and the title of his work, the abbreviation for the title appears immediately after the abbreviation for the author's name. Please note one exception: the abbreviation *Ep.* (for *Epistulae*) appears only once, although the letters of various authors are cited.

1 Clem.	1 Clement
App.	Appian
BCiv.	*Bella Civilia*
Apul.	Apuleius
Met.	*Metamorphoses* (=*The Golden Ass*)
Arch. Class.	*Archeologia Classica*
Ath.	Athenaeus
Aug.	Augustine
CIL	*Corpus Inscriptionum Latinarum*
Did.	*Didache*
Dig.	*Digest of Justinian*
Dio. Chrys.	Dio Chrysostom
Or.	*Orationes*
Ep.	*Epistulae* (=*Letters*)
Ep. Barn.	*Epistle of Barnabas*
Epic.	Epictetus
IG	*Inscriptiones Graecae*
Ign.	Ignatius
Pol.	Epistle to Polycarp
Inst.	*Institutiones*

Joseph.	Josephus
BJ	*Bellum Judaicum*
Lucr.	Lucretius
Mart.	Martial
NPNF	*Nicene and Post-Nicene Fathers*
NRSV	*New Revised Standard Version*
Petr.	Petronius
Sat.	*Satyricon*
Plaut.	Plautus
Curc.	*Curculio*
Plut.	Plutarch
Mor. Quaest. Rom.	*Moralia Quaestiones Romanae*
Sen.	Seneca (The Elder)
Controv.	*Controversiae*
Sen.	Seneca (The Younger)
Ben.	*De beneficiis*
Clem.	*De clementia*
Suet.	Suetonius
Aug.	*Divus Augustus*
Tac.	Tacitus
Ann.	*Annales*
Germ.	*Germania*
Quint.	Quintilian
Inst.	*Institutio oratoria*
Val. Max.	Valerius Maximus

Slavery in Early Christianity

Introduction

This study focuses on the impact of the ubiquitous ancient institution of slavery on the emergence and development of Christianity. I work from the understanding that both slaves and slaveholders were more pivotal in early Christian circles than has been generally acknowledged. The centrality of slavery affects not only the reconstruction of the social histories of the emerging churches but also theological and ideological analyses of Christian rhetoric. I stress the corporeality of ancient slavery. Christians who argued that true slavery was spiritual in nature often depended on somatic metaphors. Thus, even as we turn to metaphoric uses of slavery in Christian discourse, the corporeality of slavery retains priority. Early Christian slavery emerges as a significant chapter in the history of the body.

Although the earliest Christian writings are laced with images and metaphors borrowed from the rhetorical domain of chattel slavery, evidence concerning Christian slaves and Christian slaveholders is typically fragmentary. An understanding of the institution of slavery during the period in which Christianity emerged and defined itself is necessary for comprehending both the rhetoric of slavery in Christian writings and the realities of slavery in Christian communities. I have defined the relevant period quite broadly, from the early years of the Roman Empire to late antiquity, when slavery continued to be quite common.[1] Within this time frame Christianity first emerged and was eventually recognized as the official religion of the Empire.[2] Keith Bradley, who has written extensively about slavery in Roman history, refers to the "'steady state' mentality" of slaveholders throughout antiquity. Since the attitudes of slaveholders remained constant, the conditions in which slaves lived and worked also persisted from generation to generation.[3] Slaveholders in the first century characterized their slaves as bodies, and their treatment of their slaves was commensurate with that characterization. This was equally the case in the fourth century, when Constantine came to power, and a century after that.[4]

A wide variety of sources attests to the contours of slavery in the Roman Empire, from bills of sale to legal codes to literary works. However, we have to remember that the picture of slavery we derive from these sources is pieced together rather than given. Any description of slavery in antiquity is the product of multiple scholarly decisions: whether we can discern links among miscellaneous sources to tell a connected story, for example, or how much we can assume about the context of an important but obscure piece of evidence. Hayden White has argued that literary scholars often seek to "explain" texts with reference to a historical background. In doing so, they assume that this background context; "'the historical milieu'—has a concreteness and an accessibility that the work can never have, as if it were easier to perceive the reality of a past world put together from a thousand historical documents than it is to probe the depths of a single literary work that is present to the critic studying it. But the presumed concreteness and accessibility of historical milieux, these contexts of the texts that literary scholars study, are themselves the products of the fictive capability of the historians who have studied those contexts."[5]

Scholars of early Christianity often rely on a seamless picture of ancient life, which disguises the jagged edges of the documentation, as though there could exist a concrete, accessible, and coherent background picture on which we could piece together the puzzle of early Christian life. Throughout this study I have deliberately tried to expose the jagged edges of the primary sources I use. I want readers to be able to discern the weaknesses as well as the strengths of the evidence and thus to come to their own conclusions. I will be happy if the presentation of my arguments leads some readers to conclusions other than the ones I draw.

We encounter several kinds of problems as we try to draw on the disparate sources pertaining to Roman slavery throughout the Empire. An examination of a single document grants insights into both the possibilities and pitfalls of research into ancient slavery. I treat one specific document at length to demonstrate the inherent complexity of our sources for slavery. In correspondence dated 199 C.E., an Egyptian man writes to his daughter and his wife to inform them that he is manumitting a number of slaves. The author of the correspondence identifies himself as Marsisuchus, a former high priest of the temple of Hadrian in the Arsinoite nome. His wife's name is Bernice; deterioration in the papyrus has destroyed traces of the daughter's name. Among the slaves to be manumitted are two women, Sarapias and Soteria, and their offspring. Marsisuchus threatens his wife and his daughter that if they should try to block the manumissions he will take back property he has previously settled on them and instead donate the property to the temple of Serapis in Alexandria. The notices to Bernice and the daughter list different slaves, hinting that the wife and the daughter have separate claims on the slaves whom Marsisuchus wants to manumit.[6]

The correspondence offers tantalizing possibilities for insight into the emotional entanglements of family members around their slaves, yet it leaves us with few solid conclusions about that situation. We may infer that Marsisuchus anticipates resistance from his wife and daughter with respect to the manumissions, but we have no clues regarding the nature or motivation of that opposition. The purchase of replacement slaves would represent a significant expense, but other factors could also affect their reactions. For instance, if the slaves had a long tenure with the family, Bernice and her daughter might feel an emotional attachment to them. Perhaps more intriguing is the nature of Marsisuchus's relationship with these slaves. By manumitting them he will tolerate the loss of a substantial investment; the correspondence indicates that he has even borne the cost of taxes due at the time of manumission. What is more unusual is his seeming willingness to suffer—even to provoke—the anger of his wife and daughter in order to effect the freedom of the slaves. It is possible that Sarapias and Soteria were his sexual partners, and their children, in fact, his children. Ancient law did not recognize slaves as having fathers. Free men who fathered children with their female slaves had no obligation to acknowledge their paternity and only rarely did so, although we may speculate that they would have been more likely to manumit slaves they believed to be their offspring.[7] Such a scenario could explain Marsisuchus's behavior, but the absence of a more extensive documentary context limits our ability to situate this correspondence within a family narrative. Letters from the ancient world tempt the modern reader with promises of windows into the lives of real people. However, epistolary allusions to people and events are almost always cryptic, since the letter writer assumes the recipient has prior knowledge of such details. A twenty-first-century reader is thus likely to gain a glimpse rather than a panoramic view of the world of the correspondents.

We compound the interpretive problems when we try to generalize the significance of a particular document. Suppose, for example, we are trying to draw a picture of family life among slaves. Can we use Marsisuchus's letter as evidence? His plan to manumit Sarapias and Soteria along with their offspring could be construed to indicate some respect for the de facto slave family. Other categories of papyri also offer indirect evidence about the inclinations of slaveholders with respect to slave families. We have some bills of sale recording transactions that preserved the relationships of mothers and children: around 250 C.E., for instance, a twenty-one-year-old woman named Tereus was sold along with her son, specified in the contract as a nursling.[8] However, we must consider such evidence in light of the greater quantity of records that document the sales of young children without reference to their mothers and always without fathers.[9] Epigraphic evidence corroborates this overall picture. Some slave children grew up in the same household with their biological mothers, but many others were not so lucky.[10] In evaluating any single piece of evidence, such as Marsisuchus's letter to his wife and (legitimate) daughter, we need to remind ourselves of wider trends in the evidence. At the same time, our generalizations about various topics (for example, the prospects for stable family life among slaves) depend on the painstaking evaluation of numerous individual and often idiosyncratic sources.

Still more broadly, when we rely on papyrological evidence we need to consider the extent to which Egypt represents a typical province in the Roman Empire. Since the late nineteenth century, large quantities of papyri from Egypt have been recovered and published. The arid Egyptian climate preserves organic material exceptionally well. We thus have much thicker documentation from Egypt than from other sectors of the Roman Empire: personal letters, census returns, household accounts, wills, legal petitions, and so on. Earlier generations of scholars, inclined to view Egypt as an atypical province, ignored the papyrological evidence in discussions of the Roman world. Today, papyrologists argue that classicists who overlook the Egyptian evidence do so not because Egypt differs from the rest of the Empire but because the mass of papyrological evidence is unfamiliar, vast, and unwieldy.[11] However, as archaeologists slowly recover documentary evidence from other parts of the Empire—from as far away as the northern borders of Britain—Egypt increasingly seems to resemble other provinces, neither more nor less unique than other provinces in the Empire.[12] Classicists therefore increasingly turn to the Egyptian papyri for documentation of mundane details of daily life in the Empire, as I will do in this volume.

Evaluation of the contributions and limitations of other categories of evidence for reconstructing the institution of slavery and the lives of slaves is just as complex as evaluation of the contributions and limitations of documentary sources. Literary sources offer a certain thick description of the ancient world, incidentally describing minutiae of daily life. How close can ancient literature get us to an understanding of the dynamics of slavery? Literary sources furnish layers upon layers of information about a society in which slavery is ubiquitous. They depict slaves at work in mills, kitchens, and public

baths, for example. That such scenes are peripheral to plot development does not mitigate their usefulness to the social historian. Historians of ancient slavery have culled
quotidian details from works as fantastic as Apuleius's *Golden Ass* and the tales of Aesop.[13]
Nonetheless, the contemporary historian is left to sort out the degree to which novels
and plays accurately represent existence in the ancient world. Romances, for example,
depict slave women as the confidantes of their mistresses. Many freeborn women may
have relied on enslaved women for matters ranging from emotional support to the bearing of confidential messages. At the same time, devoted relationships between free and
slave women are also an established convention in ancient literature: in Greek tragedy,
Phaedra's nurse functions as her trusted and intimate advisor. The reader must be careful not to confuse an author's idealized vision of a relationship between mistress and
slave and the actual experience of such relationships for both slaveholders and slaves.[14]
Like the papyri, literary sources provide material for rich insights into daily life, but a
caveat applies. Literary sources coax the modern reader into an illusion of access to the
ancient world. Historians, grateful for these material insights, should nonetheless retain their critical judgment regarding the narrative worlds created by literary artistry.

Other categories of evidence offer distinctive perspectives on slaves and slavery in
the Roman Empire and present, in turn, distinctive challenges for the modern interpreter. Roman law codes, for example, consider multiple aspects of slavery, which arise
from the peculiarity of classifying a slave both as a person and as a thing. However,
since successive emperors issued edicts reiterating the same points of law, we may question the extent to which Roman law was consistently promulgated in all sectors of the
Empire. Moreover, only Roman citizens were bound by Roman law. Throughout the
Empire, Roman law coexisted with local laws in complicated ways, which scholars have
not entirely penetrated. The magisterial compilation of Roman law known as the *Digest
of Justinian* is a product of the sixth century. It reflects centuries of debate—often contradictory—on points of law that are, at times, academic exercises.[15] Thus, readers should
be aware as they read excerpts from the *Digest* that the opinion a jurist delivers on a
given topic may or may not reflect common practice. Fergus Millar acknowledges these
shortcomings of the *Digest* but still emphasizes its utility for social history: "In no real
sense is the *Digest* a code of law; on the contrary, it is a collection of varying opinions
on points of law. . . . the texts assembled in the *Digest* reflect with great vividness and
accuracy the world of the High Empire of the second and third centuries"[16] Despite its
limitations, the *Digest* supplies us with a wealth of information about the preoccupations and attitudes of the elite Romans who composed it. It remains an invaluable source
for any discussion of Roman slavery.

Some readers may anticipate that Jewish law on slavery will play a significant role in
the story of early Christian slavery. The direct impact of Jewish law would be potentially
most acute at the earliest levels of the tradition, even in the very sayings of Jesus. That
there is little distinctively "Jewish" in the representation of slaves in Jesus' sayings is
not, ultimately, surprising. Dale Martin has argued, "Jewishness itself had little if any
relevance for the structures of slavery among Jews. . . . Slavery among Jews of the Greco-
Roman period did not differ from the slave structures of those people among whom
Jews were living."[17] Documentary finds from Jews in the Arabian desert (extending from
Judaea to Arabia) suggest that Jews living in the Eastern Empire were influenced by
Roman family law and local custom as much or more than they were influenced by

rabbinic codes.[18] Jewish law enters this study most directly when I refer to various injunctions found in the Hebrew Bible regarding the treatment of slaves, for example, the mandate to shelter fugitive slaves. I draw on other Jewish sources, from Josephus to rabbinic commentaries, as literature that emerges from and sheds light on the practices and ideology of slaveholding in the Roman Empire.

In the course of this study I refer to the writings of a number of Stoic and Cynic philosophers, including Epictetus, Seneca, Musonius Rufus, and Dio Chrysostom. Stoic and Cynic philosophers frequently invoke problems of slavery and freedom. Little evidence supports the contention that these philosophers represented or affected wider public perceptions of the institution of slavery. We cannot assume on the basis of their writings that their philosophical positions on the relative insignificance of legally defined bondage or freedom affected their actual treatment of slaves they encountered or owned, much less that they influenced others to follow either their counsel or their example. Nonetheless, their criticisms of common assumptions about slaveholders and slaves form yet another distinct perspective on slavery in the Roman Empire.

One shortcoming endemic to all the genres I have discussed is that each accords priority to the perspectives of slaveholders rather than the perspectives of slaves. Roman law protects and promotes the interests of Roman citizens and of property owners. The slaves who excite the greatest sympathy in romances and dramas are faux slaves, who have been reduced to bondage under false pretenses; romances and dramas predictably hinge on the restoration of these faux slaves to their rightful positions as prominent freeborn citizens. Stoic philosophy speaks of the common humanity of slave and slaveholder but urges equanimity in the face of enslavement. Even the documentary evidence largely represents the concerns of slaveholders rather than those of slaves. The papyri disproportionately chronicle governmental and legal matters, and slaves had no independent access to the courts. Although we do have documentary evidence for manumissions, we encounter still more bills of sale and wills, which consider slaves not as persons but as things, as *ta sōmata doulika*, slave bodies. Letters sometimes mention slaves, and a few seem to have been written by slaves. Nonetheless, we have far more correspondence associated with wealthy, property-owning persons and families than correspondence among tradespeople, laborers, and slaves.

Acquaintance with a wide assortment of ancient writings is necessary for piecing together a picture of slavery in the Roman Empire. In every case, however, we must be wary of construing partial, biased sources as though they provide neutral overviews of what it meant to be a slave or to live in a society in which slavery was unquestioned. Still, a rich sense of the sources pertaining to slavery will help us see what is either distinctive or typical about slavery in Christian circles.

At the same time, we cannot simply compare and contrast Christian sources with the portrayal of slavery that we derive from other sources. Christian writings in fact contribute to our understanding of slavery in the Roman Empire from the first century through late antiquity. For example, discussions of child exposure, a common form of postnatal birth control, as a source for slaves in the Roman Empire frequently cite the Christian authors Justin Martyr and Clement of Alexandria. I will return to the problem of child exposure at several points in this study. A man could legally decide that he did not want the responsibility of raising an infant newly born to his wife (or another woman in his household). The infant would be removed from the household and left outdoors. Many of these children survived their exposure. Townspeople would know where infants were likely to be exposed; in Egyptian towns, babies were left on the town dungheap. Anyone who wanted to raise an exposed child could do so. Exposed infants were almost always raised as slaves. Evidence for the practice of child exposure is extensive and varied. Classicists frequently return, however, to the cautions of the Christians Justin Martyr and Clement of Alexandra.[19] Justin and Clement warn that those who expose children run the risk of later committing unwitting incest, since the children are likely to be raised as enslaved prostitutes.[20]

The relationship of Christian churches to the larger Roman society is complex and evolves dramatically over the first centuries of Christianity. Nonetheless, Christians and Christianity do not hover above or apart from everyday life. They are an integral part of the story of the Roman Empire. Christian writings supply key evidence, both direct and indirect, about the social relations of that world. To understand Christian discourse invoking the figure of the slave, we must first apprehend the figure of the slave in other discourses of the Roman Empire. At the same time, as we come to appreciate the centrality of slaves, slaveholders, and the institution of slaveholding in the emergent churches, we will better understand the place of slavery in the Roman Empire. To understand what it meant to be a slave in the first Christian centuries, we begin first of all with the bodies of slaves.

1

Bodies and Souls

The Rhetoric of Slavery

Sometime in the fourth or fifth century, a Christian man ordered a bronze collar to encircle the neck of one of his slaves. The inscription on the collar reads: "I am the slave of the archdeacon Felix. Hold me so that I do not flee."[1] Although the collar purports to speak in the first person for a nameless slave, the voice we hear is not that of the slave but that of the slaveholder. Felix, enraged by a slave's previous attempts to escape, ordered the collar both to humiliate and to restrain another human being, whom the law classified as his property. The chance survival of this artifact of the early church recalls the overwhelming element of compulsion that operated within the system of slavery, with its use of brute paraphernalia for corporal control. Contemporary sensibilities recoil from such tangible evidence for the inherent violence of ancient slavery. We are likely to consider Christian slaveholders to be hypocrites and to find the notion of Christian slavery oxymoronic. Felix exhibited no awareness of such contradiction: the slave collar he ordered even bears an incised cross. Centuries after Paul wrote to another Christian slaveholder, Philemon, counseling him to act in love toward the runaway slave Onesimus, the otherwise unknown archdeacon, Felix, apparently saw no incongruity in proclaiming simultaneously his status as a leader in the church and his identity as a slaveholder.

Slaves in the Roman Empire were vulnerable to physical control, coercion, and abuse in settings as public as the auction block and as private as the bedroom. Since slavery was identified with the body, it is not surprising that the experience of slavery was conditioned by gender and sexuality. At the same time, a person's experience of what it meant to be male or female was conditioned by the accident of slavery. A male slave, for example, had no legal connection to his own offspring, thus excluding him from the cultural status of fatherhood. Slaveholders had unrestricted sexual access to their slaves. This dimension of slave life was most likely to affect female slaves and young male slaves. Moreover, slaveholders valued female slaves for their biological capacities of reproduction and lactation. Problems emanating from the sexual and gender-specific use of slaves are central to the understanding of slavery in the early Christian era.

In the late second century, an Ephesian native named Artemidorus wrote a treatise on the interpretation of dreams, the *Oneirocritica*. Artemidorus proposed interpretations for seemingly every image that might arise in the course of a night's sleep. In Artemidorus's dream logic, slaves and bodies dissolve into one another. In dreams, he claims, slaves represent the bodies of their owners: "The very man who dreamt that he saw his household slave sick with a fever became ill himself, as one might expect. For the household slave has the same relationship to the dreamer that the body has to the soul."[2] According to this logic, the slave serves as surrogate body for the slaveholder, the experiences of the slaveholder played out in the very body of the slave.[3] This equation between slaves and bodies actually begins with the lexicon of slavery. The Greek word for body, *to sōma*, serves as a euphemism for the person of a slave. As we will see, wills and property registers were particularly likely to refer to the slaves of a household as "the bodies," *ta sōmata*.

By the first century C.E., Stoic philosophers had appropriated the trope of slavery to represent what we would describe as spiritual or moral postures, for example, in the struggle to avoid enslavement to the passions. Similarly, in a wide variety of Christian sources, the rhetoric of slavery represents the negative relationship of the human person to sin or the positive relationship of the Christian to God or to Christ.[4] Perhaps because of this theological displacement, scholars have been slow to interrogate the ideology of slavery in early Christian sources. Following the lead of the primary texts, we may be tempted to identify true slavery as spiritual bondage. Christian authors nonetheless employ conventions and cliches that construct an image of the slave body as vulnerable to invasion and abuse, reinforcing a range of other evidence from the early Empire. Ironically, even as Christian sources downplay the impact of the brutal physical realities of ancient slavery, they rely on corporal metaphors of slavery to depict spiritual identity. In the gnostic *Exegesis of the Soul*, the embattled heroine is in fact the Soul, whose trials parallel those of an enslaved prostitute: "But even when she turns her face from those adulterers, she runs to others and they compel her to live with them and render service to them upon their bed, as if they were her masters."[5] Although *Exegesis of the Soul* emphasizes the bondage of the soul, the passage is persuasive only to the extent that the reader recognizes the dangers that slavery poses to the body.

In this chapter I move from physical slavery to spiritual slavery, from bodies to souls, in order to expose the dependence of Stoic and Christian discourses of spiritual slavery on bodily metaphors. I begin with a body count, pointing to the characterization of slaves as bodies in accounting records and other documents. I argue that slaveholders rely on the bodies of slaves, themselves unprotected, as surrogate bodies to buffer their own persons. Since slaves' bodies mediated their experiences of bondage, I explore the implications of gendered identity for slaves. I conclude the chapter with readings of selected passages from the *Discourses* of the Stoic freedman philosopher Epictetus and from Paul's letter to the Galatians. Both Epictetus and Paul attempt to minimize the importance of physical slavery. The arguments of both, however, turn on the recurring equation between slaves and bodies.

Body Count

The Greek word *to sōma*, "body," functioned as a synonym for *ho doulos*, "slave." Wills and other listings of property frequently designated slaves as bodies. As part of the settlement of an estate in Egypt in 47 C.E., three sons agreed to a division of four slaves or, literally, four slave bodies, *ta doulika sōmata*. In its specification that the brothers who received female slaves as their portion of the inheritance also inherited the future offspring of those slaves, the settlement attests to the pervasive use of female slaves for breeding the next generation of human chattel.[6] In this context the designation of female slaves as (reproductive) bodies has particular resonance. Some ancient testators stipulated which slave(s) each heir inherited. Other testators allowed their heirs to divide the enslaved bodies, often constituting a significant portion of an estate, impersonally. The appearance of slave bodies in census returns is a curiosity that underscores the ambivalent legal status of slaves: classified as things, classified as persons. A household lists two enslaved bodies in its 202–203 C.E. census declaration: "Elpis . . . aged 26, having a scar on the left shin, and half of a slave Sarapammon born in the house of Isis also called Memphis, 20 years old, whose other half belongs to Kroniaine and Taorsis in the Syrian quarter."[7] Counted as a person, Sarapammon merits inclusion in the census. Counted as a thing, Sarapammon appears as jointly owned property.

In a wide variety of contexts, slaveholders relied on slaves as body doubles. We see one such instance memorialized in the bylaws of a fraternal society. The purpose of the society was to help members set aside funds, which would be used to pay the head tax levied on all adult males. In specifying the penalty for members who fell behind in payment of dues, the bylaws indicated that a slave could stand in to receive the owner's punishment. The bylaws referred to slaves who absorbed their owners' penalties as *sōmata*, bodies. "If anyone is in default and fails in any respect to pay the dues . . . Kronion shall have authority to seize him in the main street, or in his house, and hand over him or his slaves [bodies]."[8] While imprisonment of a slave deprived the slaveholder of the slave's personal services and productive labor, the slave, not the slaveholder, endured the actual privations of prison. Prison conditions could be severe. Writing in 7 C.E. to Athenodoros, a wealthy but feckless citizen, a woman named Tryphas, in a position to address him bluntly, insinuated that because Athenodoros had neglected to pay some fines, two of his slaves had been imprisoned and were in danger of death.[9] Tryphas referred to the slaves imprisoned in Athenodoros's stead as bodies, *ta sōmata*.

Although I have been translating *to sōma* literally, as "body," I am not certain that ancient audiences would have heard the expressions *ta sōmata* and *ta sōmata doulika* as references to bodies or slave bodies. If the metaphor were no longer live, those who used the expression *ta sōmata* simply intended to say "slaves." Many contemporary scholars take this position and routinely translate *to sōma* as "slave" rather than "body."[10] A diminutive of *to sōma*, *to sōmation*, is the term regularly used in the papyri to refer to the exposed infants so often raised as slaves. Again, I am not certain that ancient audiences would have heard the expression *to sōmation* literally as "little body." If the metaphor were no longer live, those who used the expression *to sōmation* simply intended to say "foundling." It may be relevant, however, that slaves are referred to literally as bodies in some contexts but not in others: when they are listed as property, for example, but not when their actions are described. In grammatical terms, *to sōma* is more likely to serve as an object than a subject. Moreover, references to plural slave bodies are more frequent than references to a single slave body. We cannot know whether such word choices distanced ancient speakers and writers from the humanity of their property. To twenty-first-century readers, allusions to human beings as bodies underscore the coldness of ancient calculations involving human property. The author of the Apocalypse may be emphasizing the bitterness of the slave trade when he lists the luxury products sold by the merchants of the earth: fine linen, olive oil, horses and chariots, bodies (*sōmatōn*), and human souls.[11]

Bodies without Boundaries

Although slaves could be referred to as bodies, the bodies of slaves were not themselves neatly bounded nor defined entities. The bodies of slaves were vulnerable to abuse and penetration. The insult suffered by a free woman who received an unwanted sexual proposition was mitigated if she were dressed in such a way that she could be mistaken for a slave. Plutarch proposed that free Roman youths wear the amulet known as the *bulla* to prevent adult men from accosting them for sexual purposes.[12] The absence of the *bulla,* by implication, marked enslaved youth as sexual prey. Roman law stated that when a third party abused or insulted a slave, the slaveholder, not the slave, suffered the injury. Abuse of a slave was an attack on the slaveholder's personal dignity, an injury from which slaves were immune because slaves did not possess dignity in their own right. In this context slaves served as surrogate bodies for their owners. The *Digest of Justinian* preserves the words of the jurist Ulpian, who wrote in the early third century. "Again, a contumely can be affected against someone personally or through others: personally, when a head of household or matron is directly affronted; through others, when it happens by consequence, as when the affront is to one's children or slave."[13] We see an application of this general principle in an early third-century petition by a slaveholder who construed the kidnapping of one of her slaves precisely as violence against herself: "For Thonis the curator of Seuthes rushed into my house and dared to carry off my slave Theodora, though he had no power over her, so that I am subjected to unmitigated violence."[14] Writing in the second century, the jurist Gaius had delivered a related opinion. He held, however, that a man was not hurt by physical or verbal insults to his slave in the same measure that he would be hurt by similar insults to his wife and children.[15]

Because slaves lacked protection against a variety of abuses their bodies were consequently ill defined. The vulnerability of slave bodies was inscribed in law. (The reader should remember that the opinions recorded in the *Digest* do not necessarily reflect legal decisions actually rendered in courts around the Empire. The *Digest* does record, sometimes with uncanny vividness, the attitudes and preoccupations of its elite contributors.) Ulpian wrote:

> Thus, the praetor does not promise an action for every affront in respect of a slave; if the slave be lightly struck or mildly abused, the praetor will not give an action; but if he be put to shame by some act or lampoon, I think that the praetor's investigation into the matter should take into account the standing of the slave; for it is highly relevant what sort of slave he is, whether he be honest, regular, and responsible, a steward or only a common slave, a drudge or whatever. And what if he be in fetters, branded, and of the deepest notoriety? The praetor, therefore, will take into account both the alleged affront and the person of a slave said to have suffered it and will grant or refuse the action accordingly.[16]

Freeborn persons had license, according to Ulpian, to speak to slaves they encountered as harshly as they pleased and even to subject them to incidental acts of physical abuse.[17] For more serious indignities, Ulpian noted that the position of the slave made a difference. In visiting the house of a friend or business associate, a guest would be more likely to vent frustration with a violent gesture directed against the slave who washed feet or disposed of household waste than against the manager of household accounts.

Ulpian observed that some slaves were marked as chattel through fetters or brand-ing, possibly a form of tattooing, often on the face.[18] A slave who ran away would be placed in fetters or permanently tattooed to forestall future attempts to flee. In the sur-viving fragments of the outrageous first-century novel known as the *Satyricon*, Petronius describes a misbegotten attempt to disguise the leading characters, Encolpius and Giton, as runaway slaves, in order to help them escape detection: "Eumolpus then covered our heads with long block letters drawing the notorious signs tattooed on runaway slaves."[19] Ulpian implies that such slaves, whose physical appearance advertised their servile (and renegade) status, warranted no respect of their persons or bodies. The thick bronze collar worn by the nameless slave of the archdeacon Felix proclaimed, "Hold me so that I do not flee." Indeed, Ulpian suggests that, by placing his slave in such a collar, Felix had granted permission to other freeborn persons to treat his slave however they saw fit.

A familiar episode from the Gospels illustrates the vulnerability of slave bodies to violence by third parties (that is, not by their owners). In the scene of Jesus' betrayal to the authorities, the four canonical Gospels agree that someone associated with Jesus cuts an ear off a member of the company that has come to arrest Jesus. The Gospels also agree that the man who loses his ear is a slave of the high priest. John gives the slave the name by which tradition remembers him: Malchus.[20] A less-familiar scene from the apocryphal *Acts of Thomas* illustrates this vulnerability of slave bodies equally well. The apostle Thomas has been enslaved, and his owner takes him to a foreign land. Thomas is seated at table with others, listening to a young woman as she plays the flute. He directs his eyes to the ground. A member of the group, a cup bearer, reaches over and slaps Thomas. Although Thomas turns his gaze to the man, no one else in the group evinces any interest in this casual act of violence against a slave.[21]

In the *Acts of Thomas*, the ghastly death of the cup bearer (who is consumed by dogs) implies that God has acted to avenge the enslaved apostle. Such literary partisanship on behalf of a slave who suffers casual violence is rare. Literatures of the Roman world consistently suggest that slaves could not protect their bodies from a range of daily in-trusions and insults. Nonetheless, evidence that slaves regularly met such treatment is elusive. We are unlikely to find extensive documentation in the papyrological record. The law permitted freeborn persons casual abuse of slaves who crossed their paths. We therefore cannot expect to discover petitions complaining about such incidents, regard-less of how common those incidents were.[22] We do, however, encounter occasional complaints by freeborn persons who experienced rude treatment that they deemed more appropriate for slaves. A fragment of a mid–second-century petition drew an explicit comparison. "Of all the injustices in life," the petitioner complained, "the most infa-mous is that free persons become the victim of overweening pride." The petitioner elabo-rated on the characteristics of overweening pride, hubris, inappropriately directed against a freeborn person: "to beat and to give a thrashing and to flog the freeborn like slaves."[23]

Apparently, then, freeborn persons were not entirely exempt from such abuse. When they were so treated, the fact that they were being handled like slaves exacerbated their mental anguish. Pliny recounts a story in which a senator accidentally received a casual slap intended for a slave. Pliny presents the incident as an omen of the senator's immi-nent and untimely death. The senator, Larcius Macedo, was in the baths. One of his slaves lightly tapped the shoulder of a man, a member of the equine order, to let him know that Macedo wanted to pass. The man turned around to slap the slave and instead struck Macedo. In Pliny's telling, incidental violence against a slave is an everyday matter. In contrast, Pliny stresses that, with the slap intended for a slave, the senator absorbed a grave insult.[24]

Differential vulnerability of free and enslaved women to insult provides a context for understanding an incident in the second-century work known as the *Acts of Paul*. Thecla is a young woman of Iconium who breaks her engagement in order to follow Paul and convert to Christianity. She is the daughter of a well-to-do family, and her fiancé, Thamyris, is a leading citizen. Thecla's household includes a number of female slaves, and her fiance is in a position to host a lavish banquet at his own home. When Thecla visits Paul in prison, she bribes the doorkeeper with her bracelets and the guard with her mirror, thus divesting herself of accoutrements that would signify her status. Paul is expelled from Iconium, and Thecla is sentenced to death by fire. When the fire is miraculously extinguished, Thecla escapes and finds Paul again. Together Paul and Thecla enter the city of Antioch, where a prominent man named Alexander spies them. Smitten with Thecla, Alexander plies Paul with money and gifts, but Paul denies that he knows Thecla—or that she belongs to him. Alexander then physically embraces Thecla publicly, in the open air, an embrace she resists. The scene becomes more plausible when we infer that Alexander has mistaken Thecla for a slave. She is no longer dressed as an elite young woman. Since Paul denies knowledge or ownership of her, she appears to be unaccompanied. Thus, Alexander exerts the privileges of the elite male, who understands himself to have sexual access to a female slave. Thecla responds with the instincts of a well-bred woman whose honor has been besmirched.

Legal consideration of the vulnerability of slave bodies to insults and affronts covered only the injuries that could be visited on the slave by a person who was not the slave's owner. The slaveholders' right to abuse their slaves at will was almost beyond question. Artemidorus considered at length the possible meanings of dancing in dream logic. He noted, "However and wherever a slave may dance [in a dream], he will get a good beating."[25] (I treat the brutal but ordinary corporal punishment of slaves at greater length in chapter four.) Rights of the slaveholder over the body of the slave did not terminate at the moment of manumission. If the boundaries of the slave body were ill defined and the boundaries of the freeborn body were clearly demarcated, we may anticipate that the freed body would not be able to maintain perfectly defined and defended boundaries. Ulpian wrote, "We allow a patron a restricted right of punishment of his freedman . . . for the praetor does not have to tolerate his slave, now a freedman, complaining against his master that the latter abused him verbally or moderately chastened or corrected him."[26] Ulpian considered the question of whether the husband of a freedwoman could lodge a complaint for insult against her patron. The problem was that both husband and patron had rights over the person of the freedwoman. The patron had an ongoing right to insult or physically correct the freedwoman; a husband was the victim of an insult to his dignity when his wife was abused. Ulpian modified an earlier opinion holding that the husband retained his right to bring an action against his wife's former owner: "For my own part, I have made a note . . . that I do not think that this holds good for every affront; for why should the patron be denied reasonable chastisement, or, provided it is not lewd, berating even of a married woman?" Of course, Ulpian noted, if both husband and wife were former slaves of the same owner, the husband had no right at all to bring complaint against the patron.[27]

Surrogate Bodies

By abrading or striking a slave, one could effect an insult against the slaveholder, and in this sense slaves served as body doubles for their owners. Slaves served in another sense as surrogate bodies for their owners: as stunt men, doubling the physical force their owners could exert. Slaveholders relied on slaves as agents of vicarious violence in order to accomplish disreputable ends. Ramsay MacMullen notes that the absence of a police force would have made it difficult to restrain slaveholders whose slaves constituted private armies.[28] Roman law equivocated on the liability of an owner for a slave's criminal activity. A free person who believed that a slaveholder ordered a slave to mount an assault could sue the slaveholder.[29] In many circumstances, however, it would have been difficult to establish that a slave had committed a criminal action as part of a work assignment. The law distinguished between a situation in which the owner was present when a slave committed an affront and a situation in which the owner was absent. The law authorized proceedings against the slaveholder who was present for the slave's assault but specified that the slave should be taken to the governor to be scourged if the slaveholder was absent.[30]

Legal petitions and letters preserved in the papyri suggest that such assaults were common.[31] As we read the petitions, we should keep in mind that the petitioners narrated events in order to minimize or obscure their own responsibility for whatever took place. We rarely have access to the version of events presented by other parties in the case or to the decision that was handed down.[32] In some cases, petitioners alleged that slaves joined slaveholders in skirmishes. In a late fourth-century petition, a creditor asserted that when he tried to collect a particular debt, the debtor and his household slaves joined forces to attack the creditor and his wife.[33] In a document dated 326 C.E., a petitioner claimed that his wife was at home when she was assaulted by a woman named Tapesis and her slave Victoria. The petitioner requested that a midwife examine his wife so that she could later testify regarding the extent of the damages sustained.[34] In these two cases, slaves served as body doubles, reinforcing the physical capabilities of their owners—or at least this is how the petitioners told their stories. Ulpian held that "the outrage is enhanced by the station of the person responsible."[35] By emphasizing that slaves were involved in an attack, petitioners emphasized the degree of indignity suffered and tried to heighten the sympathies of those who read the petitions.

In other cases, slaves participated in attacks in the absence of their owners. In 7 C.E., Stilbon wrote to Athenodoros (we have already encountered Athenodoros, whose negligence in paying a fine had landed several slaves in jail) informing Athenodoros that he had suffered an attack by man named Skaliphos, who was accompanied by a slave of Chrysippos. He explained the attack by saying that Skaliphos had grown impatient awaiting word from Athenodoros on some matter.[36] Stilbon offered no explanation for the involvement of the slave of Chrysippos in the attack. Perhaps the slave was there to support Skaliphos; perhaps the slave had his own grudge against Stilbon or Athenodoros; or perhaps Chrysippos ordered the slave to harass Stilbon in a way that could not be traced back to him. Although slaveholders had some limited liability for their slaves' actions, relying on slaves to perform disreputable actions allowed owners to accomplish their less-savory ends while protecting their reputations, livelihoods, and physical integrity. Slaveholders relied on slaves as surrogate bodies to do their dirty work when they wanted to keep their own hands clean.

We read in the *Digest* that "a slave should not obey his owner who orders him to commit a crime."[37] The jurist Alfenus addresses the situation at greater length: "A slave does not usually in all cases obey the orders of his master with impunity, for instance, where the master had ordered his slave to kill a man or to commit theft against someone. Consequently, even though a slave had committed piracy on the orders of his master, an action must be taken against him after he is freed."[38] Whether slaves or slaveholders would have been aware of such limitations on the obligations of slaves to obey their owners is unclear. The elite jurists whose opinions the *Digest* preserves evinced no interest in the difficulties that slaves would encounter should they try to pursue legitimate avenues when their owners ordered them to engage in illegitimate activities. In order to avoid possible beatings at the hands of authorities, slaves would have endured certain beatings at the hands of their owners. Nonetheless, when literary sources depict slaves aiding their owners in criminal activity, they rely on the stereotype of the servile person, naturally prone to antisocial actions. In one of Apuleius's seemingly endless tales of faithless women in *The Golden Ass*, a matron whose honorable stepson rejected her as a sexual partner turns against him and seeks to poison him. She relies on one of her slaves, part of her dowry, as an accomplice and sends him for the poison. In Apuleius's prose, the slave is as guilty as the matron. Apuleius represents the slave's obedience not as faithfulness but as the flowering of his own criminal nature. Apuleius even describes the slave's willingness to endure torture to protect his mistress as a sign of obstinacy rather than as a token of fidelity.[39]

Female Bodies

The English word *slave* is unisex; it can refer either to a male or a female slave. The English word *slaveholder* can similarly refer to a male or a female owner of slaves. Reliance on such unisex terms tends to obscure the gendered dimensions of slavery. Even in situations where the Greek word *doulos* clearly refers to a male slave, translators are likely to translate this grammatically masculine term as "slave" and not as "male slave." However, the grammatically feminine term *doulē* is typically translated as "female slave" or "maidservant" rather than "slave." (The translation "maidservant" not only highlights gender but also downplays servile status.) The plural form *douloi* is grammatically masculine. Although *douloi* can properly refer to mixed groups of male and female slaves, it can also refer to groups entirely composed of male slaves. The gender of the term is suppressed in English, however, except in rare situations, for example, in apposition to a plural feminine form. In Acts of the Apostles, for instance, Peter quotes the prophet Joel: "In those days I will pour out my spirit even on your male slaves and your female slaves."[40]

More generally, contemporary scholars often presuppose that slaves are male unless otherwise specified—yet this is hardly the case. Perhaps it is even more accurate to say that many scholars have overlooked the gender of slaves and that ancient slaves appear to the modern imagination as neither male nor female. Inasmuch as slaves were identified as bodies, however, their embodiment as male or female largely determined the conditions of their servitude. At the same time, their identity as slaves would condition their experiences and reception as male or female. Roger Bagnall has challenged scholars who assume that males dominated the servile population. Census data from Egypt during the Roman period imply that male slaves were often manumitted around thirty, but female slaves were unlikely to be manumitted until menopause, which for many women took place in their late forties (and many women would have died before they reached that age). The disproportionate number of female babies who were exposed by their parents and raised in other households as slaves may also have affected the ratio of female slaves to male slaves. Bagnall argues that female slaves constituted two-thirds of the enslaved population of Roman Egypt.[41] Bagnall has not persuaded all interlocutors of the accuracy of these numbers nor their relevance for the rest of the Empire.[42] His arguments nonetheless underscore the necessity of considering the experiences of women in any treatment of slavery during the centuries that witnessed the rise of Christianity.

Pregnancy, childbirth, and lactation were among the somatic experiences that potentially linked slave and free women. Vibia Perpetua, a freeborn woman of considerable privilege (perhaps of curial rank), kept a diary of her time in prison awaiting execution as a Christian.[43] Perpetua wrote that she hoped to keep her infant with her so that she could continue to nurse the child. Her father refused to release the baby to her care. Miraculously, her baby accepted the loss of the breast, and she did not ache for her child: "But as God willed, the baby had no further desire for the breast, nor did I suffer any inflammation; and so was I relieved of any anxiety for my child and of any discomfort in my breasts."[44] An ancient editor—perhaps Tertullian—appended some concluding narrative material to Perpetua's account. Although Perpetua did not mention her fellow prisoner Felicity, we know from the editor's additions that Felicity was a slave who was pregnant when arrested. She feared that her pregnancy would delay her execution, and her fellow Christians would go into the gladiatorial arena without her. Felicity rejoiced when she endured an early and difficult childbirth. She accompanied Perpetua and the others into the gladiatorial arena. The women "were stripped naked, placed in nets and thus brought out into the arena. Even the crowd was horrified when they saw that one . . . was a woman fresh from childbirth with the milk still dripping from her breasts."[45] Perpetua's own words stressed the primacy of the experiences of lactation and weaning for a woman awaiting death. The editor who added the account of the martyrs' deaths in the arena equally stressed the effect that Felicity's lactation had on the crowd that witnessed her death. In at least one bloody context, the capacity to produce milk dissolved differences between an elite woman and a humble slave woman.

However common the bodily experiences of childbirth and lactation were for women, though, their social and symbolic meanings differed for free and slave women. A female slave's reproductive capability made her valuable property until menopause. Women's reproductive capabilities seem to have had a pervasive influence on gender-specific patterns of slaveholding. In his manual on agriculture Columella wrote that he rewarded enslaved women who bore many children. When a woman had given birth to three sons, he lightened her work assignment. When she gave birth to another son, he considered manumitting her. (Columella did not mention miscarriages, stillbirths, or daughters in his account of these reward calculations.)[46] Petronius gave an exaggerated version of a slaveholder, the freedman Trimalchio, publicly listening to his estate accounts being read:

July 26th: on the estate at Cumae, which belongs to Trimalchio, there were born thirty male slaves, forty females; 500,000 pecks of wheat were transferred from the threshing floor to the barn; 500 oxen were broken in.

On the same day, the slave Mithridates was crucified for speaking disrespectfully of the guardian spirit of our Gaius.[47]

The situation envisioned by Columella and satirized by Petronius was, however, atypical in the Roman Empire. Large-scale reliance on slaves was characteristic of agricultural practices in Sicily and the Italian peninsula between the years 200 B.C.E. and 200 C.E. but rare outside those geographic and temporal parameters. (Slaves were nonetheless a continuous source of agricultural labor on a more modest scale around the Mediterranean throughout antiquity.) Although we may not encounter such calculated breeding practices in other circumstances, slaveholders were certainly aware of the potential of female slaves to increase household wealth by bearing future generations of slaves. As I have already mentioned, wills and bills of sale specified that the heir or purchaser of female slaves also owned the rights to future offspring of those slaves.

Orlando Patterson has defined slavery as the "*permanent, violent domination of natally alienated and generally dishonored persons*," an observation that echoes Moses I. Finley's description of the slave as "always a deracinated outsider . . . in the sense that he was denied the most elementary of social bonds, kinship."[48] In the Roman Empire, children born to enslaved mothers were themselves slaves. Unlike the paternal link, which was not acknowledged in any way, legal documents frequently named the enslaved mothers of slaves—but only as a means of identification. To say that a slave had a certain slave as a mother was an identifying marker as would be a reference to a scar, lisp, or limp. This maternal tie had no legal ramifications. The slave who was named as a mother in a legal document had no recognizable claims on the child to whom she had given birth. The slaveholder retained the fundamental right to sell either mother or child or to will mother and child to separate households in a final testament. Many slave mothers nursed and reared their own children, but these were privileges accorded by the slaveholder rather than rights enjoyed by the mother. Even as a slave woman nursed her own child, she increased the wealth of her owner by nourishing the little body that was her fellow property.

Human milk was a valuable commodity in the ancient world. The supply of human milk was inseparable from the physical presence of a woman who not only provided the milk but also held and soothed the baby who consumed it. Despite the warnings of philosophers and physicians that freeborn babies would flourish best when their own mothers nursed them, women in the ancient world who could afford wet nurses routinely relied on them. The second-century writer Aulus Gellius recorded in his *Attic Nights* the tirade of one intellectual against the employment of wet nurses. Favorinus, a eunuch, had studied with Dio Chrysostom, an eclectic philosopher who purveyed an amalgam of Stoic and Cynic ideas. Gellius recorded an incident in which Favorinus called on a family in which a young woman had just given birth. The young woman's own mother informed Favorinus that she had engaged a wet nurse so that her daughter's pains in childbirth would not be compounded by the difficulties of nursing. Favorinus begged the mother to reconsider: "For what kind of unnatural, imperfect and half-motherhood is it to bear a child and at once send it away from her? To have nourished in her womb with her own blood something which she did not see, and not to feed with her own milk what she sees, now alive, now human, now calling for a mother's care?"[49] For Favorinus, consigning care of a baby to a wet nurse was little different from abortion. He believed that a woman passed on both her physical likeness and mental qualities with her milk. Worst of all, he noted, those who wanted to engage a wet nurse were rarely selective, "for as a rule anyone who has milk at the time is employed and no distinction made."[50] He particularly condemned the use of slaves and former slaves as wet nurses, since the baby would imbibe their poor characters with the milk.

In wealthy households that included a number of slaves, a wet nurse could be chosen from among the existing slaves, or a new slave could be purchased to serve as a wet nurse. Emotional bonds formed between a nurse and her charge often survived the period of physical dependency. Literary works from the period feature nurses as the closest companions of elite young women, certainly closer than their own mothers. In Apuleius's *The Golden Ass*, Charite discovers that a bosom friend of her beloved husband had caused his death. Moreover, she realizes that the traitorous friend committed the foul deed in order to displace her husband in her bedroom. Plotting revenge against the villain, she relies on the offices of her faithful nurse. On the night appointed, the nurse welcomes the unscrupulous Thrasyllus to Charite's chambers. As Thrasyllus awaits Charite's arrival, the nurse calmly mixes a sleeping draught into wine and serves the soporific cocktail to him. When she realizes that she has successfully drugged him, she summons Charite, who blinds Thrasyllus before she publicly commits suicide.[51] Although fantastic, the story relies on the shopworn but comforting stock character of the faithful nurse. The *Acts of Thomas*, a Christian work, relies on the figure of the faithful nurse for a less sensational but equally intimate scene. The freeborn woman Mygdonia desires baptism. Like Charite, she chooses as her most trusted confidante the woman who had been her childhood nurse. Mygdonia asks Marcia, her nurse, to make the necessary arrangements for bread, wine, water, and oil. The scene concludes with the nurse herself asking to be baptized.[52]

How realistic are these works in their literary representations of relationships between freeborn women and the enslaved women who had been their childhood nurses? Epigraphic evidence from Rome memorializes the affection of wealthy Romans for their wet nurses. In a study of epigraphs dedicated to wet nurses, Sandra Joshel reminds us that these one-sided testimonials can only affirm the publicly acceptable sentiments of the elite. They yield no insights into the feelings of the women who had no choice except to dedicate their lives to foster children who were also their owners.[53] Joshel's work is a rebuttal of Joseph Vogt's celebration of relationships between freeborn Romans and their nurses. For Vogt, these relationships epitomized the humanity of Greco-Roman slavery.[54]

One of the recurring difficulties inherent in writing about slavery in the ancient world is our lack of access to texts or other materials that would help us to appreciate the perspectives of the slaves themselves. We do have such evidence, however, from more recent slave societies. Joshel writes: "I draw on the testimony of masters and slaves from the American South to indicate how the nursling's view might distort the nurse and her lived reality. Although the explicit statements of mammies [sic] cannot prove what the Roman nurse felt, their divergence from their nurslings' views suggests the need for caution in reading nurses' epitaphs solely in terms of upper-class views and underscores the value of exploring other lines of interpretation."[55] The evidence Joshel marshals suggests that, at least in the American South, enslaved nurses were ambivalent about the babies they fed with their own milk, who grew up as their owners.

Both in the ancient world and in the American South some slaves were enlisted as wet nurses after they had had a chance to nurse and wean their own children. Some women also became available as wet nurses after the death of their own children. Given high rates of infant mortality, this would hardly have been an unusual circumstance. In other cases, the mistress's baby displaced the slave's own infant at the breast. Those who followed the advice of the first-century physician Soranus would even prefer a nurse whose own child was still an infant. Soranus believed that the ideal wet nurse had been lactating for at most a few months.[56] Despite the warmth a woman might feel for the baby she suckled, she would still be concerned for the baby she had prematurely weaned or could only nurse when she was sure the little master or mistress had consumed his or her fill.

Regardless of tender emotions, an enslaved wet nurse was still property that could be alienated. In a nineteenth-century memoir, Harriet Jacobs reflects on the deceptive closeness that service as a wet nurse could foster: "My mother's mistress was the daughter of my grandmother's mistress. She was the foster sister of my mother; they were both nourished at my grandmother's breast. In fact, my mother had been weaned at three months old, that the babe of the mistress might obtain sufficient food. They played together as children; and when they became women, my mother was a most faithful servant to her whiter foster sister. On her deathbed her mistress promised that her children should never suffer for anything; and during her lifetime she kept her word."[57] At the death of this kind mistress and foster aunt, Harriet learned the identity of her new owner. She was the property of her late mistress's niece, a child of five years. Harriet quickly became the sexual prey of her young mistress's father. The parameters of slave life were similar in the ancient world. A slave beloved by household members for nurturing them in their youth could be sold to another household because of financial need or at the time of estate settlement. Even more commonly, a family that sentimentally retained the old nurse would think little of selling the nurse's own children away from her.

In less-wealthy households, the temporary services of a slave (or sometimes even a free) wet nurse could be purchased. A late second century receipt from Oxyrhynchus acknowledges that the slaveholder Chosion had received payment, including wages, oil, clothes, and other expenses, for the two years that his slave Sarapias had nursed Helena, the daughter of Tanenteris. Sarapias had weaned Helena and returned her safely to her mother. Slaveowners also purchased the services of wet nurses outside their own households to suckle enslaved children when wet nurses were not available within the household. In many cases, these wet nurses suckled infants rescued from the dungheap to be raised as slaves, but in certain circumstances slaveholders hired the services of wet nurses for slaves born within their households. A fragmentary receipt from the second century records that Thenkebkis had received payment for the services of the slave Sarapias in suckling Eudaemon, a male child of Isidorus. Eudaemon's mother was a slave belonging to Isidorus, and so Isidorus's son was also his property. We have no way of knowing why the slave mother did not nurse her own child. Perhaps Eudaemon's mother died in childbirth. Perhaps Isidorus hoped that his slave would become pregnant again and thereby expand his property. Perhaps Isidorus's wife had also given birth, and she wanted a household slave to serve as wet nurse for her own child. Or perhaps Isidorus preferred his sexual partner to be free of the burden of breastfeeding.

Sexual Surrogates

Sexual access to slave bodies was a pervasive dimension of ancient systems of slavery. Both female and male slaves were available for their owners' pleasure. In the *Oneirocritica*, Artemidorus writes, "If a man dreams that he is masturbating privately, he will possess either a male or female slave, because the hands that are embracing his penis are like attendants."[58] Artemidorus's dream logic identifies slaves as sexual body doubles, surrogates relieving the slaveholder of the inconvenience of having to provide his own sexual pleasure. This oneiric reasoning depends on the widespread ancient recognition of slaves as benign sexual outlets for their owners.

In Petronius's *Satyricon*, the freedman Trimalchio famously boasts, "To do your master's bidding is nothing to be ashamed of. And I gave my mistress equal time!" He also notes, however, that when his master became aware that Trimalchio was sleeping with his wife, he banished the slave to his farm.[59] Although some matrons exploited their male slaves sexually, constraints on the sexuality of freeborn women rendered this practice less acceptable than the sexual exploitation of male or female slaves by male slaveholders. The consequences of conception varied in these two sets of circumstances. A householder who impregnated a female slave increased his stock of slaves. A matron who gave birth to the child of a slave disrupted the household; the event would likely be the occasion for a divorce. The child, though freeborn, would be illegitimate.

In a petition for divorce submitted in the late first century B.C.E., a woman named Tryphaine alleges that her husband, Asklepiades, "abused me and insulted me, and laying his hands on me, he used me as if I were his bought slave."[60] Tryphaine implies that as a wife she should be exempt from certain kinds of treatment, which female slaves were not in a position to protest. Although a husband might be able to overpower his wife to exact sexual favors, the terms of many marriage contracts gave women financial leverage over their husbands. Knowledge that his wife could initiate a divorce and block his access to her financial resources would curb the behavior of at least some men. Slaves, however, had no such leverage.[61] In a letter speaking sympathetically of a free woman who divorced her husband, Jerome wrote that her husband "was a man of such heinous vices that even a prostitute or a common slave would not have put up with them."[62] Jerome's words confirm the impression that slaveholders relied on slaves to provide sexual pleasures that freeborn women would find shameful. Leukippe, the heroine of Achilles Tatius's *Leukippe and Clitophon*, is a freeborn woman whose enslavement puts her at the mercy of Thersandros, who at first attempts to seduce her. When Leukippe resists his fantasy of seduction, Thersandros responds by calling attention to her vulnerability as a slave to his sexual desires: "But since you are unwilling to feel my passion as your lover, you shall feel my power as your lord!"[63] Plutarch recommends that men demonstrate respect for their wives by relying on slaves to sate their erotic appetites.[64] In this respect, a wife who wished to limit and control her sexual activities could rely on household slaves to serve as surrogate bodies available to satisfy her husband's particular appetites without endangering her own status or her children's position as heirs.

The *Acts of Andrew*, dating from the second or early third century, includes the story of a Christian woman named Maximilla, who uses her slave Euclia as an erotic body double. Maximilla was under the influence of the apostle Andrew, who decried all sexual activity as polluting. The proconsul Aegeates, Maximilla's husband, was not a Christian and was unhappy with her resistance to his sensual overtures. Seeking to preserve her own purity, Maximilla sends Euclia to assume her position in Aegeates' bed. By serving as surrogate body, Euclia pays the price for Maximilla's personal purity: "Just as a woman customarily adorns herself to look like her rival, Maximilla groomed Euclia in just such finery and put her forward to sleep with Aegeates in her stead. . . . By so doing, Maximilla escaped detection for some time, and thereby got relief, rejoiced in the Lord, and never left Andrew."[65] According to ancient mores, Euclia responds inappropriately to her relationship. She boasts of her position and demands from Maximilla payment that includes not only money and jewelry but also her freedom. Other slaves in the household grow increasingly bitter toward the favors Euclia receives. They eventually inform Aegeates of the deception. Again Euclia serves as a surrogate body for Maximilla as Aegeates directs his anger toward the freedwoman rather than the matron: "The proconsul, furious at her for boasting to her fellow slaves and for saying these things in order to defame her mistress—he wanted the matter hushed up since he was still affectionate for his spouse—cut out Euclia's tongue, mutilated her, and ordered her thrown outside. She stayed there without food for several days before she became food for the dogs. The rest of the slaves who had told their story to him—there were three of them—he crucified."[66] The *Acts of Andrew* condemned Euclia's behavior but did not condemn the sexual use of slaves, at least if that practice permitted an elite Christian woman to remain unsullied by sexual contact. Rather, the *Acts of Andrew* condemned the hubris of a slave who overestimates the significance of a sexual relationship with her owner.

Andrew S. Jacobs argues that the denigration of marriage in the apocryphal acts is a rejection of upper-class ethics. The period of composition of the apocryphal acts roughly coincides with an era of increasing pressure throughout the Empire for elite men and women to marry and produce children. During this same period, Roman law increasingly codified restrictions against marriage between people of different social echelons.[67] As support for his argument, Jacobs includes the story of Euclia. He writes, "The marriage bed is evidently a dangerous place for slaves." But in the *Acts of Andrew*, the danger for a slave is not sexual contamination but the possibility that she will forget her proper place, a conclusion that is hardly a protest against upper-class ethics.[68] The *Acts of Andrew* seems to exempt Maximilla of any moral culpability in the subterfuge, implying that Euclia's actions are completely explicable in the context of her nature, depicted as both lascivious and greedy. Her own curves indict her. "She [Maximilla] summoned a shapely, exceedingly wanton servant girl [*paidiskē*] named Euclia and told her what she delighted in and desired. 'You will have me as a benefactor of all your needs, providing you scheme with me and carry out what I advise.'"[69] The *Acts of Andrew* does denigrate one version of upper-class sexual ethics, which posits procreative, conjugal sex as a civic duty. However, it promotes another version of upper-class sexual ethics, in which abstinence from polluting sexual activity is a distinctively elite prerogative. This latter ethical system served not only upper-class interests but also explicitly Christian interests.

We should not extrapolate from the *Acts of Andrew* that married women generally promoted sexual associations between their husbands and slaves nor that slaves universally understood such relationships as grounds for boasting. All evidence suggests that the sexual use of female and young male slaves was widespread. The typical range of reactions by slaves to their carnal duties is much harder to assess, as are the reactions of slaveholding women to their husbands' erotic dalliances with slaves. Ancient sources yield no insights into the actual reactions of slaves to their masters' sexual initiatives. Some slaves may have genuinely cared for their masters; others may have hoped that sexual liaisons with their masters would constitute a route to freedom; but regardless of slaves' affections, ambitions, or misgivings, they had no control over the master's decision to use them sexually.[70]

Tales of women who found respite in their husbands' sexual engagements with slaves are balanced by stories about women enraged at the slaves they perceive to have seduced their husbands. In *An Ephesian Tale* by Xenophon of Ephesus, a woman finds out that her husband has acquired as a slave the novel's heroine, Anthia, with whom he is infatuated. The woman responds by accusing Anthia of scheming against her marriage and arranges the sale of Anthia.[71] Valerius Maximus records the virtue of Tertia Aemilia, whose tolerance was so great that she ignored the sexual liaison between her husband, Scipio Africanus, and a household slave. Even after her husband's death, she resisted the urge for revenge, instead freeing the slave and arranging a marriage for her.[72] In this anecdote, what is unusual is not the sexual relationship between a prominent Roman man and his slave—but that the man's wife does not attempt to make the slave's life miserable.

Roman cultic practices ritualized the division between slaveholding women and enslaved women. The Matralia, celebrated on June 11, was a holiday on which well-born matrons worshiped Mater Matuta. The myth of Ino associated with Mater Matuta's cult includes the story of a sexual relationship between Ino's husband and her female slave. Plutarch's account of the Matralia includes a curious detail. Although slave women were in general forbidden to take part in the festivities, during the course of the celebration one slave woman was escorted onto the premises. The matrons ritually beat the helpless slave.[73] Ross Kraemer argues that the female slave served as a scapegoat. The matrons enacted the hostility and jealousy they felt toward their husbands' enslaved sexual partners by ritually abusing a token female slave.[74] A variety of evidence thus suggests that many matrons viewed their husbands' reliance on slaves as carnal surrogates not as relief but as threat.

A matron's jealousy might extend not only to female slaves but also to male slaves her husband found beguiling. When Trimalchio begins to kiss a beautiful little slave boy (in Latin, *puer*) in Petronius's *Satyricon*, his wife responds immediately and violently.[75] In a wedding song Catullus teases the young male slave who will no longer be the bridegroom's concubine, offering mock lamentation that the young slave has recently begun to shave his formerly whiskerless cheeks. Noting the bridegroom's weakness for "smooth-skinned boys," Catullus warns the bride that if she is reluctant to satisfy her husband's sexual desires he will readily turn elsewhere.[76] Greco-Roman sexual and aesthetic norms celebrated the beauty of young males whose bodies had not gone through the changes of adolescence. While adult men would find the sons of elite households as sexually desirable as the enslaved children of these households, their access to freeborn males was considerably more restricted than their access to boyish slaves. Beautiful boys in Roman love poetry are usually slaves: descendants of Ganymedes pouring wine at dinner parties or vamps displaying boyish charms on the auction block.[77] In an epigram Martial even personifies his penis as grief stricken and whining over his refusal to pay the high price demanded at a slave auction for a *puer*.[78] An abundance of evidence suggests that slave dealers not only marketed attractive young boys on the basis of their physical charms but also produced the kinds of bodies that would realize high returns. Quintilian complains that the slave dealer "regards strength and muscle, and above all, the beard and other natural characteristics of manhood as blemishes, as at variance with grace, and softens down all that would be sturdy if allowed to grow, on the ground that it is harsh and hard."[79] Castration was the ultimate somatic modification inflicted by slave dealers on their human merchandise, a modification intended to preserve the puerile traits of the slave by inhibiting the development of the physical attributes of a mature man.

Of course, the majority of enslaved boys were *not* castrated, and convention suggests that their sexual attractiveness to other men diminished as their bodies became hairy and muscular. Nonetheless, both Greek and Roman vocabularies continued to assimilate them to the status of boys.[80] Regardless of whether his owner still desired him sexually, an adult slave remained vulnerable to his master's carnal whims and disciplinary practices. Jonathon Walters argues that in Latin, *vir*, "man," implies social status as much as gender identity. "Male slaves, too (and ex-slaves), even if adult, are not normally called *viri*. The preferred designation for them is *homines* (which is also used in elite literature for low-class and disreputable men), or *pueri* [boys]."[81] In Greek the expression *pais* was entirely ambiguous: it could refer equally to a child or to a slave of any age.[82]

Male Bodies

Beyond an accident of language, the male slave endured the permanent status of a boy, excluded from maturing into the category of manhood. Indeed, later slave systems, such as those of the American South and the Caribbean, have also characterized male slaves as "boys" and thereby refused to acknowledge their manhood.[83] In the context of the Roman thought world, the slave remained forever under the *potestas* (power) of the owner-patriarch.[84] An incident from the ministry of Jesus illustrates the ambivalent position of the *pais* (child or slave) in the master's household.[85] One context in which rural provincials would come in contact with large slaveholding households would have been encounters with military personnel, many of whom amassed large numbers of slaves as they moved around the Empire. According to Matthew, as Jesus entered Capernaum a centurion approached him to ask Jesus to heal his ailing *pais*. Whether Matthew's *pais* is a child or slave is unclear. Luke's version is unambiguous: the centurion wants Jesus to heal his dying slave, his *doulos*.[86] The slaveholding Roman military official exhibits a paternal persona, caring for his slave, who is implicitly represented as vulnerable and childlike. The story functions as a companion piece to the story of Jesus' encounter with the synagogue leader Jairus, whose daughter Jesus raised from the dead.[87] Although the centurion expresses paternal care for his *pais*, he also proclaims the subordinate status of slaves. Drawing an analogy to the power of his own commands, the centurion announces that a word from Jesus should be sufficient to effect a cure of the *pais*: "For I also am a man under authority, with soldiers under me; and I say to one, 'Go,' and he goes, and to another, 'Come,' and he comes, and to my slave, 'Do this,' and the slave does it" (Matt. 8:9). The centurion's world was also Jesus' world. In that world, a freeborn man would be protective of his legitimate son. The son, in turn, would grow up to assume the role of protector toward others, a manly role. A slave, however well cared for by his owner, remained in a dependent and secondary position. Although he might display the somatic characteristics of the adult male, he nonetheless had the social standing of a *pais*—a slave, a child.

The exclusion of slaves from the category of manhood was thus implicit in ancient Mediterranean conceptions of masculinity.[88] Stephen Moore and Janice Anderson summarize a current that has prevailed in classical studies since Michel Foucault's influential work:

> Mastery—of others and/or of oneself—is the definitive masculine trait in most of the Greek and Latin literary and philosophical texts that survive from antiquity. In certain of these texts, as we shall see, a (free) man's right to dominate others—women, children, slaves, and other social inferiors—is justified by his capacity to dominate himself. Moreover . . . this hegemonic conception of masculinity was less a dichotomy between male and female than a hierarchical continuum where slippage from most fully masculine to least masculine could occur. The individual male's position on this precarious continuum was never entirely secure.[89]

The practice of rhetoric among elite men provides an example of a domain where freeborn men found themselves precariously close to emulating the manners of slaves. Since women and slaves were stereotypically associated with persuasive and perhaps deceptive speech, a man who sought to inculcate his own capabilities to sway others through his oratorical style entered a tenuous territory. Thus Quintilian championed styles of oratory that eschewed artifice, which he explicitly linked with slavish practices of somatic presentation ranging from excessive hand motions to castration. The command of voice and posture that freeborn men tried to develop in their rhetorical training was founded on a hatred of the servile, which was exacerbated by its proximity to the stratagems of the disempowered.[90] Elite ideology insisted that men should master and control the boundaries of their bodies as slaves could never do.

Legally, a male slave could not experience paternity. In the eyes of the law, he neither had a father nor could he father a child. Obviously, male slaves did impregnate women and produce biological progeny, but this biological kinship escaped legal recognition and legitimation.[91] Physically, the male slave had a penis, although the vulnerability of his other sexual organs to the modifications of castration at an owner's whim underscored the degree to which his body was not his own. Rather, he was another's body, counted among the slaveholder's *sōmata* in the context of a will or other tabulation of property. Symbolically, no slave had a phallus. No slave had the legal right to a patrimony, to inheriting or transmitting a family name or other symbolic capital. Artemidorus's dream logic spells out the connection between the phallus and a man's name: "The penis signifies, moreover, the enjoyment of dignity and respect. . . . I know of a slave who dreamt that he had three penises. He was set free and, in place of one name, he had three, since he received in addition the two names of the master who had freed him."[92] A slave was unaffiliated, outside the system of filiation in which fathers recognize and legitimate sons, thereby enabling them to assume their places within society.[93] Indeed anthropologists acknowledge natal alienation as a defining characteristic of slavery crossculturally.[94]

In the twenty-first century courts accept genetic testing as definitive evidence for or against paternity. Not so under Roman law. Of course, we have no way of knowing whether scientific advances would have altered the conventions of paternity laid down in Roman legal codes. According to Roman law, paternity could only be established when a free man acknowledged a child as his own. A free man had the right to "decline" fatherhood; he alone could legally make the decision to rear a child. A free man who decided not to acknowledge his offspring would order the infant to be exposed in a public place. The child might die. The child might also be taken from that public place by another person and raised as a slave. (For further discussion of child exposure as a source of slaves, see chapter three.) When a man died during his wife's pregnancy, the child had to be reared with the family, since the only person who could make the decision to disavow the child could no longer speak.[95] Although a divorced man might be compelled to provide financial support for a child his wife conceived during the marriage, he was not obliged to recognize the child, that is, to extend to the child his symbolic patrimony, including the family name. An enslaved man was not in a position to decide whether or not to raise a child. A legal nonperson, he had no patrimony to extend to biological offspring. A free man who chose to acknowledge and raise an infant thus marked the child as his own. An enslaved man, legally and culturally outside the phallic economy, lacked the ability to mark offspring as his own. In the matrix of Roman thought, fatherhood was not conceived at the genetic or the spermatic level but at the level of language, the symbolic, the bequeathing of a name and a status recognized by law. As Richard Saller concludes, "One of the things that most sharply distinguished the *paterfamilias*' child from his slave was that only the former stood to inherit the father's position."[96]

Although the law did not recognize slaves as fathers, it did recognize freedmen as fathers, and freedmen who were married could even father legitimate, freeborn children. We cannot know, however, what proportion of male slaves actually had this opportunity. Returning to the best-documented geographic region of the Roman Empire, the Egyptian evidence suggests that male slaves were commonly manumitted by age thirty. However, many slaveholders seem to have retained their female slaves in bondage for at least another decade, that is, until they had passed their peak reproductive years. Who were the sexual partners or potential wives of freedmen? If they had slaves as sexual partners, the law designated any progeny as the property of the woman's owner rather than as the son or daughter of the biological father. Freedmen might also have freedwomen as sexual partners or legally recognized wives, but the data suggest that the numbers of still-fertile freedwomen may have been relatively small. Cultural and, in some cases, legal norms discouraged partnerships between freedmen and freeborn women.[97] Thus, although freedmen could legally be the fathers of legitimate children, and ample evidence attests that this was not uncommon, we nonetheless have reasons to suspect that many freedmen were never able to establish themselves as fathers within their own families.[98]

Shame, Honor, and Slave Bodies

The gender-specific liabilities of slaves placed them "outside the game of honor," in Orlando Patterson's words.[99] At its simplest level, honor is a "socially recognized claim to worth."[100] Honorable people guard their honor by protecting their persons from both physical and symbolic affronts. As we have seen, the slave is vulnerable to both. Consider, for example, Bruce Malina's synopsis of male honor in the New Testament world: "First of all, male honor is symboled by the testicles, which stand for manliness, courage, authority over family, willingness to defend one's reputation, and refusal to submit to humiliation."[101] A slaveholder's claim to the body of a male slave certainly extended to possession of his testicles, and in certain circumstances the slaveholder might assert that right to the testicles through castration. More broadly, the sexual availability of the (young) male slave signified his exclusion from the category of honor. Correspondingly, the male slave had no authority over a family, had no reputation to defend, and was permanently liable to humiliation. A male slave's inability to protect the sexual integrity of his biological female kin further underscored his lack of honor, his dearth of what the Romans called *dignitas*, a peculiar combination of birth, character, virtues, access to power, material resources, and legal status. (A person's legal status included citizenship status and whether he or she was freeborn, freed, or enslaved.[102]) In the *Acts of Paul*, Thecla makes the prominent citizen Alexander a laughingstock when she rips his cloak and removes the wreath from his head, an assault that is precisely an attack on his *dignitas*.

Since sexual exclusiveness is the mark of female honor, female slaves lived with a state of perpetual shame.[103] The ancient Roman festival of slave women, the *ancillarum feriae*, exploited the distinction between the honor of freeborn women and the inherently dishonored state of slave women. According to Plutarch, the festival originated in the fourth century B.C.E., when Latin allies of Rome demanded Roman virgins and widows in marriage as a sign of Roman submission. At the suggestion of a slave woman, the Romans instead sent a cadre of slave women dressed as free women, who spent a night in the Latin camp and then signaled the time for a Roman attack.[104]

Anxiety over protecting the *dignitas* of elite households motivated Roman emperors to draft elaborate legislation regulating and in some cases prohibiting sexual and marital arrangements between free persons and slaves. Although sexual relationships between free women and male slaves were especially suspect, marital relationships between free men and female slaves also attracted the wary eye of the emperors.[105]

Slaves were certainly not the only persons in the Roman world outside the game of honor. Actors, gladiators, and prostitutes were among those considered infamous. Their infamy, however, suggests an adaptation to the category of slaves, rooted ultimately in a condition they shared with slaves: corporal vulnerability. Catherine Edwards argues:

> One striking feature of the legal position of the infamous [actors, gladiators, prostitutes] is their assimilation to slaves, in particular, as regards their liability to corporal punishment. . . . Probably the majority of those who followed those professions were slaves or free noncitizens. But this does not explain the legal stigma attaching to those who were Roman citizens. Many Roman citizens worked alongside slaves as builders, agricultural workers, shopkeepers. What made the infamous like slaves was that they too served the pleasures of others, they too had no dignity, their bodies too were bought and sold.[106]

That actors, gladiators, and prostitutes shared the dishonored state of slaves, then, ultimately underscores the source of the slave's dishonor: the slave, conceived as a *sōma*, or body, was nonetheless unable to guard her or his body from insult or violation.

By tracing the dishonor of slaves and the exclusion of male slaves from the category of masculinity, have I thereby reinscribed this lack or, more properly, this perceived lack? Because we do not possess a body of literature from the ancient world that we can reasonably attribute to slave authorship, we have few clues to help us understand how slaves perceived their own personhood, in particular, how they perceived themselves as women and men. We do not know how they absorbed or resisted discourses that excluded them from the game of honor. Clement of Alexandria described free women whose male slaves washed and massaged them in the baths.[107] The suitability of male slaves as attendants for women in the baths was predicated on the exclusion of those slaves from the category of manhood. Did male slaves who served as attendants in the baths appreciate this logic? If so, did it affect their self-images? In the *Acts of Thomas*, Charisius is the husband of Mygdonia, who has been drawn into the orbit of the apostle. Charisius mistakenly believes that the apostle is his wife's lover and torments himself: "But that I should suffer such a thing at the hands of a stranger! And perhaps he is a slave who has run away, to my hurt and that of my most unhappy soul."[108] The elite man perceives that his shame would be greater if his wife's lover had the status of a slave. Did slaves share or resist such attitudes?

Bits of scattered evidence suggest that many slaves throughout antiquity did form family bonds, including marriages. Such marriages existed at the whim of the slaveholder and had no legal status but would still have been important to enslaved spouses. Our sources again limit our ability to comprehend whether married slaves understood their unions to be subject to the informal rules of honor and shame that governed the unions of freeborn men and women. Under the *potestas*, or power, of their owner(s), married slaves would have found it difficult to maintain the boundaries of privacy necessary for building or sustaining a sense of personal or family honor. A particularly lurid story that Apuleius recounts in *The Golden Ass* hinges on the ability of slaveholders to meddle in slave marriages. A slave entrusted by his master with the management of an estate is married to a fellow slave. The male slave-manager has an affair with a free woman, who does not live on the estate. When his wife learns of the affair she avenges herself by burning his account books and then committing suicide. The slaveholder holds the manager responsible. He punishes the slave by covering his body with honey and binding him to a tree trunk. Ants attracted to the honey slowly consume the slave's body.[109] Apuleius's interest in the story centers on the slave's gruesome death, leaving other questions unanswered. The story does not specify whether the slaveholder is angry because he disapproves of the slave-manager's extramarital affair or because the affair led to the destruction of estate property: the burning of account books and the suicide of a slave. The slaveholder's arrogation of the right to judge another man's conduct in his marriage is a denial of the enslaved man's masculinity and honor. Apuleius represents the slaveholder not only as owner of the couple but ultimately as owner of their marriage. Again, we have no ancient sources that would help us understand how such attitudes affected slaves' perceptions of their own marriages and families.

Orlando Patterson has argued that there is "absolutely no evidence from the long and dismal annals of slavery to suggest that any group of slaves ever internalized the

The Rhetoric of Slavery   29

conception of degradation held by their masters."[110] The sources do not permit us to reconstruct in any meaningful way the psychology of ancient slaves, and I am reluctant to project my own voice through them. In a careful study of an obscure event of 101 B.C.E. recorded in an equally obscure book of prodigies by one Julius Obsequens, Shane Butler attempts to decode one slave's act of autocastration, which led to his exile from Rome. Butler's essay illustrates the uncertainties inherent in the reconstitution of voices of ancient slaves. Although castration technically refers to removal of the testicles, popular imagination and occasional practice associates castration with removal of the penis. Butler argues:

> A slave's penis was not entirely superfluous, for it was at least valuable as a source of *vernae*, slaves born within the household. But it was not a phallus—that is, it did not signify the sexual and political domination exercised by adult male Roman citizens. The *symbolic* superfluousness of a slave's penis was translated into its sexual insignificance, from the master's point of view, from which the only penis that really mattered was the phallus, that is, the one he shared with the other free men of Rome. . . . In such an account of Roman sexuality, penises that are not phalluses are meaningless loose ends, and the slave of Caepio is to be thanked for neatly trimming one away.

To read the slave's gesture of autocastration in this manner, however, merely reinforces the cultural norm of the slave's corporeal subordination. Butler suggests an alternate reading of the slave's act: "Suppose that the slave borrowed the metaphor that made him an extension of his master, but that he used it for the purposes of his own analogy, in order to see himself in his own genitals at the moment that he made himself master of his own body."[111] We are left with a vivid image: a slave cuts off his own penis. However, we do not know whether to read that act as a somatic inscription of the slaveholder's diminishment of slaves' masculinity, or as one slave's rejection of that ideology.

Marilyn Skinner has written, "Clearly, further research on the rhetoric of slavery is in order, with special attention to finding evidence of how marginal populations—women, slaves, and noncitizens—designate themselves in respect to the conjunction of class and gender."[112] The bodies of slaves populate the pages passed down to us from the centuries that witnessed the rise of Christianity. These same pages, however, yield little insight into how slaves understood themselves and their agency in the world. We know that slavery marked the body: through shaved heads, tattoos, fetters, and the visible scars of physical discipline. We do not know, however, how slavery marked the person whose body bore these stigmata.

Spiritual Slavery and Somatic Metaphors

Throughout antiquity, and certainly throughout the decades and centuries that witnessed the emergence of Christianity, every level of documentation represents slaves as bodies. The writings of early Christians are no exception. Corporeality conditioned the circumstances and experiences of slaves, ranging from their vulnerabilities to restraint and abuse to gender-specific dimensions of their servitude. Even a person's identity as a woman or a man in a patriarchal and honor-conscious society was modified by the fact of enslavement. Nonetheless, contemporary scholars often minimize the liabilities of slave status, downplaying the consequences of literal, physical slavery. In doing so, scholars follow the lead of ancient writers who insisted that the only true slavery was spiritual slavery. The history of Western philosophical and theological thought has, more broadly, subordinated matters of flesh to matters of the spirit. Given the ancient equation of slaves with bodies, it is not surprising that historians and theologians have so often overlooked the conditions and consequences of enslavement. In doing so, they can draw on a number of ancient writers who in turn minimize the impact of corporeal slavery while stressing the dangers of spiritual, mental, or volitional slavery.

In the *Acts of Thomas*, the apostle looks with compassion at a band of slaves who carry the litter of a wealthy woman who desires to hear him speak. He notes that the slaves are heavy laden, treated by their owner as beasts of burden. He insists that God does not distinguish according to status, slave or free. He then tells them what God requires of them: to abstain from murder, theft, avarice, and other vices. He reserves his strongest language for his warning against sexual activity, which he represents as a vice which has the power to enslave.[113] The passage moves from the opening recognition of the physical burdens of the enslaved litter bearers, carrying their owner on their backs, to its climactic insistence that the worst slavery is the bondage of sexual desire.

The remainder of this chapter analyzes the arguments and rhetoric of two ancient works, which proclaim the relative insignificance of physical slavery and the overarching perils of spiritual slavery. Even here, I argue, we cannot escape the pervasive identification of slaves and bodies. Epictetus, a freedman and Stoic philosopher, argues that the freedom of moral choice is the only liberty of any consequence. To Epictetus, the body is a burden-bearing donkey, and what happens to the body is of no consequence. Since all a slaveholder can own or affect is the body of a slave, legal subjugation cannot compromise a person's liberty. In his letter to the Galatians, Paul points to a life in Christ that is beyond the divisions of slave and free, male and female. Having enunciated the dissolution of these identities, however, Paul redoubles his reliance on somatic and gendered metaphors of slavery. For both Epictetus and Paul, the rhetoric of physical slavery haunts the claim that the only real bondage is the servility of will, of mind, or of spirit.

Discourses of Epictetus

Epictetus lived during the early years of the Christian movement, from the mid–first century C.E. until 135 C.E. As a child he was a slave of Epaphroditus, a freedman and an officeholder under Nero and Domitian. Epictetus studied philosophy with Musonius Rufus. Eventually, Epaphroditus manumitted him. His student Flavius Arrianus (Arrian) recorded his teachings in the work now known as the *Discourses*. Although Epictetus is not himself the author of this work, the *Discourses* bring us closer than most other ancient literature to the insights of a (former) slave, albeit an exceptional slave. Throughout this discussion I treat the *Discourses* as though they accurately record the words of Epictetus, although I acknowledge that the words we read have inevitably been filtered and shaped by Arrian. According to Epictetus, the situation of the slave is no different from the situation of the free person in the only respect that he thinks matters: the freedom of judgment and moral decision making. By proclaiming that the liberty of the (legally) free person is a chimera, Epictetus denies the essential distinction between slave and free. However, a corollary of this proclamation is a refusal to acknowledge that the toll of slavery on the human person is genuine.[114]

For Epictetus, people's ability to decide between what is right and wrong defines their liberty, so that we may most accurately refer to "volitional" bondage or freedom. Epictetus recognizes that many things are outside the control of the individual. Because a person cannot control external circumstances, it is impossible to choose wealth, a good reputation, physical well-being, or a happy family. But liberty is unrelated to riches, a good name, health, or kinship:

> "Have you nothing that is free?" "Perhaps nothing." "And who can compel you to assent to that which appears to you to be false?" "No one." "And who can compel you to refuse assent to that which appears to you to be true?" "No one." "Here, then, you see that there *is* something within you that is naturally free. But to desire, or to avoid, or to choose, or to refuse, or to prepare, or to set something before yourself—what man among you can do these things without first conceiving an impression of what is profitable, or what is not fitting?" "No one." "You have, therefore, here too, something unhindered and free." (3.22.42–44)

Not only does Epictetus stress the dangers of volitional indenture, but he also argues that the condition of legal servitude does not and cannot damage a person. Epictetus acknowledges that he lives in a culture that allows one person to hold legal title to another, but he insists that such title is insufficient to enable one person to be master of another: "For what is a 'master'? One man is not master of another man, but death and life and pleasure and hardship are his masters" (1.29.61–63). Epictetus ridicules the notion that papers or rituals could determine whether a person is slave or free. The only evidence of a person's liberty is that person's behavior, particularly in the exercise of discernment between what is good and what is evil.

All persons have the capacity to distinguish and choose what is right because human beings are the children of Zeus, imbued by Zeus with a spark of divinity. Who are you, asks Epictetus, and why are you in this world? Zeus has brought you into this world and equipped you with senses and reason (4.1.104). What ultimately horrifies Epictetus about enslavement to the passions—subjugation to love, to fear, to greed for wealth or power—is that such bondage compromises Zeus, who is carried inside each person: "But you are a being of primary importance; you are a fragment of God; you have within you a part of Him. . . . You are bearing God about with you, you poor wretch, and know it not!" (2.8.9–15). Epictetus believes that as children of one father, Zeus, we should acknowledge our kinship to other human beings, ignoring such artificial barriers as the claims of nationality or even the formalities associated with slavery: the buying, selling, and possession of human bodies.

On one level there is nothing controversial about Epictetus's definition of freedom: "He is free who lives as he wills, who is subject neither to compulsion, nor hindrance, nor force, whose choices are unhampered" (4.1.1). However, Epictetus's definitions of compulsion, hindrance, and force diverge from common interpretations of these concepts. Is the threat of physical injury, or even death, relevant to compulsion or force? Not according to Epictetus: "Come, can anyone force you to choose something that you do not want?—He can; for when he threatens me with death or bonds, he compels me to choose.—If, however, you despise death and bonds, do you pay any further heed to him?—No.—Is it, then, an act of your own to despise death, or is it not your own act?—It is mine" (4.1.65-74).

Even as the *Discourses* provide evidence about the harsh conditions of slavery in the first and early second centuries, they discourage the reader from considering those conditions as liabilities for persons who endure them. Epictetus views the slaveholder's weapons as feeble. A master or mistress can ask a slave to perform immoral actions and can beat, maim, or kill the slave who refuses to comply. But this is all the slaveholder can do. Epictetus argues that a slave who does not cower before physical abuse or death is therefore free to act as he or she chooses: "How, then, does it come about that he [a slave] suffers no harm, even though he is soundly flogged, or imprisoned, or beheaded? Is it not thus—if he bears it all in a noble spirit" (4.1.127). A slave who compromises behavior or judgment because of the threat of punishment is nonetheless still culpable, because he or she has valued physical well-being over moral well-being. A slaveholder controls only the body of a slave, but to have power over a body is to dominate a thing which is of no value in itself. Epictetus can thus recognize that the slaveholder's dominion over the enslaved body is absolute and still deny that the slaveholder has any real mastery over the one who is called a slave.

The *Discourses* reinforce the ancient rhetorical association of slaves and bodies. We find this association repeated, for example, in the writings of another Stoic philosopher. Seneca writes, "It is a mistake for anyone to believe that the condition of slavery penetrates the whole being of a man. The better part of him is exempt. . . . It is, therefore, the body that Fortune hands over to a master; it is this that he buys, it is this that he sells; that inner part cannot be delivered in bondage."[115] However, while other ancient works characterize slaves as bodies, the *Discourses* characterize bodies as slaves: "'Is the paltry body [to *sōmation*] you have, then, free or is it a slave?' 'We know not.' 'You do not know that it is a slave of fever, gout, ophthalmia, dysentery, a tyrant, fire, iron, everything that is stronger?' 'Yes, it is their servant'" (3.22.40-41). According to Epictetus, a person should demonstrate no concern for what is external, and he includes one's very body among the external circumstances that are peripheral to personal identity. Dissociating oneself from one's body is liberating, claims Epictetus, since one is no longer subject to tyranny:

> When the tyrant threatens and summons me, I answer, "Whom are you threatening?" If he says, "I will put you in chains," I reply, "He is threatening my hands and my feet." If he says, "I will behead you," I answer, "He is threatening my neck." If he says, "I will throw you into prison," I say, "He is threatening my whole paltry body; and if he threatens me with exile, I give the same answer."—Does he, then, threaten *you* not at all?—If I feel that all this is nothing to me—not at all; but if I am afraid of any of these threats, it is I whom he threatens. (1.29.6-8)

The body is servile, external to the true person, and burdensome—like a donkey, says Epictetus. Ancient law and custom stated that the body of the slave belonged to another. Epictetus goes still further. A slave does not possess his or her own body, but neither does a free man or a free woman. I have noted that ancient documents refer to the little bodies lifted from dungheaps to be raised as slaves with a diminutive of the word for body: to *sōma*, the body, to *sōmation*, the little body. Thus, when Epictetus describes his own body as a negligible thing, a *sōmation*, he underscores once again the slavish nature of the body, the *sōma*: "my paltry body, something that is not mine, something that is by nature dead [*to sōmation, to ouk emon, to physei nekron*]" (3.10.15).

In many respects, Epictetus's arguments assume great respect for the integrity of those persons whom others designated slaves. Like every other human being, the slave is a son or daughter of Zeus, who carries Zeus within. Slaves consequently share with the rest of humanity a boundless potential for moral discernment and action. One may differentiate slaves from free persons on grounds of utility ("For there is some use in an ass, but not as much as there is in an ox; there is use also in a dog, but not as much as there is in a slave; there is use also in a slave, but not as much as there is in your fellow citizens" [2.23.24]) but not on moral grounds. Epictetus concedes the legal division of slave from free but questions the significance of this division. The formal Roman ceremony associated with manumission requires the slaveholder to turn his slave around. Epictetus assesses the import of this ritual:

> When, therefore, in the presence of the praetor a man turns his own slave about, has he done nothing?—He has done something.—What?—He has turned his slave about in the presence of the praetor.—Nothing more?—Yes, he is bound to pay a tax of five percent of the slave's value.—What then? Has not the man to whom this has been done become free?—He has no more become free than he has acquired peace of mind. You, for example, who are able to turn others about, have you no master? Have you not as your master money, or a mistress, or a boy favorite, or the tyrant, or some friend of the tyrant? If not, why do you tremble when you go to face some circumstance involving those things? (2.1.23–28)

In his insistence that the slaveholder controls only the body of the slave, Epictetus denies the slaveholder any meaningful victory over another person. Hegel argues that in subjugating the slave the master seeks to force another consciousness to acknowledge his superiority. But Epictetus argues that the master tames neither the consciousness nor the conscience of the slave. In achieving victory over the slave's body the master has merely subdued an inanimate object. Epictetus characterizes the body not only as slavish but as clay, a lifeless thing. Not only, then, do Epictetus's arguments seem to dignify the humanity of the slave, but they also controvert the slaveholder's claim to a higher status.

Epictetus's dismissal of the importance of corporeal slavery, however, is in no way a rejection of the institution of slavery. Epictetus insisted that people should not try to change the circumstances in which they found themselves but should accept their situations as given by Zeus. Rich or poor, free or slave, each person should only care about what is within the control of every person, that is, proper discernment and alignment of the will with what is right. Acceptance of this ethical framework would prevent a slave from running away or rebelling against a slaveholder, two alternatives that untold numbers of slaves pursued throughout antiquity.

To accept Epictetus's arguments today is to disavow the gravity of slavery in the Roman Empire. For Epictetus, the slave who disposes of the household's human wastes is a slave on a small scale (*mikrodoulos*), and the governor or consul who has abased himself before the emperor to achieve his position is a slave on a large scale (*megalodoulos*). On this view, the fact of a person's legal manumission is inconsequential; the kidnapping and sale of a free person into slavery is equally inconsequential. The slaveholder who inflicts physical abuse on the slave suffers harm from the act, while the slave who is beaten suffers no harm. The association of slaves and bodies is crucial for Epictetus's arguments. If my body is not my own, it is a slavish thing of no consequence, and what happens to my body should not affect who I am as a person. But what happens to my body surely is part of my story. While Epictetus ridicules the impact of beatings or even threats of death, at no point does he acknowledge that slaves' bodies were also sexually vulnerable. Unlike Epictetus, I do not think that people who alter behavior in order to avoid physical abuse compromise themselves morally. Moreover, extreme physical assaults such as torture have the potential to erode the very structure of personhood.[116] Somatic injuries are real injuries, and corporeal pain is real pain. Given the time-honored devaluation of the body in Western thought, Epictetus's arguments can seem persuasive. Respect for the bodies of ancient slaves, coupled with acknowledgment of the harm that enslavement caused them, demands that we ultimately reject those arguments.

Paul's Letter to the Galatian Christians

In his letter to the Galatian Christians, Paul quotes a baptismal formula to remind his readers that their new identity in Christ abrogates the claims of other status markers: "For when all of you were baptized into Christ, you put on Christ as though he were your clothing. There is neither Jew nor Greek; there is neither slave nor free; there is no 'male and female'; for all of you are One in Christ Jesus" (Gal. 3:27-28). Commentators agree that Paul quotes the baptismal formula in this verse because he is concerned with the dissolution of the categories of Jew and Greek. However, having incidentally announced that within the Christian community *slave* and *free* are not relevant categories, Paul introduces imagery that stresses acknowledged legal and cultural differences between slave and free. Moreover, despite his dismissal of the categories *male* and *female*, the tropes of slavery and freedom that pervade Galatians 4 are gendered tropes. We have seen that, in Greco-Roman culture, status as well as gender affected the articulation and practices of "masculinity" and "femininity." Although Paul instructs the Galatian Christians to concern themselves with spiritual rather than corporeal slavery, his rhetoric ironically underscores the somatic structure of ancient slavery. Elizabeth Castelli argues, "The very notion of difference works in the passage as a conceptual problem for Paul, something that his argument requires, and yet that his philosophical framework cannot sustain."[117]

Paul writes, "There is neither Jew nor Greek; there is neither slave nor free; there is no 'male and female'; for all of you are One in Christ Jesus." He continues, "And, if you are Christ's, then as a result of that, you are seed of Abraham, heirs in accordance with the promise" (3:29).[118] In order to tease out the significance of the trope of the heir, Paul contrasts the heir with the slave. Having explicitly introduced this opposition, the distinction between the heir or son and the slave suffuses Paul's argument. That the heir is only a son by adoption in no way minimizes the impact of Paul's analogy. The symbolic or phallic configuration of paternity, rather than the biological relationship, distinguishes the relationship of a freeborn father and son from the relationship of an enslaved father and/or son.

Galatians 4 begins: "What I mean can be made yet clearer by a picture: So long as the heir is a child, he is no different from a slave, even though, in prospect, he is lord of the entire household. He is under the authority of guardians and managers until the arrival of the time set by the father for his passage to the status of an adult" (4:1–2). Paul then speaks of God's ransoming the Galatians from the enslaving powers of the cosmos and even adopting them as sons: "So then, you are no longer a slave, but rather a son; and if you are a son, you are also an heir by God's act of adoption" (4:7). Paul's metaphors make sense only in the context of some peculiar dimensions of first-century practices of slavery. First, Paul's comparison of the underage heir with the position of the slave points to the assimilation of slaves, perhaps especially male slaves, to the position of children, of boys. Within Greco-Roman systems of gender, the slave could not grow into the full status of a man. Second, Paul's contrast between the son or heir and the slave emphasizes the exclusion of the slave from systems of paternity or filiation and thereby the slave's lack of a phallus. Third, Paul's introduction of the Hagar-Sarah allegory reminds his readers of the sexual vulnerability of slaves, especially female slaves.[119] (Sarah, the infertile wife of Abraham, encouraged her husband to conceive a child with the Egyptian slave Hagar. After Sarah gave birth to Isaac she engineered the expulsion of Hagar and Hagar's son into the wilderness.) Fourth, and finally, the passage relies on a peculiar confusion between slave and prospective heir. Imagine a little body, an indeterminate body, perhaps lifted off a dungheap, that may be raised as a slave or may be adopted as a son. Thinking about this little body and its potential as son or as slave will help us come to terms with the extent to which first-century intimations of gender escaped biological definition, rooted as they were not in carnal bodies but in symbolic bodies, in networks of status and power.

As I have already argued, the tenure of the slave in the household of the master enshrined his position as *pais*. The subordinate status of the slave prevented him from claiming the position or prerogatives of manhood. Paul evokes precisely this dimension of the ancient ideology of slavery in his assimilation of the slave to the underage child, the heir. A *pais* who is an underage heir may be the legal master of the household, but at this time the household guardians and managers—who themselves may be slaves—function as his masters. Nonetheless, the day will come when he will assert his masculinity by exerting his mastery over the household retainers. A *pais* who is a slave, however, cannot look forward to this transition and is thus no different from a child, although he may sport a full beard and other somatic markers of the adult male. The point of contrast between slave and heir is that of potential. The heir expects that he will eventually attain the status of manhood, but the slave does not. Although Paul does not point explicitly to the sexual vulnerability of the slave, his first-century audience was familiar with that liability. A slave's inability to master the borders of his own body was a corollary of his subordinate status and his permanent exclusion from the category of manhood into which the heir would grow.

Peter Garnsey has noted that Paul seems to have Roman law on slaves, sons, and inheritance in mind in the third and fourth chapters of Galatians.[120] Indeed, the apparent erasure of division between slave and free that Paul proclaims in 3:28 is only a cover-up, as Paul goes on to reinscribe customary and legal distinctions between slave and free. These distinctions are gender-laden. In contrasting the experiences of the slave and the heir, Paul assumes the exclusion of slaves from an important dimension of masculinity: the experience of being acknowledged as a father or as a son. Once he has reintroduced the division between slave and free, Paul insists on its significance through his use of the Hagar-Sarah allegory.

Paul offers a cryptic summary of the story of Sarah and Hagar: "Abraham had two sons, one from the slave girl and one from the free woman, [but] the crucial point is that the son from the slave girl was begotten by the power of the flesh, whereas the son from the free woman was begotten from the power of the promise" (4:22b–23). The son of the slave woman is begotten by the power of the flesh alone. The son of the free woman is recognized as the son of the father because he is begotten by the power of the spirit into a place in the legal and symbolic nexus. Paul thus subordinates biological to symbolic dimensions of fatherhood, the flesh to the phallus. Abraham sires two sons, but he is only a father to one of them. Biological reproduction does not exhaust the meaning of fatherhood. The freeborn man, the patriarch, can choose whether or not to recognize his offspring. The enslaved son is excluded from the transmission of symbolic capital. Indeed, this division between slave and free comes down to a potential property dispute, that is, the fear that the child born to the slave woman will assert a claim against the estate. To forestall this contention, Paul quotes Genesis: "Throw out the slave girl and her son. For the son of the slave girl will certainly not come into the inheritance along with the son of the free woman" (4:30b). Acknowledgment of kinship between a patriarch and his biological progeny who is more property than son threatens the clearly etched claim of the legitimate son to his patrimony. Better to disavow the relationship entirely: throw out the mother, expose the son.

To develop his analogy of the child born into slavery, Paul relies on the expectation that his readers, the Galatian Christians, will know that the status of the child follows the status of the mother. His audience may or may not have heard the story of Hagar and Sarah from other preachers,[121] but they are certainly familiar with the sexual vulnerability of female slaves and the destiny of their offspring. Despite Paul's repetition of a baptismal formula that promises an end to the division between slave and free and between male and female, his rhetoric throughout Galatians 4 relies on tropes of inheritance that presuppose a gender-marked division between slave and free. The adult male slave can beget children, yet these children are not counted as his own in the phallic economy. The boy born to an enslaved mother is likewise recorded in the property register as a possession of his mother's owner, rather than as the son of his biological father, even when owner and father refer to the same person. To protect the patrimony of the heir, writes Paul, we must expel the threatening bodies of the slave woman and her son. To the uncanny and threatening little bodies of exposed children we now turn.

In the opening verses of Galatians 4, Paul compares an underage heir to a slave and thus parallels the situation of slaves to that of children: "When we were children, we were held in a state of slavery" (4:3). Although in 4:1–2, Paul seems to speak of the heir and the slave as separate figures, as he works through the implications of his imagery the metaphor changes or perhaps becomes more focused. Through the legitimating power of the spirit, those formerly enslaved by the law are redeemed (that is, bought out, manumitted from slavery) and adopted as sons. Paul concludes, "So then, you are no longer a slave, but rather a son; and if you are a son, you are also an heir by God's act of adoption" (4:7). A decision of a patriarch determines whether the little body of the child is adopted and acknowledged as son or raised as human chattel.

We may find Paul's mixing of metaphors confusing. Surely one would know whether a little body was destined to be an heir or a slave. The documentary evidence, however, implies that the distinction was not always so clear. For example, a fourth-century contract arranging the adoption of a two-year old-boy as an heir to a formerly unrelated man speci-fies that under no circumstances may the adoptive father reduce him to slavery.[122] Enun-ciation of this prohibition hints that the parents who permitted the adoption harbored some fear that the adoptive father might later attempt to alter the terms of his relationship with the child. Identities of the infant bodies lifted off dungheaps appear to have been even more fluid. Documents that refer to these infants typically use the term *sōmatia*, little bodies, to describe them. The term *sōmation* is an appropriate epithet, a diminutive for the word *sōma*, which refers not only to the human body but also to the slave as thing or property. In the papyri such bodies appear to be interchangeable, devoid of personality. Contracts for wet nurses who are hired to nourish and raise these little bodies emphasize the indeterminate quality of these *sōmatia*. Wet-nursing contracts sometimes specify that if the infant being nursed dies, another *sōmation*, another little body, should be raised from the dungheap to take its place. Some contracts ascribe the responsibility for raising a substitute body to the nurse or her owner, and some contracts ascribe this responsibility to the owner of the original little body.[123] In itself the *sōmation* has no identity but re-quires inscription into a will, a property register, or a bill of sale.

Alternately, the *sōmation* may be inscribed as son, as heir. A mid–first-century legal dispute records such confusion over the identity of a little body. A woman named Seraeus had contracted to nurse an enslaved foundling belonging to a man named Pesouris. At the same time, her own son was quite young, newly weaned. One of the little bodies in her care died. Seraeus claimed that the child who died was the foundling lifted off the dungheap and that the surviving child was her own son. Pesouris claimed that the child who died was Seraeus's son and that the surviving child was hence his property. Pesouris brought the matter to court to decide whether the *sōmation* should be marked as his property or as the legitimate son of Seraeus and her husband, Tryphon. The court sided with Tryphon, who was willing to acknowledge the little body, the *sōmation*, as his son and heir.[124] At a distance of almost two thousand years we cannot say for sure whether the infant who survived had been born to Seraeus and Tryphon or secretly adopted by them after the death of their own son. The little body was not intrinsically slave or free, but his inevitable assignment to one of these statuses would legally and culturally con-dition his reception as a man and hence his experience of masculinity.

Mireille Corbier writes of adoption in Roman law: "Just as he had the right to de-cline paternity, the 'legal' father had the right to transfer his paternity by adoption," and "Adoption was governed by strict rules, namely those of the transmission of a col-lection of real and symbolic possessions, the first and foremost of these being the family name."[125] Although Roman men who had not produced legitimate sons sometimes chose to adopt close relatives, under some circumstances even a slave or an infant raised from a dungheap could be ascribed the status of a son. Paul's allusion in Galatians 4:7 to the adopted son who is no longer a slave is thus not entirely idiosyncratic. Paul does not use the word *sōmation* in Galatians, but his logic at the beginning of chapter 4 indicates familiarity with such indeterminate little bodies, whose future identities were contin-gent on the decision of a man who could designate himself either father or owner. That decision would determine whether the *sōmation* would be translated into an heir or an inheritance, listed as a body, a *sōma*, in the property register of the heir himself.

As we consider a *sōmation*, a little body pressed against a woman's breast for nour-ishment, we see a little body not yet defined by the categories of slave and free. At this moment the little body's identity is fluid, undefined. The patriarch has not yet decided its destiny as slave or son. The patriarch has not inscribed the infant into a symbolic body where it will be designated slave or free. Paul promises a suspension of the categories of slave and free, male and female, within the Christian community. His rhetoric, however, insists on the consignment of human persons to places in society that are defined by these very categories. Even as Paul dismisses the relevance of legal, corporeal slavery among Christians, he warns his Galatian audience that they are once again being spiritually enslaved by their submissive participation in ritual practices. The metaphors he chooses to dramatize his admonition recall the real limitations and perils of first-century slavery: relegation to a childish and dominated position in the household, sexual vulnerability, alienation from one's biological kin, and exclusion from any inheritance, including the inheritance of a name. Because Paul subordinates the power of the flesh to the power of the spirit, generations of readers have been convinced that the hazards of mundane slavery must pale in comparison to the evils of spiritual bondage. However, the structure of Paul's argument is contingent on the somatic configuration of first-century slavery.

Throughout the Roman Empire, slavery was understood in corporeal terms. Nonetheless, some thinkers of that era, who have continued to be influential over the millennia, insisted that legal, physical slavery was not nearly as great a threat as bondage of the will, the mind, or the spirit. In the course of their arguments, however, both Epictetus and Paul draw our attention to the conditions and practices that affected slaves in the first century. In his insistence that blows to the body should not affect a person's will, Epictetus reminds us of the vulnerability of the slave to physical abuse. In his desire to convince the Galatian Christians of the pitfalls of spiritual enslavement, Paul relies on imagery that evokes the somatic liabilities of servile status. My discussion of Galatians has focused on Paul's inability to sustain rhetorically the dissolution of the categories of slave and free that he signals in 3:28. I have not, however, explored the relations between enslaved and free members of the Galatian community. Did those baptized into the body of Christ experience a life beyond the status distinctions of slave and free? We therefore turn to a consideration of the impact of slavery on Pauline communities and the impact of Christianity on the lives of slaves and slaveholders in Pauline circles.

2

Body Work

Slavery and the Pauline Churches

Travelers to the towns and cities of the Roman Empire customarily sought shelter with those they knew, or they carried letters of introduction from families and friends. When Lucius, the hero of Apuleius's *Golden Ass*, arrives in the town of Hypata in Thessaly, he inquires at a public inn for the home of Milo. Lucius is previously unacquainted with Milo, but a friend has provided him with a letter of introduction. The old woman who directs Lucius to Milo's house notes as a sign of Milo's meanness that, although he is a wealthy man, the only inhabitants of his house are his wife and a single female slave. Lucius knocks at Milo's gate and his knocking brings the slave, Photis, to the gate. The rudeness of the house is apparent in her interrogation of the visitor. When Lucius presents her with the letter of introduction, she again bars the gate as she brings the letter inside to Milo.[1] Acts of the Apostles presents a scene with similar details, set in another urban environment in the Eastern Empire, Jerusalem. After King Herod orders the killing of James, the brother of John, he orders the arrest of Peter. The night before Peter is scheduled to appear before Herod, an angel appears in his cell and releases his chains. The angel leads Peter past the guards. The iron gate opens for them, and they go into the city. Realizing where he is, Peter proceeds to the house of his fellow believer Mary. A prayer meeting is in progress at her house. When Peter pounds on the gate, Rhoda, a slave, arrives at the gate to see who is causing the disturbance. Like Photis, she leaves the visitor at the gate while she runs into the house to report the appearance of the visitor, although the text attributes her behavior not to rudeness but to flustered joy (12:2–14).[2]

The appearance of these two slaves when visitors knock at the gates of the houses in which they dwell ushers us into the world of urban slaves in the Eastern Empire. Both Photis and Rhoda live in modest slaveholding establishments. Households with a hundred or more slaves existed but were far less numerous than smaller slaveholding establishments, families that held one or two slaves or a half dozen slaves. In contrast to the miserly Milo with his single slave, the traveler Lucius is eventually joined even on his travels by two of his own slaves, who follow him on foot. Milo's hospitality to Lucius extends to these two slaves. This is only a minor act of generosity; hosting a few extra slaves causes Milo little trouble. Apuleius mentions the crude mattress shared by Lucius's slaves when its relocation to a place in the courtyard farther from Lucius's door signals that Photis has been preparing for an evening of erotic activity with the visitor. One of these slaves later arises from a heap of straw in the stable to beat a troublesome ass, whom he fails to recognize as his master, Lucius, transformed. Acts of the Apostles does not specify the extent of Mary's slaveholdings, but we may infer that she does not have an opulent household. Rhoda does not seem to be exclusively a gatekeeper: she must come to the gate when she hears the knocking.

By contrast, a grander household would feature a slave for whom gatekeeping was an exclusive duty. For example, in the Gospel of John a woman who seems only to serve as a gatekeeper guards the entrance to the high priest's complex.[3] The *Acts of Paul* includes a reference to the enslaved doorkeeper of Thecla's household because he serves as a witness to her nocturnal comings and goings.[4] Seneca remarks on a surly door-keeper who expects visitors to drop a small coin in his hand as he lets them cross the threshold. The wise visitor placates the doorkeeper, says Seneca, "as one quiets a dog by tossing him food."[5]

Gatekeepers, cup bearers, hairdressers, *paedagōgi* accompanying young masters through the streets to school—roles played by domestic slaves in antiquity may seem at odds with images of slaves' work influenced by the paradigm of heavy slave labor on the cotton-producing plantations of the American South. Domestic slaves did not always contribute to the wealth of the household, while the costs of maintaining the household increased with every slave. ("The only servant he [the miserly Milo] feeds is one young girl," says the innkeeper as she supplies the traveler Lucius with information about his prospective host.[6]) Reliance on slaves as a source of wealth or income, however, is only one dimension of the anthropology of slavery.[7] Paul Bohannan, who defines slavery in terms of a servile antikinship relationship in which the slave is subject to sale, notes: "The content of the master-slave relationship may vary greatly. One or the other aspect may be emphasized: economic, domestic, religious, sexual, or whatever. Any attempt to classify systems of servility in terms of the economic obligations and positions of the slave is to assume that this one point provides an index for the rest, when in fact such a situation must be shown empirically to exist or not to exist."[8]

Pauline Christianity was an urban phenomenon. The relationships of slavery with which Paul was acquainted would have been principally the relationships of urban slavery. Slaves in Corinth or Philippi would not have been miners or agricultural laborers but, for example, craftspeople, prostitutes, managerial agents, and domestic slaves, including those whose domestic duties included sexual obligations. How would a new identity as a Christian affect an urban slave, and how did the presence of slaves and slaveholders in the population affect the growth and practices of the churches? Ancient understandings of slaves as bodies will again inform my analysis. I situate the slaves and slaveholding households of the Pauline orbit in the context of the practices of slavery in the early Empire before I narrow my focus to a consideration of the (in)compatibility between enslaved and thus sexually vulnerable bodies and the strictures of purity demanded within the Christian body.

A Walk through the Streets of a Provincial City

Who were the slaves that Paul encountered in the course of his travels? Where and in what contexts did he encounter them? Acts of the Apostles includes one account of a slave whom Paul met in the streets of Philippi. The unnamed female slave (*paidiskē*) was possessed by a "Pythian" spirit, who spoke through her. The slave's oracular powers were a source of income to her owners and a source of annoyance to Paul and his companions. The woman followed after them, calling out that they were "slaves of the most High God." A first-century traveler like Paul would not have been surprised to run across a fortune-teller plying her trade in the street. Fortune-telling was a common phenomenon in antiquity. Scraps of papyri record the questions that unknown persons from antiquity posed to fortune-tellers: questions about love and marriage, trade, gambling, and childbirth.[9] Residents of Mediterranean cities would routinely have chanced on fortune-tellers. In *The Golden Ass*, for example, Lucius tells Milo of the predictions he received from an itinerant fortune-teller, and Milo replies by sharing the story of his own encounter with the same seer.[10] According to Acts of the Apostles, Paul responded to the enslaved fortune-teller by performing an exorcism, which rid her of the possessing spirit and thus deprived her owners of a sure source of revenue.[11]

The slave practiced her lucrative trade publicly, in the streets. Evidence that female slaves and other women of humble status moved freely in urban streets and squares modifies the scholarly generalization that public spaces were "male" whereas private spaces were "female." In the Hellenistic Jewish narrative of Judith, for example, Judith's confinement to her home at the beginning and end of the story establishes her status as a respectable free woman of considerable means. It seems natural, however, for her female slave to travel through the streets, with no apparent companion, to invite the elders to a meeting in Judith's house. In an article on Jesus' conversation with the Samaritan woman at the well (John 4), Jerome Neyrey argues that the woman's presence in a public space, at noon, and engaged in conversation with a stranger, marked her as "deviant." Neyrey's assessment of the Samaritan woman as deviant because of her presence in a public place at midday can only be sustained if we label as deviant all women of lower statuses (slaves, freedwomen, poor freeborn laborers), a considerable percentage of the female population. To support his characterization of a cultural division between public/male and private/female spaces, Neyrey quotes Philo: "Market-places and council-halls and law-courts and gatherings and meetings where a large number of people are assembled, and open-air life with full scope for discussion and action—all these are suitable to men. . . . The women are best suited to the indoor life which never strays from the house, within which the middle door is taken by the maidens as their boundary, and the outer door by those who have reached full womanhood."[12] Neyrey fails to note that Philo's articulation of the division between male and female worlds was expressly marked by status considerations. According to Philo, the woman who confined herself to her home except when she went to temple and then chose the hours when the market would be quiet deserved the honorable name of "freeborn lady" (Greek, *eleuthera*). Other literary references that associate women with interior spaces reinforce the impression that gender segregation was a phenomenon based on status and class. In the *Acts of Thomas*, for example, Charisius asks his wife sadly, "Why did you not have regard to your position as a *free woman* [emphasis added] and remain in your house, but go out and listen to vain words?"[13] Indeed, Philo's commentary on the symbolic division between male and female spheres devolves into a condemnation of women who behave in unseemly ways in public spaces, specifically, women who argue and fight in the marketplace.[14] Philo's censure hinges on the everyday presence of women in markets and other public places—and many of the women buying, selling, bargaining, and fighting in the marketplace would have been slaves.

As Paul traveled from city to city, then, he would have found it impossible to avoid contact with slaves. When he went to the marketplace to find other craftspeople or to purchase food for dinner he would have mingled with both male and female slaves. A wide variety of evidence attests to the ubiquitous presence of slaves in marketplaces. In the *Life of Aesop*, for example, the slaveholder Xanthus orders his slave Aesop to cook dinner for a gathering of his pupils. Not only does Aesop serve as cook, he also goes to the marketplace to buy the provisions for the meal. The other shoppers he encounters in the marketplace would have included male and female slaves, freedmen and freed-women, as well as freeborn folk of the lower economic strata. The merchants would have been of equally modest status. Funeral epitaphs of slaves as well as freedmen and freedwomen list such occupations as fishmonger, salt vendor, and grain merchant.[15] Kathleen E. Corley has argued that the saying of Jesus comparing his generation to children in the marketplace may refer more plausibly to slaves sent by their owners to the marketplace to look for work as entertainers at a banquet.[16] "They are like children [*paidiois*, which Corley proposes translating as "slaves"] sitting in the marketplace and calling to one another, 'We played the flute for you, and you did not dance.'"[17] Paul would have encountered slaves in the homes of the men and women who offered him hospitality. Even before he entered those homes, however, he would have interacted with slaves as he made his way around urban streets throughout the Empire.

Working Bodies: Occupations of Slaves

Slaves could be found in every occupation in Greco-Roman cities.[18] The men who maintained the furnaces in the baths were often slaves. The women who served beer in beer shops were often slaves and, for that matter, often prostitutes. Slaves worked in pottery factories and on farms, in mines and as shepherds. In smaller establishments a slave might have multiple jobs. Slaveholders provided official notifications of the deaths of slaves in order to avoid capitation taxes. These death notices typically referred to the slave's trade. They sometimes stated the deceased slave was not skilled in any particular trade.[19] The staffs of larger households included slaves who managed the accounts and oversaw other slaves as well as slaves who carried household waste to public dump sites.

Evidence is extensive for the involvement of slaves in the production of commodities, where they typically worked alongside free laborers. For example, during the early Empire, Arezzo was a center for the manufacture of red-glazed pottery. In workshops ranging in size from a dozen to sixty workers, slaves crafted pottery, which they marked with their own names.[20] Slaves were ubiquitous in all ranks of garment workers, from weavers to dyers to seamstresses. Papyri that listed the occupations of slaves often cited weaving as a trade. An early third-century guardian's account of the financial status of his wards, two minor boys, listed the wages earned by a female slave employed as a weaver. The text's modern editor notes that the slave's wages were sufficient to lift the account into the profitable range.[21] A sheaf of apprenticeship contracts suggests that slaveholders often sent female slaves, less often male slaves, to learn the trade of weaving.[22] Such contracts delineated responsibilities for feeding and clothing the enslaved apprentice and specified the holidays the slave would enjoy while working under the weaver. Benefits to the slaveholder were multiple. The slaveholder received remuneration for the slave's labor during the time of the apprenticeship. At the same time, the slave became more valuable to the slaveholder as she became more skillful in the designated craft.

Along with labor in workshops, fields, and markets, slaves advanced their owners' financial ends through serving as financial agents and managers of all kinds. Ostraca document the activities of slaves who served as financial agents, often with some autonomy. At least in Egypt, Roman families living abroad, including members of the imperial family, were most likely to rely on slaves as agents.[23] Jesus alluded in the parables to slaves who managed other slaves, some serving their owners more faithfully than others.[24] As overseers, slaves could exercise considerable power over other slaves within the household, but even outside the structure of the household a slave could manage a slaveholder's fortune. A well-documented example of a slave heavily involved in financial management comes from a villa in the vicinity of Pompeii. Wax tablets excavated there record the activities of a slave named Hesychus, who acted as his owner's agent in loaning 10,000 sesterces to an importer of foodstuffs named C. Novius Eunus. Hesychus also coordinated the rental of extensive food storage facilities. Moreover, this trove of tablets reveals some of the material benefits that could accrue to a slave entrusted with financial affairs. Within months of expediting his master's loan in 37 C.E., Hesychus became a creditor in his own right through a loan of 3,000 sesterces to C. Novius Eunus.[25] Only a minority of slaves had such lucrative opportunities. The overseer parables, for example, call attention to the (praiseworthy or culpable) activities of the slave entrusted with affairs of the household. The parables allude to a greater number of other household slaves, under the supervision of the overseer, who held less-responsible positions. The ascendancy of a Hesychus was thus neither a norm for slaves nor an anomaly. (Chapter four, which analyzes the parabolic figure of the slave, examines at greater length the evidence regarding managerial slaves.)

It is difficult to assign a single job title to capture the work obligations of a slave in a small slaveholding establishment. A second-century contract from Oxyrhynchus gives an idea of the range of duties a slave who belonged to a more humble master or mistress might have to perform. Glaukos leased his slave Tapontos, a weaver, to Achillas for a period of a year. The lease specified that Achillas would be responsible for Tapontos day and night. However, Glaukos retained the right to send for Tapontos during the night to make bread.[26] Clearly, Glaukos's establishment was not large enough to include a full-time baker, as one would expect to find in a wealthy household.

Our sources typically distinguish between urban and rural slaves. The opening act of Plautus's *Mostellaria*, for example, features banter between a country-bumpkin slave and a scheming city slave with a superior attitude. The distinction between urban slaves, belonging to the *familia urbana*, and rural slaves, belonging to the *familia rustica*, was predicated as much on the slaves' duties as on their place of residence.[27] Smaller slaveholding households would not have included sufficient staff to maintain this demarcation. The Gospel of Luke includes a parable of Jesus in which an agricultural slave doubles as a cook and domestic attendant: "Who among you would say to your slave who has just come in from plowing or tending sheep in the field, 'Come here at once and take your place at the table'? Would you not rather say to him, 'Prepare supper for me, put on your apron and serve me while I eat and drink.'"[28]

Jesus' parable does not evoke a vision of life on a vast estate, such as the extensive landholdings that dominated the landscape in Sicily and the Italian peninsula, but a smaller slaveholding household in which a slave's multiple and varied duties ranged from agricultural and pastoral tasks to food preparation and service. In larger slaveholding establishments, slave labor could be highly specialized. Clement of Alexandria, for example, disapproved of bloated household staffs, with some slaves "to prepare and make the pastries, others to make the honey cakes, and still others to prepare the porridges."[29] Josephus mentioned that Herod the Great was especially fond of three of his eunuchs, each of whom had extremely limited duties. One eunuch did nothing but pour Herod's wine. Another served his food. A third eunuch, who shared Herod's bedchamber, helped Herod as he prepared for bed.[30]

Domestic slaves probably outnumbered slaves engaged in productive or managerial work.[31] The horrors of life in the mines or on the vast agricultural estates of Sicily in many ways dwarfed the indignities of life as a domestic slave. Nonetheless, Keith Hopkins has argued, "Roman literature abounds with stories of incidental cruelty to individual domestic slaves. . . . Domestic slaves stood in the front line. They were more privileged and pampered than the tens of thousands of slaves who labored without hope in the fields and mines. . . . But domestic slaves also had more contact with their owners, and were more often subjected to their despotic whimsy."[32]

In smaller households the very slaves who contributed to the production of commodities would also have been involved in household tasks, including food preparation, cleaning, removing waste, and caring for children. Along with producing clothes for sale, a slave skilled in wool working could also produce clothing for members of the household. In larger households the tasks performed by domestic slaves would be highly specialized. Thus, on a continuum, the slave in the Lukan parable moved from work in the fields to waiting on the master at the table. Aesop not only shopped for food but also prepared and served it to his master and his master's guests. A wealthier household would have multiple slaves dedicated to particular cooking specialties. In *The Golden Ass*, for example, Lucius the ass eventually falls into the hands of two kitchen slaves, one specializing in sweets and the other in sauces.[33]

Descriptions of banquets suggest that elaborate household staffs would enhance the self-image of some slaveholders. The more frivolous a slave's task, the clearer the evidence of the owner's wealth. In the *Satyricon*, Encolpus describes the scene as he enters Trimalchio's banquet, where Trimalchio is playing a ball game with some boys:

> If the ball hit the ground, he [Trimalchio] didn't chase it, but had a slave with a bag full of balls give the players a new one. We noticed some other novelties: there were two eunuchs stationed at different points in a circle; one was holding a silver chamber pot, the other was counting the balls. . . . While we wondered at the extravagance of this, Menelaus ran up and said, "This is the guy who's throwing the party! What you see is only the prelude to dinner." As Menelaus spoke, Trimalchio snapped his finger as a signal to the eunuch to hold out the chamber pot for him as he continued to play. After emptying his bladder, he called for water for his hands, sprinkled it lightly on his fingers and then wiped them dry on the head of a young slave.[34]

Trimalchio has set up this scene as a tableau for his guests so they can witness the extent of his wealth. As Menelaus pointedly observes, "This is the guy who's throwing the party!"

Jesus and his followers encountered the slaves of opulent households on those occasions when their activities came to the attention of civil or religious authorities. For example, during the events surrounding the arrest of Jesus, he and his followers had dealings with slaves belonging to the grand household of the high priest. One of the high priest's male slaves had an ear severed during the arrest of Jesus; several of the high priest's female and male slaves accosted Peter to accuse him of accompanying Jesus.[35] The Pauline letters and Acts of the Apostles include references to a number of households that included slaves.[36] However, on the basis of these texts, we cannot reach firm conclusions about the size of those households nor the degree to which their slaves specialized in productive, managerial, domestic, or sexual duties. We have no evidence to suggest that Paul interacted with slaves or slaveholders in households as lavish as Trimalchio's. Still, when he accepted hospitality from a slaveholder, domestic slaves would have tended to his needs, from washing his feet upon entering the household to preparing the food for communal meals.

Domestic Bodies: Family Life among Slaves

Our sources help us detect the shadowy ghosts of slaves proceeding through the streets of Mediterranean cities in the course of their varied duties or laboring in workshops and kitchens. The sources are less helpful when we try to reconstruct the domestic arrangements of slaves. What kind of quarters did slaves occupy? How did the layout of ancient houses facilitate or impede family ties among slaves? Moreover, how did residential layouts shape the quality of relationships among slaves who succeeded in establishing, at least for a time, stable family ties? Literary sources afford scant cues. Archaeological remains are in need of interpretation.

Sometimes slaves lived outside the households of their owners. We have a glimpse into such living arrangements in a legal petition submitted in 60 C.E., in which a slaveholder named Theon complained that thieves had twice broken into the living quarters of his slave Epicharis, who lived in an apartment of some kind in a house in another district.[37] More often, slaves lived with their owners. Larger houses had separate slave quarters—dark, cramped, far less ornamented than the rooms in which the head of the household received guests or conducted business. Smaller households did not have separate accommodations for slaves. Regardless of whether the slaves had their own quarters, however, no corner of the household was off limits to slaves. Attending children, preparing food, working on accounts—the slaves, who were integral to every aspect of the household's function, would have been found in every nook and cranny of a house during the hours of work.[38] At night, a slave might have slept in a closet that was also used for food storage or curled up in a corner of an owner's bedroom.

The information we have about ancient slave quarters is, at best, minimal. Evidence so fragile cannot sustain generalizations about the quality of domestic life among those slaves fortunate enough to establish (at least temporarily) family bonds. Michele George notes, "The development of slave families is also problematic. In large households separate suites for slaves with considerable responsibilities may have been usual. However, in houses of average size this would have been impossible, and here slave families must have evolved despite proximity to the free household, and in a cultural context with notions of intimacy and personal space which were different from our own."[39] (It seems worth noting that if slaves lived with less privacy than families in modern industrialized societies, so too did slaveholders.) Envisioning the domestic configurations of a family of slaves owned by a modest slaveholding establishment is difficult. Did they enjoy common leisure time? Where did they congregate? Were they able to spend time with one another without intrusions from their owners or, for that matter, from other slaves in the household? The questions become still more complex when we try to imagine the domestic relations among a family of slaves with multiple owners or the domestic relations among a family that included freedpersons as well as slaves.

Our inability to envisage how slaves arranged their family time and space should not be construed as evidence of a failure on their part to do so. Dale Martin has reviewed funeral epitaphs from various regions in the Empire. The dedications of these epitaphs most commonly indicate that an immediate family member (spouse or child) of the deceased was responsible for the memorial. This held true for slaves and freedpersons as well as for freeborn persons. Martin encourages caution, however, in drawing conclusions based on the epitaphs. We cannot easily infer from epitaphs, which employ stereotyped formulas of affection and respect, the actual feelings that ancient family members had for one another. Most slaves from antiquity were not remembered in formal epitaphs, which suggests that the slaves so memorialized represented an atypical cross-section of ancient slaves. Nonetheless, the picture sketched by the epitaphs is remarkably consistent. At least in death and most likely in life, the slaves who dedicated epitaphs to one another valued their life partners and their offspring.[40] We do not know when slave families made time for one another or how they managed to find a place for that time together, but epigraphic evidence suggests that many did so.

Martin concludes that "these [epigraphic] studies illustrate the existence and importance of the immediate family for a significant minority of slaves."[41] Many more slaves, however, lived and labored under conditions that did not enable them to sustain stable family connections. For example, the sexual demands that slaveholders made on female and young male slaves may have strained family relationships among slaves themselves. Or perhaps not—slaves who cared about other slaves in demand as their owners' sexual playthings did not leave diaries recording their emotional reactions to the intimate violation of their loved ones. Studying architectural remains of private dwellings in Italy and the Eastern Empire tells us only that slaves and slaveholders often shared remarkably close quarters. It does not tell us how the resultant lack of privacy impinged on the ability of slaves to construct their own lives and worlds of meaning.

The Head of the Body: The First Christian Slaveholders

Paul's encounter with the slave possessed by an oracular spirit led to conflict with her owners rather than to an opportunity to evangelize her household, although Acts of the Apostles does include four accounts of household conversions. In each case, Peter or Paul gained entry through contact with the head of the household. A dream of Cornelius led him to send two slaves and a soldier to find Peter (10:7). Peter decided to baptize the household when the holy spirit descended on the assembled members, including, presumably, those enslaved (10:44-48). When Paul encountered Lydia, the Lord opened her heart, which led not only to her own baptism but also to the baptism of her entire household (16:14-15). A jailer's experience of God's power in opening the doors of the prison precipitated his invitation to Paul and Silas to preach to his household and then to the household's baptism (16:27–34). Brief mention of the conversion of the synagogue official Crispus notes that his entire household followed his lead (18:8).

The historical accuracy of these summaries is difficult to assess. Luke's theological emphasis is on the power of the spirit at work building the church. Luke supposed that his readers would find nothing amiss when a slaveholder determined the religious practices of the household. Indeed, even contemporary scholars evince little concern about the legitimacy of conversion and baptism of slaves in such circumstances.[42] Scholars debate whether the household baptisms represented in Acts of the Apostles involved children, but they do not debate whether household baptisms included slaves. They assume and assert that this was the case. Moreover, they do not seem troubled by this assumption. For example, as James Dunn reviews the household conversions in Acts, he equivocates on the inclusion of children in household baptisms but not of adult slaves. Dunn writes of Lydia's situation, "Household here need not include children since the term was commonly used to include household slaves and retainers." Of the conversion of the jailer's household, Dunn writes, "It is equally unclear whether household slaves and other adults *alone* [emphasis added] are in view or also children." Finally, regarding the conversion of Crispus's household, Dunn notes, it is "not clear whether a family is in view or simply the household slaves and retainers."[43] Like Dunn and other commentators on Acts, ancient readers would have understood these households to include slaves. Unlike these commentators, however, I think that household baptisms masterminded by slaveholders raise uncomfortable questions about the social dynamics within the Pauline churches, as well as questions about the reception of the gospel by those who participated in the ritual of baptism.

Paul's initial contact in Philippi, according to Acts of the Apostles, was a dealer in purple goods named Lydia. She was a godfearer, that is, a Gentile who worshiped the God of Israel but had not converted to Judaism. Her openness to Paul's message, we have noted, led not only to her own baptism but also to the baptism of her household (Acts 16:13–15). Paul and his companions accepted her invitation to stay with her, so her house was large enough to accommodate visitors. Whether she was a wealthy woman or a relatively small business agent is not clear, further muddied by the difficulty of identifying social strata of ancient society in terms familiar to modern readers. She could have been a freedwoman who first entered the garment trade when she was a slave.[44] Perhaps some of those who lived in her house were slave apprentices. Perhaps she owned her workers, or perhaps they were freedmen and freedwomen.

Ivoni Richter Reimer has advanced the hypothesis that Lydia's house was a "contrast society" in a Roman colony. As a female head of household, Lydia was not a *pater familias*. The citizen *pater familias* (Latin, "father of the family," or more generally "head of household") possessed, at least according to law, near total powers over members of the household, especially his offspring (including adult offspring) and slaves. Despite an earlier mention in Acts of the Apostles of a female Christian slaveholder, Mary (12:12–14), Reimer minimizes the likelihood that Lydia was a slaveholder, seeing her instead as an "independent woman. . . . who provides shelter for other people in her house." Even conceding that Lydia's home could have included slaves, Reimer claims that Lydia's home was an egalitarian retreat: "Because, for example, there is no longer a *pater familias*, there is no more patriarchal subordination, and all can be equal sisters and brothers."[45]

A later papyrus from Karanis offers a glimpse into a household headed by a female garment worker, which hardly conforms to Reimer's hypothesis that a female-headed household would constitute a contrast society. An apprenticeship contract for a female slave to learn the trade of weaving identified Aurelia Libouke as a weaver who had the right to act without a guardian because she had raised three children. Aurelia Libouke agreed to teach the slave the craft of weaving and promised that the slave would attain proficiency suitable for a girl her age. Unlike most apprenticeship contracts, which specified regular holidays throughout the apprenticeship period, this contract stipulated that the slave would be available for labor with no days off for leisure or even illness.[46] The mere presence of a woman such as Lydia as head of household did not, therefore, transform a household from a hierarchical to an egalitarian structure.[47] Richard Saller notes, "Though the head of the household was stereotyped as male by use of *pater familias*, in reality Roman women owned property and must often, in the absence of husbands, have wielded power over households with dependents. This gendered language causes historians to lose sight of female heads of households, even when they know better."[48]

The baptism of her household was Lydia's initiative. Luke does not suggest that the motivations or reactions of other household members concerned either Lydia or Paul. Acts of the Apostles does not present the Christian message as a challenge to slaveholding authority. Through the representations of household baptisms in Acts of the Apostles, Luke reinscribes the power of the head of the household over the lives of those in the house, including resident adult slaves. Chris Frilingos has argued that, in his letter to Philemon, Paul employed the vocabulary of family in such a way as to establish himself as the affectionate and commanding *pater familias* with authority over both slave and slaveholder. In this picture of Christian origins, the new Christian community unsettled existing hierarchical modes of relating among members of Christian households, even between slaveholders and slaves.[49] In contrast, by suggesting that the spirit responded to the invitations of slaveholders, household by patriarchal household, Acts of the Apostles treats enslaved members of households as dependent bodies subject to the intellectual and spiritual authority of slaveholders.[50]

An authorial propensity to identify with the viewpoint of slaveholders rather than slaves may also influence two summaries of the exodus event in Acts of the Apostles that, curiously, lack any reference to the enslavement of the Israelite people. When Paul preaches at the synagogue in Antioch, he encapsulates the events surrounding the liberation of the Israelites without even a cryptic allusion to the coercive nature of their continuing sojourn in Egypt: "The God of this people Israel chose our ancestors and made the people great during their stay in the land of Egypt, and with uplifted arm he led them out of it" (13:17). In Stephen's speech before the council, he represents the kings of Egypt as evil not because they enslaved the Israelites who had been their guests but because they promoted infanticide: A king who had not known Joseph came to power, declares Stephen, and he "dealt craftily with our race and forced our ancestors to abandon their infants so that they would die" (7:19). Although in the nineteenth century African-American abolitionists would celebrate the exodus story as a narrative of God's historical intervention against slavery, these first-century synopses of the exodus expunge any memory of the enslavement of the Israelites.

Paul identifies the Christian community as the body of Christ. Descriptions of household conversions in Acts of the Apostles suggest that slaveholders played a disproportionate role in the baptisms of their households and therefore a role in the Christian body that derived not from a gift of the spirit but from their secular status. In 1 Corinthians Paul refers to a message he received from "Chloe's people," members of Chloe's household, probably her slaves.[51] Since Paul expected his readers to be familiar with Chloe, he had no reason to specify whether she was herself a Christian. She may well have been. If she was a believer, Paul's reference to "Chloe's people" hints that Christian slaveholders had a higher profile within the church than enslaved members of their households who were also baptized, an impression entirely consistent with Luke's depiction of the movement of the spirit in Acts of the Apostles. According to Acts, Peter and Paul gained access to households not through humble members of the household— children or slaves—but through their heads. Slaveholders chose baptism not only for themselves but also for others who belonged to them, including, presumably, enslaved adult members of the household. What was the position of these enslaved bodies within the Christian body? Given the circumstances of a household baptism, could slaves' experiences as members of the Christian community obliterate the disadvantages of their slave status, even within the cult?[52]

Obstacles to Slaves' Participation in Pauline Churches

Paul claimed that membership in the body of Christ dissolved barriers between slave and free.[53] Largely on this basis, scholars have inferred that slave status did not entail any special liabilities for participation in the Christian community. However, because slaves were their masters' sexual property, their obligations to their masters would at times have included actions defined as polluting or aberrant in the Christian body. Slaves whose owners were not members of the church would have been especially vulnerable, since their owners would not have been subject to the community's censure. The argument of the remainder of this chapter has two stages. The first stage analyzes evidence concerning slaves and their lack of control over sexual activity in the ancient Mediterranean world. Ancient texts record acceptance of masters' control over their slaves' sexuality and establish a strong link between slavery and prostitution. The second stage of the argument analyzes Paul's discourse on *porneia*, or sexual immorality, in 1 Thessalonians 4:3–8 and 1 Corinthians 5–7 in light of evidence concerning the sexual vulnerability of slaves.

No New Testament text details the sexual obligations of slaves to their masters.[54] Nonetheless, consideration of the sexual demands of first-century slavery requires that we revise, or at least qualify, our claims about the composition and practices of Pauline communities. Wayne Meeks's assessment that "a Pauline congregation generally reflected a fair cross-section of urban society" has dominated recent reconstructions of Pauline circles.[55] To assume that these congregations never encountered potential converts among the many urban slaves who numbered sexual activities among their duties would modify our picture of Pauline communities in an erratic manner. How Pauline communities responded to these slaves is another question. Either the community excluded slaves whose sexual behavior could not conform to the norms mandated within the Christian body, or the community tolerated the membership of some who did not confine their sexual activities to marriage. The first possibility challenges the assumption that slavery did not jeopardize the standing of individuals in the Christian community; the second possibility suggests that Pauline communities viewed some sexual activities as morally neutral.

In 1 Thessalonians Paul advises as an antidote to *porneia* the acquisition and control of a vessel, *skeuos*. What he means by this counsel remains notably obscure. Some commentators believe that he is urging (male) members of the Thessalonian congregation to acquire wives. Other commentators believe that he is urging the Thessalonian Christians to control their own bodies or, perhaps more specifically, their sexual organs. The Christian men of Thessalonika who first received this letter were accustomed to thinking of slaves as morally neutral sexual outlets. I suggest that we revisit Paul's advice to the Christians in Thessalonika to ask how the first male recipients of this letter would have understood Paul's instruction that each man should acquire a vessel for himself.

We do not know the extent to which the Corinthian community adapted Paul's teachings in 1 Corinthians. I argue, however, that his teachings on sexuality in 1 Corinthians 5–7 would have complicated and even barred the participation of many slaves in Christian life. The passage 1 Corinthians 5 establishes parameters for the discourse, raising the question of what constitutes *porneia*. Paul situates *porneia* as a problem not only for individuals engaged in such behavior but for the entire community. In 1 Corinthians 6:12–20, Paul explains why a Christian community cannot include a man who frequents prostitutes. Paul's logic is predicated on the incompatibility of prostitution with the Christian life. Enslaved prostitutes who had no control over their owners' decisions to profit from their bodies would thus have been excluded from membership in the Christian body. Finally, Paul's insistence that sexual activity should be confined to marriage (1 Cor. 7) posed difficulties for slaves whose masters insisted on sexual relations with them.

In Paul's understanding, could the Christian body accommodate the sexually available bodies of slaves? That is, would the inclusion of Christians who were legally and culturally unable to protect the boundaries of their own bodies have threatened the maintenance of clear boundaries for the Christian body? Or does the presence of urban, domestic slaves and slaveholders among the congregations of the Pauline orbit require that we revise our estimations of the Pauline definition of *porneia*, sexual impurity?

Body Work: Sexual Availability of Slaves

Concerning the sexual availability of slaves, Moses I. Finley writes, "This is treated as a commonplace in Graeco-Roman literature . . . only modern writers have managed largely to ignore it, to the extent that the fundamental research remains to be done."[56] Modern scholars usually overlook the problem of whether slaves' sexual availability affected their membership in the Christian community. The ancient church, however, explicitly considered this question by (at the latest) the third century. *The Apostolic Tradition*, usually attributed to Hippolytus, included in its discussion of baptism a list of those whose participation in the Christian community was proscribed or otherwise regulated.[57] The situation of enslaved concubines received particular attention. Men who kept concubines could only join the community if they formalized those relationships through legitimate marriages. Enslaved concubines were welcome in the community if they had been faithful to their masters and if they had raised their children. (A complicating factor unrecognized by Hippolytus is that the owner rather than the enslaved concubine would have decided whether to rear or expose any child born to her.[58]) Contemporary scholars should exercise caution in asserting the relevance of a third-century document to the first-century church. What is striking is that an ancient Christian source articulated separate sexual standards for female slaves (who did not own nor control their own sexual activity) and free men (who did control their own sexual activity), thus calling attention to a moral conundrum intrinsic to the situation of enslaved Christians, which modern biblical scholarship has neglected.

In Finley's formulation, a chief characteristic of ancient slavery was that slaves were answerable with their bodies.[59] Such answerability manifested itself in three major ways. First, corporal punishment was largely restricted to slaves, and slaves were in constant danger of corporal punishment. Although others, including sons and daughters of elite Roman families, were legally subject to beatings by the *pater familias*, corporal punishment was symbolically linked to servile status in Roman thought.[60] Indeed, the nexus between slaves and the whip is a leitmotiv of the comedies of Plautus, as in this exchange between two slaves in *Persa*:

Sagaristo: Down at the mill I've been promoted
        To first sergeant in charge of flogging.

Toxilus: Oh, you're an old hand at that; you've earned your stripes.[61]

A second sense in which slaves were answerable with their bodies was the practice of requiring all testimony by slaves to be given under torture.

Finally, Finley observed, "The third, qualitatively different and ubiquitous, manifestation of the answerability of slaves with their bodies, [was] their unrestricted availability in sexual relations. . . . Prostitution is only one aspect. More interesting in the present context is the direct sexual exploitation of slaves by their masters and the latter's family and friends."[62] Finley adduced as evidence an aphorism of the elder Seneca, which referred to the moral position of the receptive partner in male homosexual encounters: "Unchastity [*impudicitia*] is a crime in the freeborn, a necessity for the slave, a duty [*officium*] for the freedman."[63] While the (im)moral evaluation implicit in the saying is satirical, its presupposition of the availability of slaves for sexual service is germane. Enslaved girls, women, boys, and young men were frequently sexual targets for their masters. Moreover, as Susan Treggiari writes, "The assumption seems implicit in Roman society that intercourse with a slave, who had no moral responsibility and no choice, was morally neutral for the free initiator."[64]

Freeborn Roman men typically married in their late twenties or early thirties.[65] Since Roman society placed little value on men's sexual abstinence, young men often satisfied their sexual desires with household slaves or prostitutes (who were typically slaves). From the man's perspective, one important benefit of such sexual encounters would be that any children conceived in those circumstances would not compete with legitimate children, conceived later, for claims to the estate. For the same reason, many Roman men chose sexual partners who were slaves or freedwomen after their wives' deaths.[66]

Enslaved women were additionally vulnerable to retaliation from wives who knew or suspected their husbands' sexual involvements with household slaves. While some women may have appreciated their husbands' circumspection in seeking other sexual outlets, a variety of evidence suggests that wives often reacted negatively to slaves who attracted such attention. Sexual jealousy might prompt a wife's resentful notice. A wife might also be angry if she thought her husband had squandered household resources to purchase a sexual partner or to pay for the partner's upkeep. Annalisa Rei notes of the comedies of Plautus, "Characteristically, a wife takes action to avenge not a husband's infidelity, but his violation of the property which the couple shares or which even belongs to the wife entirely. The pursuit of courtesans, both by married and by unmarried men, was not considered immoral in Roman society."[67]

The mistress of a household had a variety of means at her disposal for harassing slaves, including physical abuse. In *Genesis Rabbah*, several rabbis commented on the scriptural observation that "Sarai dealt harshly" with her slave Hagar (Gen. 16:6). Rabbi Berekiah speculated that Sarai (Sarah) attempted to humiliate Hagar by requiring her to carry towels and water buckets for bathing or that Sarai slapped Hagar's face with a shoe.[68] Galen claimed that his mother used to bite female slaves when she was angry with them; Augustine recorded an incident in which his paternal grandmother ordered the household slaves to be beaten because she perceived them to be disloyal to her daughter-in-law, Augustine's mother, Monica.[69] Given the ancient stereotype that women are less able than men to control their passions, writers may have exaggerated the violence of slaveholding women against their slaves.[70] Still, we should guard against the equally distorting assumption that a slaveholding woman and a woman she owned would have naturally presented a joint front because of their shared gender identity. Potentially faced with retaliation by their mistresses, many slaves might have preferred to avoid sex with their masters. The choice, however, was not theirs to make.

In the world constructed by the romances, noble young women who were enslaved in unfortunate circumstances were typically able to resist the sexual overtures of their owners. Still, the threat of sexual compromise was constantly present for them. In Chariton's *Chaereas and Callirhoe*,[71] for example, the title characters consummate their marriage before being torn apart. Callirhoe finds herself the slave of Dionysius, a good man who is desperate to sleep with her. She manages to resist until she realizes that she is pregnant, whereupon she sends a message to Dionysius that she is willing to be his wife but not his concubine. Dionysius joyously accepts. Callirhoe convinces her new husband that the child she is carrying is his. What rings true about the episode is the master's desire for an attractive young slave. However, Dionysius's deference to Callirhoe's sexual reluctance is implausible, as is his acceptance of her marriage proposal. Livy's version of the story of Verginia assumes the inability of a woman with the legal status of a slave to protect the integrity of her own body. In Livy's version, Appius Claudius has Verginia legally declared a slave so that her father cannot defend her chastity. Elaine Fantham writes, "It is telling that Verginius should protest in terms of his daughter's status, 'his daughter would have been dearer to him than life itself if she had been allowed to live free and chaste; but . . . he saw her dragged off to be raped like a slave girl.'"[72] While the romances drew attention to the sexual vulnerability of their enslaved heroines and heroes, the genre's insistence on happy endings necessitated that those heroines and heroes should preserve their chastity through utterly implausible stratagems. Slaves did not have the legal right nor cultural power to say "no" to their owners' sexual demands.

In her dissertation on women in Greek novels, Brigitte M. Egger notes that although the preservation of the sexual integrity of enslaved protagonists is a recurring theme, the romances do not evince concern for the sexual integrity of other enslaved characters.[73] Masters in the romances take for granted that their slaves are their sexual property. The excitement of the stories builds on the possibility that noble young women separated from their protective environments will be treated in a way considered appropriate for common household slaves. So too on the stage. In Plautus's *Persa*, a young woman who is caught in a scheme of her father's that involves selling her into slavery in order to reveal that the slave dealer is trafficking in freeborn "merchandise" worries that even a temporary enslavement will deter any decent man from later marrying her. No matter how brief her period of (pseudo)enslavement, for a short time she will not be in a legal or cultural position to guard her chastity.[74] In Plautus's *Curculio* the slave Palinurus responds with alarm to his master's announcement of plans to seduce a young woman until Phaedromus, his master, specifies that the object of his lust is a slave rather than a proper young woman. Palinurus proclaims, "No one bans or prohibits you from buying what's for sale from this place, if you have the cash. No one prohibits a man from using the public street, so long as you don't cut a path through an enclosed property: so long as you keep off wives, widows and virgins, young men and boys of free birth, make love to anyone you choose."[75]

The frequency of manumission inscriptions that imply that the freed slave was the master's sexual partner indicates the prevalence of such liaisons in Greco-Roman societies.[76] One manumission inscription from Delphi in the late first century B.C.E. illustrates the asymmetry in power that persisted even after a master freed his concubine. Kleomantis manumitted Eisias, the mother of his sons. However, he stipulated that she had to remain with him his entire life, "doing everything that is ordered like a slave. . . . If Eisias does not remain or does not do what is ordered, let Kleomantis have the power to punish her in whatever way he wishes, by beating her and selling her."[77] Far from the respect accorded the heroines of the romances, many slaves (and even former slaves) would have encountered physical abuse and the threat of being sold should they resist their masters' advances.[78]

Resistance of male or female slaves to sexual overtures sanctioned by their owners was not acceptable servile behavior. A scrap of papyrus from Oxyrhynchus records a crude proposition or, more accurately, a threat from two males to a third. It reads: "Apion and Epimas proclaim to their best-loved Epaphroditus that if you allow us to bugger you it will go well for you, and we will not thrash you any longer." Epaphroditus typically appears in the papyri as a name associated with a slave. Here, a young slave, or perhaps a freedman, seems to have two "options": to submit to unwanted sexual activities or to allow two other men to (continue to) beat him.[79] The bluntness of the message highlights the implausibility that a slaveholder such as Chariton's Dionysius would respect a slave's privacy and sexual integrity. On the other hand, for every Epaphroditus who resisted such sexual advances and perhaps even saw them as rape, there may have been another slave who accepted sexual overtures with equanimity. For some slaves, cohabitation with a master or, very occasionally, a mistress was certainly a route to what we would recognize as upward social mobility.[80] Our sources are silent regarding the actual reactions of slaves to their sexual obligations. The silence is revealing. Ancient societies were not concerned with the reactions of slaves to sexual coercion, since the slave had no legal or cultural right to say "no."[81]

Bodies for Rent: Slavery and Prostitution

Just as the typical slave had little opportunity to resist a master's sexual advances, prostitutes who were slaves had little if anything to say about the work their owners required
of them. A suggestion by Margaret Y. MacDonald that Christianity represented an economic threat to slaveholding pimps would require enslaved prostitutes to be in a position to refuse their assigned labor.[82] This is highly improbable. By the late second century, Tertullian even complained that a persecution of Christians had extended to forcing
a Christian woman into prostitution, the first known instance of a practice that lasted
until the fourth century.[83] Aline Rousselle asks, "Can we say that slaves and prostitutes
enjoyed sexual freedom in this sense when we know that the *leno*, or procurer, took
them to the ports when he heard that a ship had arrived? We should not imagine that
all the young girls who were abandoned and then brought up to be slaves or prostitutes
or both, and later freed by a procurer, were *demi-mondaines*."[84] Roman law and custom
suggested that female prostitutes enjoyed a sexual freedom parallel to that of men, but
such freedom was more apparent than real. Prostitutes did not choose their sexual partners; they were chosen as sexual partners. In his work on prostitution in ancient Rome,
Thomas A. J. McGinn concludes, "This is a reflection of the unequal distribution of
power implicit in the exchange of sex for money, an inequality especially notable when
the woman [or the male prostitute] is a slave."[85]

Roman law recognized the validity of certain restrictive covenants in the sale of slaves.
One of those covenants, *ne serva prostituator*, forbade the buyer (including subsequent
buyers) from forcing the slave into prostitution. A buyer who violated a *ne serva prostituator*
covenant faced several potential penalties. In some instances the seller would reclaim
ownership of the slave. In other instances the buyer would be forced to pay a financial
penalty to the seller, who presumably had taken a financial loss in selling the slave under
a restrictive covenant. In still other instances the slave would be manumitted as a Junian
Latin, without benefit of citizenship. Although the *ne serva prostituator* covenant bene-
fited the slave, the law was essentially concerned with the rights of the original vendor.[86] Why would a slaveholder impose the *ne serva prostituator* covenant? Slaveholders
may have had widely divergent motivations. A promise that a slave would never be
prostituted could function as either an incentive or a reward for hard work. A slaveholder
who sold his lover could be reluctant for that person to become a prostitute. A slaveholder
who sold a son or daughter might have some qualms about the prostitution of his progeny. A slaveholder who sold a slave who had worked as an intimate attendant for his
wife might feel that the slave's later work as a prostitute could taint the household. Some
slaveholders may have been genuinely concerned about the well-being of slaves with
whom they had interacted on a daily basis. All of this, however, is speculation, since
slaveholders did not record their reasons for imposing the covenant.

The very existence of such covenants highlights Roman awareness both that many
slaveholders compelled their slaves to work as prostitutes and that slaves were not themselves in a position to resist such work. Dio Chrysostom described newly enslaved women
forced to work as prostitutes who "feel shame and revulsion."[87] Slaves would have been
aware that the decision whether or not to prostitute them belonged to the master. McGinn
points to the practice of forcing Christian women into brothels as evidence that compulsion to work as a prostitute loomed as a potential punishment for slaves: "If some

slave women might be rewarded for their loyal service through exemption from forced prostitution through the imposition of the covenant, others might be punished for their failings through installation in a brothel. We have a glimmer of what might be described as the [*ne serva prostituator*] covenant's 'evil twin': a practice perhaps more widespread as a private form of punishment than the sources allow us to see."[88]

In the Hellenistic world and later during the Roman Empire, exposed infants constituted one supply of enslaved prostitutes.[89] Clement of Alexandria and Justin Martyr warned against frequenting prostitutes for fear of committing incest with a daughter one had abandoned in infancy.[90] Slave dealers had a stake in promoting trade in prostitutes. Prostitutes commanded a higher sale price than other female slaves.[91] Indeed, slave dealers moved easily between the role of *leno* (pimp or procurer) and auctioneer of female flesh.[92] In the comedies of Plautus, for example, the figure of the *leno* schemes alternately to make money as a pimp and to strike it rich by selling a few prized slave prostitutes to men infatuated with them.

Although Ulpian extended the definition of pimp to include someone who maintained free prostitutes, he primarily defined a pimp as a man who dealt in the services of enslaved prostitutes. McGinn writes, "The pimp who keeps slave prostitutes is emphasized either because this type was more significant as a socio-economic phenomenon or because a special legal reason (not evident to us) required this." However, he regards the former reason—the high proportion of slaves in the population of prostitutes—as more likely.[93] Although contemporary scholars do not have the data necessary to calculate what percentage of prostitutes were slaves, all available evidence suggests a strong correlation between prostitution and slavery.[94]

Whether *most* prostitutes were slaves is a more difficult question. McGinn expresses agnosticism on this point but adds, "It is safe to say that most prostitutes in the provinces were peregrines or slaves before A.D. 212."[95] Dominic Montserrat suggests that the documentary evidence is likely to downplay the percentage of slave prostitutes: "Since their 'bodies' were entirely at the disposal of their masters, a slave forced to work as a prostitute would need only to be recorded by social rather than professional status—the potential status as prostitute (or dancer or wet-nurse or wool-worker) was implicit in the designation as slave."[96] In her study of female prostitution in the Roman Empire, Rebecca Fleming emphasizes the substantial intersection between slaves and prostitutes. She characterizes the institution of prostitution in the Roman world as "part of the slave economy, so though the labor is hers the profits are not."[97] Artemidorus's dream logic provides a thoroughly nonscientific confirmation that ancient writers expected prostitutes to be slaves: "A prostitute dreamt that she had entered the holy place of Artemis. She was freed and gave up her prostitution. For she would not enter the temple unless she were to abandon her profession."[98] And she could not abandon her profession as prostitute while she still belonged to another.

Although I am stressing the evidence that links prostitution and slavery, I am not thereby implying that free persons who became prostitutes willingly chose the occupation with any regularity. The documentary evidence from Greco-Roman Egypt suggests that free persons who engaged in prostitution often entered the trade under duress, through dire economic necessity. An indigent woman would not typically establish herself as a prostitute. Rather, another family member, often a father, would set her up as a prostitute because of the family's destitution. Fleming writes, "Female bodies clearly counted among the economic resources, not only of slave-dealers and owners, but also of any family network."[99] Not until the rise of Coptic Christian literature is there any intimation that women enter the ranks of prostitutes to satiate their own lusts.[100] This literature, we may safely surmise, reflects the preoccupations of its authors rather than the erotic appetites of prostitutes.

In 40 C.E., Caligula instituted a tax on prostitutes. This was not a "vice tax," designed with the ulterior motive of curbing the widespread practice of prostitution. The goal of the tax was to raise revenue. The tax was collected throughout the Empire. In Egypt, the levy on prostitutes was ten times higher than other occupational taxes, suggesting that prostitutes (or their owners or brothel keepers) had sufficient income to pay a very high tax.[101] Prostitutes and prostitution were thus common and visible throughout Greco-Roman cities in the first century. Through collection of the tax on prostitutes, the emperor directly profited from the trade.[102] Furthermore, even the tax code recognized that many prostitutes were slaves: in some locales, records specify how to collect the tax from enslaved prostitutes and their owners.

Popular literature of the ancient Mediterranean often features the character of the enslaved prostitute. Fleming observes that "with one partial exception, slaves fill all literary brothels where the status of their denizens is clear."[103] In *An Ephesian Tale*, the heroine, Anthia, is sold as a prostitute and forced to display herself outside the brothel. She manages, improbably, to retain her virginity by pretending to have epileptic seizures.[104] The enslaved prostitute is a familiar figure in the Plautine corpus. The *pseudo-meretrix*, a free woman of good reputation whose virtue prevails despite her temporary enslavement, is a stock character.[105] In several plays (*Rudens, Poenulus*), a freeborn female is rescued by her long-lost father just before her sale by a *leno*. In another plot line, a clever slave arranges the sale of a woman already enslaved as a prostitute to a man who cares about her (*Pseudolus*). These plots converge in *Persa*, in which a conspiracy entraps Dordalus, a *leno*, into buying a young freeborn woman. When her identity is revealed, she is freed and Dordalus ruined. Through the fraudulent sale, a slave named Toxilus acquires the money he needs to buy from Dordalus the prostitute Lemniselenis, who he desires. Although the formulas of the romances and comedies dictate happy resolutions to these stories, the vast majority of enslaved prostitutes in the Greco-Roman world could not reasonably expect to retain nor regain control over their own sexual practices.

In general, Greco-Roman societies expected that men would frequent prostitutes and did not morally condemn them for doing so. Susan Treggiari writes, "Objections to intercourse with a common prostitute were aesthetic rather than moral or prudential."[106] Nor was *moral* condemnation of prostitutes themselves common, although prostitutes did occupy a position in society distinct from that of respectable matrons. In a culture whose definition of honor emphasized the preservation of a woman's sexual integrity and a man's sexual inviolability, prostitutes had no honor to preserve.

Nonetheless, many in the ancient world perceived prostitution as pivotal to the smooth operation of the honor-shame system. By diverting the sexual energies of men away from those whose honor mattered, prostitution protected the honor of respectable families.[107] The Greek Anthology includes an epitaph attributed to Marcus Argentarius: "Psyllus, who used to take to the pleasant banquets of the young men the venal ladies that they desired . . . who earned a disgraceful wage by dealing in human flesh, lies here. But cast not those stones. . . . Spare him, not because he was content to gain his living so, but because as keeper of common women he dissuaded young men from adultery."[108] Dio Chrysostom, the orator and philosopher who synthesized Stoic and Cynic ideas, offered a rare condemnation of prostitution. In doing so, he claimed that many of his contemporaries espoused the view that prostitution was a "wonderful elixir to produce chastity in our cities, your motive to keep those open and unbarred brothels from contaminating your barred homes and inner chambers, and keep men who practice their excesses abroad and openly at little cost from turning to your free-born [*eleuthera*] and respected wives!"[109] Acceptance of prostitution as an inevitable support for the honor-shame rubric was not universal, but many were willing for enslaved women and men to pay with their bodies the price of the chastity of freeborn wives, daughters, and sons.

Traditional Roman religion ritualized the division between prostitutes and other women. Prostitutes claimed a number of Roman holidays as their own.[110] April 23, the Vinalia, was the first of two wine festivals; prostitutes celebrated by sacrificing to Venus at her temple outside the Colline Gate. The Floralia (or Ludi Florae) on April 27, dedicated to Flora, the goddess of flowers and fertility, was another festival for prostitutes. More striking perhaps were the celebrations of April 1, the Veneralia, when prostitutes and respectable matrons separately worshiped the forces of love. Prostitutes (and possibly other base-born women) went to the men's baths to worship Fortuna Virilis, while respectable matrons worshiped Venus Verticordia. As Sarah Pomeroy summarizes these Roman ritual practices, "Thus the dichotomy between respectable women and whores was dramatized: the former worshipping an apotheosis of conjugal ideals, the latter worshipping sexual relationships having nothing to do with wedlock."[111]

These holidays were associated with the city of Rome and were not celebrated elsewhere in the Empire. They are therefore of limited relevance for understanding the structure of religious life in the cities of the Greek East where Paul evangelized. I mention these holidays because they dramatize social (not moral) distinctions between prostitutes and respectable matrons, which pertain throughout the Empire. Roman cultic practice offers a narrow window into the complexity of social relations in ancient Mediterranean societies. During the Matralia, from which enslaved women were generally barred, freeborn matrons ritually beat the single slave woman ushered into the assembly. Scholars of early Christianity often assume the gospel message broke down walls between slave and free. In what follows we consider the challenge that the sexual availability of enslaved bodies poses to that assumption.

Enslaved Bodies and the Body of Christ

Paul was active in the mid–first century in cities of the Eastern Empire, although he also had contacts in the Western Empire, even in Rome itself, where he spent his final days. Those attracted to his preaching included male and female slaves, freedmen and freedwomen, and freeborn men and women, some of whom were slaveholders. Paul insisted that authority within the congregation was a gift of the spirit, given for the building up of community. Nonetheless, as we have seen, Acts of the Apostles records several stories in which Paul's entry into a household occurred when he had contact with the head of the household. Corresponding stories in which Paul's entry into a household occurred through contact with a subordinate member of the *familia* (Latin, "family," implying not only biological kin but also slaves and freedpersons attached to the family unit) do not appear in Acts. How accurately Acts of the Apostles represents the history of the early Pauline communities is difficult to ascertain.

As these communities struggled to define themselves as one body in Christ, Paul specified the limits of behavior, sexual and otherwise, compatible with membership in that body. Given the ubiquity of the sexual use of slaves, Paul would inevitably have encountered slaves whose obligations included sexual relations with their owners and those to whom their owners permitted sexual access, including enslaved prostitutes. In this section I examine Paul's advice on sexual matters in light of these wider contexts. I argue that recognition of the somatic obligations of ancient slaves leads us to revise or modify commonly held positions in Pauline studies. We do not have sufficient evidence to determine whether the sexual obligations of slaves were an obstacle to their participation in the Christian community, or whether, like others in the first century, Paul and the churches regarded some sexual activity as morally neutral. Two interrelated questions structure the inquiry. First, how does a recognition that slaves were treated as available bodies affect our interpretation of Paul's instructions on sexual ethics? Second, in light of what we have learned about the sexual use of slaves, how does Paul's discourse on *porneia*, or sexual immorality, affect our reconstruction of primitive Christianity as a social movement, especially among slaves?

In the late third century, Lactantius proclaimed that Christian men and women should adhere to the same sexual standards. Christian men should not have sexual partners other than their wives, not even slaves. Such an idea was not utterly unprecedented. The Stoic Musonius Rufus, for example, had argued that by engaging in sexual activities with slaves, freeborn men exhibited less self-control than women, who avoided such entanglements. He therefore thought that men should refrain from sexual relations with slaves.[112] However, no evidence suggests that this Stoic advice had an appreciable impact on behavior in the Roman world. In contrast, later Christian writers repeated versions of Lactantius's mandate, although they often acknowledged that the reality of people's behavior did not always conform to these scrupulous standards. Ambrose urged men to avoid sexual relations with slaves in order to avoid giving their wives grounds for divorce. Jerome contrasted Christian with pagan morals by alluding to the tolerance that the latter exhibited for liaisons between free men and their female slaves.[113] Jerome wrote, "Among the Romans men's chastity goes unchecked; seduction and adultery are condemned, but free permission is given to lust to range the brothels and to have slave girls, as though it were a person's rank and not the sexual pleasure that constituted the offense. With us what is unlawful for women is equally unlawful for men."[114]

Does this view of sexual ethics arise over the course of several centuries' development of Christian thought? Or is this view of sexual ethics implicit in the earliest Christian moralizing on sexual matters as preserved in the letters of Paul? Modern commentators have assumed that Paul found the sexual use of slaves immoral. However, unlike Lactantius, Ambrose, and Jerome, Paul does not refer explicitly to sexual relations between slaveholders and their human property. Given the ubiquity of the assumption that slaves were sexually available to their owners with no moral consequences for the slaveholder, we cannot simply assume that Paul's audience implicitly understood that participation in the body of Christ precluded such sexual activity. We must return to the Pauline texts themselves. We must see what they say and, perhaps more important, what they do not say.

In several places, Paul exhorts newly formed Christians to abstain from *porneia*. To assume that this instruction includes a tacit prohibition on (consensual or nonconsensual) sexual contact between slaveholder and slave begs the question. The question precisely at hand is whether Paul understands such relations to constitute *porneia*. Is Paul silent on the question because the sexual use of slaves is abhorrent to him and he expects other Christians to share his perspective? Or is Paul silent on this question because he does not challenge cultural norms regarding the sexual use of slaves?

Musonius Rufus, Lactantius, Ambrose and Jerome all address the moral position of the slaveholder. What of the moral position of the slave? Sensitivity to the moral position of persons who are not in a position to say "no," who are unable to maintain their bodies as sexually inviolate, invites us to reconsider the consequences of Pauline sexual ethics for slaves who sought membership and full participation in the Christian body. If indeed Christian communities understood Paul's exhortations on sexual matters to preclude carnal contact between slaveholders and slaves, consequences would have differed for those in a position to control their own bodies and those not in a position to protect the integrity of their own bodies. Paul insisted that *porneia* was not primarily a matter of individual conscience. He argued that in order to avoid pollution the Christian community should expel any person who engaged in *porneia*. If we conclude that Paul included carnal relations between slaveholders and slaves under the umbrella of *porneia*, slaves whose owners insisted on using them sexually could be seen as a source of potential contamination in the pure Christian body. Under these circumstances, a slave owned by a non-Christian would be at greater risk than a slave owned by a Christian. A non-Christian slaveholder would have found a request that he abstain from using a slave sexually to be laughable.

Still more tenuous would be the position of an enslaved prostitute who heard the gospel preached and sought baptism and communion with a Christian community. The business of a prostitute (Greek, *pornē*) was *porneia*. In 1 Corinthians, Paul reacts with horror to the presence in the Christian community of a man who had frequented a prostitute. It seems unlikely that he would have responded more warmly to the presence of a prostitute. For at least some denizens of the Roman Empire, the conditions of their enslavement would have created barriers to participation in the life of the Christian body.

1 Thessalonians 4:3–8

The earliest Christian document that we possess, 1 Thessalonians, offers guidance on sexual matters. In giving that advice, Paul refers explicitly to counsel on sexual ethics that he had previously delivered to the Thessalonian church in person. Introducing his advice in 4:3–8, Paul reminds his readers that "you learned from us how you ought to live. . . . you know what instructions we gave you" (4:1–2). Although twenty-first-century readers find aspects of this advice to be obscure, the Thessalonian Christians had the benefit of hearing these remarks in the context of Paul's prior exhortations.

The NRSV translation renders the passage with artificial clarity, lending cogency to Paul's advice that is not warranted by his own phrasing: "For this is the will of God, your sanctification: that you abstain from *fornication* [=*porneia*]; *that each of you know how to control your own body in holiness and honor*, not with lustful passion, like the Gentiles who do not know God; that no one wrong or exploit *a brother or sister* in this matter, because the Lord is an avenger in all these things, just as we have already told you beforehand and solemnly warned you" (4:3–6; emphasis added). This translation glosses over several difficulties. First, Paul instructed the (male) Thessalonian Christians to abstain from *porneia*, or sexual immorality. Whether Paul understood *porneia* to encompass precisely the field of activities connoted by the modern concept of "fornication" is unclear and even unlikely. Second, by supplying gender-neutral language in place of Paul's gender-specific language, the NRSV translation artificially abstracts Paul's advice from the patriarchal culture in which he wrote. Paul expressed concern that some Christians might wrong their *brothers* in sexual matters, an uneasiness that derived its particular charge from its patriarchal context. The NRSV neutralizes and obscures this context by implying that Paul was concerned with injuries to men *or women* in the community. Third, and most problematically, in the NRSV translation Paul tells the Thessalonian Christians that it is important that "each of you know how to control your own body." What Paul actually wrote is that each (male) Thessalonian Christian should know how to "obtain his own vessel." While some translators and commentators understand this as an idiomatic expression for controlling one's own body or, possibly, sexual organs, other translators take "vessel" (*skeuos*) as a euphemism for wife, so that the passage would encourage the (male) Thessalonians to avoid sexual immorality by obtaining wives.[115] I propose a third possibility. Paul's advice could be construed as instructions to the male Thessalonian Christians to find morally neutral outlets for their sexual urges. And in the first century, domestic slaves were considered to be morally neutral outlets for sexual urges—vessels, we might say.

Ernest Best notes, "The attitude of the Christian is now contrasted with that of the pagan, which had been his own only a few months before and which he could not be expected to forget completely on becoming a Christian."[116] Reflecting on the immediacy of that pagan context for the Thessalonian Christians, I find it surprising that Paul did not explicitly reinforce a prohibition on the sexual use of slaves, if he believed that Christianity demanded such a discipline. Commentators and critics typically insist that 1 Thessalonians 4:3–8 restricts sexual activity to marriage. David Williams writes, for example, that *porneia* "regularly means to have dealings with a prostitute (*pornē*), but it was also used of any form of illicit sex—illicit from the Jewish/Christian point of view— that is, of any sexual relationship outside of marriage."[117] This reading, however, is a construction of what Williams believes Paul must have meant, rather than a straightforward exposition of what Paul actually said. Paul warned against *porneia*, but he did not define the parameters of *porneia*. As Williams acknowledges, a "restriction of sex to marriage struck the pagan world of that day as odd, for it tolerated and even encouraged, at least in the case of men, various forms of extramarital sexual activity."[118] Indeed, Paul urged the (male) Thessalonian Christians to adhere to more careful sexual standards than those tolerated by the Gentiles. Unfortunately, he did not clarify in what ways the newly formed Christians were to differentiate their behavior from that of their Gentile neighbors. The insistence of contemporary scholars that this advice required Christians to restrict their sexual activity to marriage exceeds what Paul wrote to the Thessalonians.

O. Larry Yarbrough assimilates Paul's advice in 1 Thessalonians 4:3-8 to the proscription against adultery, "which was of course fundamental to Jewish paraenesis, being one of the Ten Commandments."[119] G. P. Carras argues more broadly that Paul's instruction to the Thessalonian Christians to distinguish their sexual behavior from that of their Gentile neighbors was an admonition to follow Jewish sexual norms. Thus, Carras suggests, Paul would expect the newly formed Christians to avoid incest, homosexual practices, prostitution (although it is unclear whether first-century Judaism univocally condemned prostitution), and adultery.[120] In the ancient world, however, adultery referred specifically to sexual activity between an honorable married woman (therefore, not a slave) and a man who was not her husband. Carras's argument addresses the behaviors that Paul's counsel would exclude but does not address those behaviors still implicitly permitted by a call to observe the Jewish sexual code, which did not call into question a man's casual sexual access to his own slaves.

The crux of this difficult passage is Paul's advice to "obtain a vessel." Since antiquity, commentators have debated whether Paul advised the (male) Thessalonians to control their bodies/sexual organs or to acquire wives. Both possibilities present difficulties to the interpreter. What does it mean to obtain or acquire one's own body or sexual organs, for example? While the perfect tense of the verb *ktasthai* could be extended to denote "to possess," the present tense (which Paul uses) does not have this denotation. On the other hand, referring to a wife as a *skeuos*, a vessel, does not accord her a particularly dignified position. Since neither translation is the obvious choice, Beverly Gaventa advocates translating *skeuos* neither as body/sexual organs nor as wife but literally, as vessel, to preserve the inherent ambiguity of Paul's phrasing.[121] Moreover, translating *skeuos* as vessel leaves open the possibility that the Thessalonian Christians would have understood Paul's counsel to be consistent with the pursuit of other sexual options, which did not infringe on the honor of other free men in the community. (I am not insinuating that Gaventa espouses this final possibility. She writes, "Whatever Paul means in this particular text, it is certain . . . that Paul was opposed to all sexual expression outside of monogamous marriage."[122])

Despite the desire of some critics to see in 1 Thessalonians a representation of "marriage in the sense of full partnership," Paul's words do not evoke such an elevated view of sexual relations between men and women.[123] An appreciation for mutuality and reciprocity in marriage informs 1 Corinthians 7. However, critics should demonstrate and not simply assume continuity between the earlier letter and the later letter. *Skeuos* is a term used to refer to inanimate objects, household goods. Ernest Best rightly suggests that the "rendering wife [which he prefers] appears repulsive to modern thought, but this should not deter us if on other grounds it is the better meaning [as opposed to body], for it would not have been so abhorrent to the ancient world with its very different view of women."[124] However, Best then assimilates the passage to the later text in 1 Corinthians: a Christian man is "not to look on her [his wife] as a tool to satisfy his lusts but to appreciate her as a being who with himself is part of God's holy people (1 Cor. 7.2-6)."[125] Best insists that Paul did not want men to consider their wives as tools. Nonetheless, Paul's advice that, in order to control his sexual urges, a man should "obtain his own vessel" does promote an instrumental attitude toward women.

Some commentators cite the concern that viewing Christian wives as vessels would diminish the significance of marriage to support the argument that the vessel to which

Paul refers is the body/sexual organs.[126] My suggestion, that Paul's advice to men "to take a vessel" could encompass sexual access to slaves in one's own household, acknowledges that referring to sexual partners as vessels treats them not as ends but as means. Given the pervasive assumption in the ancient world that slaveholders had free sexual access to their human chattel, Paul's failure to iterate, or reiterate, a prohibition on such behavior is peculiar, but he may have delivered a stern warning to the Thessalonians on this matter when he was among them: "you know what instructions we gave you" (4:2a). Modern readers of 1 Thessalonians, however, did not hear those instructions, and we should be wary of assuming that we have easy access to their content. Perhaps Paul instructed the Thessalonians that participation in the body of Christ precluded sexual exploitation of slaves. Perhaps he did not deliver such a charge. However, an admonition to avoid sexual contact with one's slaves would have been sufficiently countercultural that Paul would have done well to return explicitly to the matter when he urged the Thessalonian Christians to contain their sexual urges.

Against this argument, Paul does admonish the Thessalonians that their actions should be "in holiness and honor, not with lustful passions like the Gentiles" (4:4b–5a). Would a man's sexual use of his slaves violate the holiness of the Christian body? If so, how would a newly formed Christian man come to understand that sexual use of slaves would pollute his body? Assuming for a moment that Paul had delivered such instructions in person, would later generations of Christians, who passed this letter along, have preserved and respected that mandate? I emphasize the question of pollution and holiness because a man's sexual use of his own slaves would emphatically *not* have violated first-century notions of honor. Male slaves were considered to be without honor, and female slaves without shame.

Furthermore, Paul supplies as a rationale for his sexual advice that the new Christians are to avoid infringing on each other's sexual rights: "that no one wrong or exploit a brother in this matter" (4:6a). Scholars sensitive to feminist concerns have resisted the tendency to neutralize the gender-specific language of the passage.[127] Gaventa writes, "Engaging in sexual intercourse outside marriage involves violating the property rights of another male. On this reading, verse 6 refers to the injustice done a male when another male engages in sexual intercourse with a woman whose sexual activity "belongs" to him."[128] However, in the first century, a slave's body, and thus her sexual activity, 'belonged' to the slaveholder. A slaveholder was not infringing on any other male's property rights when he had sexual relations with his own slave.

New Testament critics uniformly assert that in 1 Thessalonians Paul urges male members of the community to avoid sexual immorality by restricting sexual activities to marriage. This is not, however, what Paul says. Whether his words in 1 Thessalonians built on explicit earlier instructions to the community, which specified these behavioral parameters, is a matter of speculation rather than evidence. What Paul actually says is that male members of the Christian community should avoid immorality by "obtaining a vessel." In the first century, many who heard such counsel would understand it as consistent with reliance on slaves as morally neutral sexual outlets. Moreover, the motivations that Paul offers for confining one's sexual urges are, to a significant degree, consistent with a slaveholder having sexual relations with his own human chattel: the preservation of honor, for example, and respect for the rights of Christian brothers.

Whether a slaveholder's sexual relations with his own slaves would be consistent with the preservation of the holiness of the Christian body is less clear.

Paul expresses no concern for the feelings, experience, or moral struggles of the vessel. Does his silence betoken an indifference to the subjectivity of (free) women or of slaves? How we answer this question may depend on whether we assume that there was continuity or development between Paul's sexual ethics in 1 Thessalonians and in 1 Corinthians. In 1 Corinthians Paul speaks sympathetically of the wife's role in marriage, but even there, he does not address a practice that was universally tolerated in the first century: the sexual exploitation of slaves as bodies.

1 Corinthians 5:1-13

Chapters 5-7 of 1 Corinthians constitute Paul's most extended discussion of sexuality and Christian living. Paul cautions against *porneia*, sexual immorality, in 1 Corinthians 5:1-13 and 6:12-20.[129] In chapter 7 Paul responds to questions the Corinthians had written him about marriage and life in the Christian body. Many commentators suggest that chapter 7 begins a new section in the overall structure of the letter.[130] Other commentators note that, as Paul begins his response in chapter 7 to the Corinthians' questions, he takes his cue from the previous discussions of *porneia*. A preoccupation with sexual immorality inaugurates and governs Paul's discussion of marriage. Antoinette Clark Wire argues that Paul rehearses the arguments of chapters 5-6 so that his readers will understand the urgency of his concern in chapter 7. For Paul, Wire contends, marriage is the antidote to *porneia*.[131] What relevance did any of this discussion have for enslaved members of the congregation, who could neither resist their masters' sexual demands nor contract legitimate marriages?

Paul begins his discussion of the Corinthians' sexual practices by condemning the community for tolerating a man who had a sexual relationship with a woman who had been (and perhaps still was) his father's wife. Paul labels the relationship an instance of *porneia*. He furthermore claims that this kind of *porneia* is not even found among Gentiles. He expresses surprise that the church has been less scrupulous than the surrounding pagan world in delineating the boundaries of appropriate sexual conduct: "It is actually reported that there is sexual immorality among you, and of a kind that is not found even among pagans; for a man is living with his father's wife."[132] Paul advises, "When you are assembled . . . you are to hand this man over to Satan for the destruction of the flesh, so that his spirit may be saved in the day of the Lord."[133] Drawing on the metaphor of yeast permeating an entire batch of dough, he encourages them to remove the incestuous man from their midst. In the future, he says, they should not tolerate the presence of immoral persons in their community: "I wrote to you in my letter not to associate with sexually immoral persons—not at all meaning the immoral of this world, or the greedy and robbers, or idolaters, since you would then need to go out of the world. But now I am writing to you not to associate with anyone who bears the name of brother who is sexually immoral or greedy. . . . For what have I to do with judging those outside?"[134]

The phrasing of Paul's complaint implies that individuals and groups could vary in their perceptions of what constituted *porneia*. Even in the first century this was a category open to interpretation. Paul's purpose is not to provide an exhaustive treatment of *porneia*. Not surprisingly, then, he does not address a question immediately relevant to the present discussion: whether sexual relationships between slaves and their masters constitute *porneia*.[135] As I have argued, a positive answer to this question would not have been self-evident to a Christian congregation whose members had grown up in a social context that accepted the normalcy of such behavior.

The target of Paul's accusation is the Corinthian church rather than the individual man involved in the transgression.[136] In fact, Paul demonstrates less consternation about the incestuous man than about the community that accepted and perhaps applauded his actions.[137] Hans Conzelmann suggests, "Paul does not explicitly state the ground of his judgment, because the ground is self-evident: the community is the temple of God (6:19)."[138] The presence of the incestuous man in the community threatens the soundness of the whole, a threat Paul represents with the metaphor of leavening (5:6–8). Paul alludes to his instructions from an earlier letter to avoid *pornoi*, sexually immoral men, and, presumably, women and clarifies these earlier instructions. The Christian community cannot cut itself off from the world, but it should avoid the intrusion of the world into the community. The church is not a refuge for anyone who practices immorality, and he catalogs those whom he considers immoral, from the sexually immoral to greedy persons to thieves. (See also 6:9–11, in which Paul asserts that the Corinthian community includes some who had *formerly* numbered among such unsavory characters. Here, as well, Paul lists *pornoi* before other categories of wrongdoers.) Since *porneia* represents such a threat to the well-being of the community it would seem the entire community would have an interest in eliminating it. However, the boundaries of behavior Paul defines as *porneia* remain unclear. Would slaves who submitted sexually to their owners number among the *pornoi*? At stake, although not explicitly addressed, is the status of slaves in the community.

Although Paul is primarily concerned with the health of the community, he is also concerned with the destiny of the transgressing man (5:4–5). However, he expresses no interest in the moral status or destiny of the woman involved.[139] Commentators generally agree that Paul's lack of interest in the issue indicates that the woman was not a member of the Christian community.[140] Lending credence to this position is Paul's insistence in the same passage that Christians have no business judging those outside the community (5:12–13). Extending this logic, one might ask whether Paul's silence on the sexual position of slaves indicates that he believes that slaves who are sexually involved with their owners are therefore alienated from the Christian body. Wire proposes that Paul is silent about the stepmother's complicity because she is not in a position to be responsible for her actions, either because of extreme youth or enslavement.[141] Wire's proposal recognizes the lack of clarity that surrounds the early Christian community's treatment of slaves' sexual activity, and she may be right. Paul may have believed that the forced sexual activity of slaves was beyond moral judgment. His surviving words do not help us decide the question.

The passage 1 Corinthians 5:1–13 offers a variety of challenges for understanding the impact of Pauline Christianity on slaves. Recognition that Greco-Roman slaveholders regarded their slaves as bodies in turn complicates our reading of the chapter. The first-century category of *porneia* does not map neatly onto modern categories of sexual impropriety. The question of whether Paul thought that sexual relations between slaves and their owners fell in the category of *porneia* (for *both* slaveholder and slave or for *either* slaveholder or slave) is especially important. Paul insists that *porneia* represents a threat to the entire community and not only to the individuals immediately involved. A focus on the sexual dimensions of slavery opens the question of why Paul remains silent concerning the woman's complicity in the case of incest he reports in 1 Corinthians 5.

1 Corinthians 6:12–20

From the earlier discussion of *porneia*, broadly defined as sexual irregularity, Paul moves to a discussion of *porneia*, more narrowly defined as prostitution. In the centuries before the Roman occupation of Corinth, the city's temples legendarily enslaved a thousand prostitutes.[142] The practice of sacred prostitution disappeared long before Paul arrived in the city, but in the first century Corinth was still associated with secular prostitution. Many Corinthian coins bore the image of Aphrodite, a kind of early advertising for a popular service industry in the city.[143] As a port city Corinth attracted travelers, a group well known in antiquity for their patronage of prostitutes. Perhaps it was inevitable that a member of the Corinthian church would find his way to a brothel. In 1 Corinthians 6:12–20, Paul relies on the language of economics and the slave trade to condemn the buying and selling of bodies in prostitution. Given the high proportion of prostitutes who were slaves, the passage raises questions about the implications of Pauline Christianity for slaves.

Paul quotes what seems to be a slogan among some Corinthian Christians: "All things are lawful for me." He supplies a retort: "but not all things are beneficial."[144] Paul writes:

> The body is meant not for *porneia* [sexual immorality/prostitution] but for the Lord, and the Lord for the body. . . . Do you not know that your bodies are members of Christ? Should I therefore take the members of Christ and make them members of a prostitute? Never! Do you not know that whoever is united to a prostitute becomes one body with her? For it is said, "The two shall be one flesh." But anyone united to the Lord becomes one spirit with him. Shun *porneia*! Every sin that a person commits is outside the body; but *porneia* sins against the body itself. Or do you not know that your body is a temple of the Holy Spirit among you, which you have from God, and that you are not your own? For you were bought with a price; therefore glorify God in your body.[145] [All second-person pronouns in the passage are plural.]

The focus of 6:12–20 is on a Christian male who visits a prostitute. Jouette Bassler writes, "The prostitute is merely a vehicle for sexual freedom; Paul shows no theological interest in her."[146] Paul reminds the Corinthians that the body is made for the Lord and will ultimately share in the Lord's resurrection. His lack of interest in the prostitute suggests that, unlike the body of the believer, her body "is not destined for resurrection."[147] Although commentators tend to assume that Paul's lack of interest in the stepmother in 5:1–13 indicates that she was not a member of the community, the thought that a prostitute might be a member of the Christian body seems almost absurd. Dale Martin writes that, for Paul, a prostitute "is not a person in her own right (as if such a thing were imaginable for Paul) but a representative of the cosmos that is estranged and opposed to God and Christ."[148] The possibility that the Corinthian church might embrace women or men still working as prostitutes is not considered in the secondary literature. Wire writes: "The fact that Paul does not censure the prostitutes themselves suggests that they are not to his knowledge participants in the community. Yet most cross-class urban groups would include some prostitutes. Paul does say that many Christians practiced immorality before their freedom was purchased by Christ (6:9–11), and among those could be prostitutes living single or married lives in the community."[149] Perhaps freeborn or freed prostitutes attracted to the Christian message were able to seek other means of supporting themselves, although this is doubtful.[150] However, enslaved prostitutes would certainly lack such control over their occupation. The scholarly consensus that Paul understood membership in the Christian body to be incompatible with prostitution thus has unrecognized implications for understanding the difficulties that slaves would face in joining the church.

The language that Paul uses to challenge the common assumption that a sexual encounter with a prostitute has no lasting effects on the customer has broad implications for reconstructing his understanding of the nature of sexual activity.[151] Paul claims that whoever has sex with a prostitute becomes one body with her and supports his position by quoting Genesis 2:24: "The two shall be one flesh" (1 Cor. 6:16). Such a union, Paul says, is incompatible with spiritual union with the Lord (verse 17). Fee clarifies, "It is not the sexual union that is incompatible with Christ, it is such a union *with a prostitute.*"[152] The believer belongs to Christ as a member, so his sexual activities affect the Lord to whom he belongs (verse 15). Martin graphically writes, "The man who has sex with a prostitute is, in Paul's construction, Christ's 'member' entering the body of the prostitute. Since her body is only part of a larger whole, the cosmos, the simple act of copulation between a man and a woman becomes for Paul copulation between Christ and the cosmos."[153] It is hard to see how, on Paul's view, *any* sexual relations involving a believer could be morally neutral. All sexual relations would affect the Lord and indeed the entire Christian body (6:19–20).[154] Again, the moral status of slaves (including, but by no means exclusively, prostitutes) whose owners insisted on using them sexually remains an urgent question.

Paul relies on the metaphor of buying and selling bodies, of slave trading, to exhort the Christian community to avoid prostitutes. Ironically, Paul configures the male Christian body and the body of the church as objects of sale. The participle that Paul uses to express the Christian's relationship with a prostitute or with the Lord, *kollōmenos* (6:16–17), implies economic obligation or subordination.[155] In Paul's view a man who patronizes a prostitute abridges his own freedom by obligating himself to her. Paul urges members of the community to obligate themselves instead as slaves to the Lord.

The image of the slave market becomes more explicit. Paul informs the Corinthian community, "You [pl.] are not your own. . . . You were bought with a price" (6:19b–20a).[156] The price paid is Christ's death, yet the metaphor also positions Christ as a customer at a slave auction, purchasing the Christian body.[157] This use of language seems ironic in light of the economic realities implicit in the exchanges of prostitution, in which sexual access to a woman's (or man's) body is bought and sold. The bodies of enslaved prostitutes were of course subject to an additional kind of sale, that of slave trading. Paul expresses concern for the vulnerabilities of the Christian body (the body of the individual male and the body of the community) without expressing concern for the vulnerabilities of the (frequently enslaved, usually female) prostitute's body.

S. Scott Bartchy seems accurate in his assessment that "Paul did not want any Christian who was in slavery to think . . . that his slave-status was any disadvantage in his relation to God."[158] Although scholars debate the extent to which "the liminal transcendence of societal oppositions that was declared in baptism" affected patterns of social interaction and hierarchy among early Christians,[159] the assumption that the message of the gospel extended without prejudice to slave as well as free has largely gone unchallenged. However, Paul's insistence on the fundamental incompatibility between the body of prostitution and the body of Christ seems to leave even those prostitutes who were enslaved beyond the boundaries of Christian community. Paul draws on the metaphor of slave trading to warn the Christian community that it imperils itself when members frequent prostitutes rather than to express concern for the involuntary sexual use of the bodies of slaves, even in prostitution.

1 Corinthians 7:1–24

In 1 Corinthians 7, Paul addresses, at some length, questions pertaining to Christians and marriage. Although Paul writes explicitly of the situation of slaves in 1 Corinthians 7:21–24, the relevance of chapter 7 as a whole to the lives of slaves is problematic, since slaves were unable to contract legal marriages. J. Albert Harrill observes that, on the standard view, "Paul's entire response to the Corinthian congregation on marriage, therefore, has little relevance to slaves."[160] At the same time, by limiting the legitimate range of sexual expression to marriage, Paul implicitly suggests that slaves who oblige their masters sexually are engaged in *porneia*. This section considers how Paul's advice on marriage shapes our understanding of the challenges faced by enslaved Christians. It also reconsiders Paul's ambiguous directive to slaves in 7:21 in the context of the sexual dimensions of first-century slavery.

Paul introduces his discussion of marriage by allowing that matrimony protects men and women against *porneia* (7:2). He reinforces this declaration by conceding that, although a single life is desirable, marriage is nonetheless preferable to sexual incontinence (7:9). Continence, then, encompasses both celibacy in the single life and fidelity in the married life; the alternative, it seems, is *porneia*. Although later Christian tradition has often assumed that this demarcation of sexual practice was normative, we have seen that the majority of those living in Greco-Roman cities viewed a wider range of sexual practices as acceptable and ordinary. As we have seen, the master's right to have sexual relations with one of his slaves was not accompanied by moral judgment against the master or the slave. Christian slaveholders who heard Paul's words could choose to redirect their sexual attention to their wives. The same is not true for enslaved Christians. According to Wire's reconstruction, the church at Corinth included a number of powerful women ascetics. She writes, "The life-support arrangements of these women— where they live and what they do—are suggested only indirectly in the various domestic situations Paul describes. Slave women . . . probably retain traditional domestic responsibilities."[161] Wire does not consider the complicating factor that the "traditional domestic responsibilities" of many enslaved women included sexual obligations.

Indeed, Paul seems to assume that those whom he addresses in 7:1–16 could freely choose to marry or not to marry.[162] He offers specific advice to various categories of married and unmarried persons.[163] After addressing those who are married to believing partners and those who are not married, he addresses "the rest" (verse 12). The advice he then delivers pertains particularly to Christians whose spouses are not believers, and commentators accordingly delimit the range of "the rest" to those whose spouses do not belong to the Christian community.[164] Most commentaries do not consider who else *could* be included in "the rest." They assume that Paul's list exhaustively covers persons in all possible situations. According to this view, Paul has nothing to say about the options open to enslaved Christians, who could not contract marriages and could be used sexually by their owners. Commentators interpret Paul's silence about the moral status of the stepmother in a case of incest (5:1–13) and the prostitute (6:1–12) as evidence that these women are not participants in the Christian body. Paul's silence about the plight of sexually exploited slaves could be construed as evidence that he perceives their (compelled) behavior to place them outside membership in the Christian body.

Harrill has offered the intriguing suggestion that "the rest" in verse 12 includes not only those married to unbelievers but also "those not empowered to marry at all unless enfranchised (7:21–23)," that is, slaves.[165] He makes this proposal as he discusses 7:21, which he translates: "You were called as a *slave*. Do not worry about it. But if you can indeed become *free*, use instead [freedom]."[166] Because of the difficulties of this text, an overview of Harrill's position is essential.

He begins his discussion of 7:21 with a summary of the long-standing debate over the translation of the verse.[167] As he says, scholars base their translations not only on the syntax of the passage and its immediate context in the letter but also on their understandings of ancient slavery. These understandings often minimize the brutality of Greco-Roman slavery. Fee, for example, who offers a careful discussion of the syntax of the passage, asserts that slavery "provided generally well for up to one-third of the population in a city like Corinth or Rome. The slave had considerable freedom and very often experienced mutual benefit along with the owner."[168] Along with an analysis of the syntax of verse 21,[169] Harrill provides a discussion of seventeen philological parallels that support his contention that Paul urges slaves to "use instead [freedom]."[170]

He concedes that his translation requires Paul first to establish (in verses 17 and 20) and then violate a principle: each should remain content with the state in which he or she was called. Throughout chapter 7, however, Paul offers exceptions to the rule he has laid down. Although he says that spouses should be content to remain married, for example, he establishes guidelines for spouses seeking separation (verse 11). He encourages those who are single to be content with that status but states that they do not sin if they choose to marry (verse 28).[171] This rhetorical pattern helps clarify Paul's logic in 7:21. He encourages slaves not to be disturbed by their bondage but then offers an exception to this principle: "If you can indeed become free, use instead [freedom]."

I find Harrill's argument that in 7:21 Paul urges slaves to take advantage of opportunities for freedom to be convincing. Moreover, I find it plausible that Paul gives such advice in the midst of his discussion of marriage because he is aware that slaves, who are unable to contract marriages, are the sexual property of their owners. Harrill observes that "seizing such opportunities for liberation would have enabled a slave to escape a master's violent coercion and, as a freedman/woman, to secure more control over his or her own body and daily activities to pursue asceticism.[172] (Harrill does not explicitly address the question of sexual vulnerability, although such awareness may be implicit in his formulation.) Some forms of manumission still gave a master control over the freedperson, but freedpersons were in general less vulnerable than slaves to the demands (including sexual demands) of their masters. (Note that this reading of 1 Corinthians 7:21 does not include any claim about how Paul would respond to slaves or freedpersons who were still being used sexually by their owners or former owners—whether he would believe that such activity excluded the slave or freedperson from the Christian body or whether he would perceive coerced sexual activity as morally neutral.)

However, I do not support Harrill's argument that Paul intends to include slaves among "the rest" of verse 12: "To the rest I say—I and not the Lord—that if any brother has a wife who is an unbeliever, and she consents to live with him, he should not divorce her." With the majority of commentators, I categorize verses 17-24 as Paul's articulation of his governing principle with two examples: circumcision/uncircumcision and slavery.[173] His governing principle, again, is that each should be content with the state in which he was called. To include slaves among "the rest" awkwardly leaves an articulation of a general principle with a single illustration (circumcision/uncircumcision) followed by advice to slaves, which only obliquely pertains to the overall topic of the chapter, marriage. I follow the generally held view that when Paul refers to "the rest" in verse 12, he is referring narrowly to the case of Christians whose spouses are not Christians. In articulating the governing principle of the chapter he provides two examples. As he sets forth the second example, however, he is aware of the problematic ramifications of slavery with respect to sexual expectations and marital status, so he also offers one of the many exceptions that he scatters throughout the chapter.

We have seen that Paul rejects the idea that sexual couplings can be a matter of moral indifference (1 Cor. 6:16), and he furthermore implies that all sexual unions involving Christians have implications for the entire community (1 Cor. 6:15-20). The passage 1 Corinthians 5-7 is marked by a concern for the integrity of the Christian body, which encompasses a desire to confine sexual activity to marriage, a standard to which many slaves would not have been able to adhere. Despite Paul's belief that servile status should not affect one's life in Christ, many slaves may well have found that sexual demands made by their masters complicated their membership in the Christian body. We simply do not know how Paul responded to the situation of slaves who were used sexually by their owners. Perhaps, however, concern over this vulnerability prompted him to advise slaves to take advantage of opportunities for freedom as they arose.

Body Politics

Bartchy writes that, according to Paul's understanding, God's call in Christ "had made irrelevant every particular social and religious status."[174] The assumption that servile status was in no way a disadvantage with respect to one's membership in the church has been pervasive in discussions of New Testament texts pertaining to slavery. James D. G. Dunn argues, "If 'Christ is everything and in everything,' then nothing can diminish or disparage the standing of any one human in relation to another or to God."[175] J. N. Aletti claims that Galatians 3:28 and Colossians 3:11 indicate that there was no disparity in the "capacité éthique des croyants."[176] F. F. Bruce asks, "What real difference could there be for a Christian between bond and free?"[177] In making such statements, New Testament scholars ignore the ancient equation between slaves and bodies.

Even if we assume—and it is a major assumption—that Christian masters did not force their slaves to provide them with sexual services, pagan masters would not have shared such scruples about the bodies they owned.

Although New Testament texts are silent on the sexual availability of slaves, a vast array of Greco-Roman sources assume that masters had unlimited sexual access to their slaves. In 1 Thessalonians Paul urges male Christians to avoid *porneia* by obtaining their own vessels. Accustomed to relying on slaves as morally neutral sexual outlets, the newly converted Thessalonian Christians could easily have construed these words as advice to maintain the honor of respectable freeborn Christians by turning to slaves to satisfy their sexual inclinations. Indeed, it is strange that Paul does not explicitly condemn the sexual use of slaves if he believes this practice to be inconsistent with the Christian ethos. New Testament scholars have uncritically assumed that later Christian rejections of the sexual use of slaves are already implicit in the earliest Christian document we possess.

A slaveholder had the right to profit from a slave's body by forcing her or him into prostitution. Paul's unequivocal separation of the body of prostitution from the body of Christ would seem to exclude all prostitutes, even enslaved prostitutes, from membership in the church. More subtle would have been the problems faced by slaves whose masters used them sexually. In 1 Corinthians Paul distinguishes sexual relationships within marriage from all other sexual relationships, and he encourages the Corinthian Christians to confine their sexual practices to marriage. Perhaps this is one reason he encourages slaves to seek a change in their status when possible, taking advantage of opportunities for freedom. We do not know precisely how Paul responded to the situation of slaves whose masters insisted on sexual relations with them. However, attention to this dimension of ancient slavery makes it impossible to maintain both that servile status was no impediment to full involvement in the Christian body *and* that within the Christian body the only sexual relations tolerated were those between husband and wife.

Paul believes that baptism breaks down the barriers between slave and free (Gal. 3:28; 1 Cor. 12:13). (It may be useful to differentiate between the claim that for those in Christ there are no distinctions between slave and free and the claim that slavery presents no obstacles to those who want to join the Christian body. In fact, Paul never clearly makes the latter claim, which has been repeatedly made for him by modern scholars.) Bruce notes that it would have been easier for Paul than for an enslaved person to maintain the position that slave status was irrelevant for those in the church.[178] John M. G. Barclay has argued that masters and slaves in the same church would have found it difficult in practice to transcend those roles. For example, a slave might have found it very hard to follow Paul's advice to admonish a member of the community who had transgressed, if that transgressor were his or her owner.[179] We have seen that Acts of the Apostles accords householders (who would have been slaveholders) a disproportionate role in fostering the growth of the church, a picture that raises even more questions about the dynamics between slave and free members of the Christian body. Although Paul himself minimizes the significance of servile status, we do not have the coeval words of slaves, describing their own attempts to live a new life in Christ. In a society that represented and treated slaves as bodies, ecclesial incorporation of slaves would have exposed the body of Christ to the somatic vulnerabilities of enslaved members.

3

Body Language

Corporal Anxiety and Christian Theology

In several letters written early in the fifth century, Augustine confronted some problems he perceived with the slave system. What he found disquieting was not the institution of slavery itself.[1] Indeed, in these letters he explicitly acknowledged that scriptural tradition enjoined slaves to submit to their masters. What disturbed him was what he identified as a North African trend toward the enslavement of free persons. The details of his concerns were specific to his particular geographic and chronological location. For example, he asked about the extent of control enjoyed by the purchaser when a tenant farmer sold his son. Such a question reflected the context of agricultural conditions in the provinces in late antiquity, where tenant farming was common, rather than farming practices in Italy in the early Empire, where massive reliance on slave labor was the norm. Other details supplied by Augustine contribute to a picture of the breakdown of social order often seen as characteristic of his period: fathers sold children into permanent slavery. Men reduced themselves to slaves to accept positions as managers, not understanding the consequences of this lessening of status. Perhaps worst of all, Augustine claimed, were the kidnappings that seemed to be happening on a massive scale. These kidnappings were so common, alleged Augustine, that they were reducing the population of North Africa, as free people were captured and sold across the seas into a slavery from which they could never escape: "Whatever authorities or offices have responsibility for this law [punishing those who traffic in free persons] . . . it is up to them to see to it that it is enforced in order that Africa will cease being emptied of its native inhabitants and that in large groups, like a never ending stream, a great multitude of people of both sexes will no longer lose their freedom in a form of captivity worse than that experienced among the barbarians. Many are brought back from the barbarians but, transported to provinces across the sea, these have scant possibility of such a form of rescue."[2]

Each of Augustine's charges invites further layers of investigation. For example, do Augustine's perceptions accurately represent conditions in North Africa in late antiquity? To what extent can we move from his observations of a particular place and time to an understanding of the movement between free status and slave status elsewhere and earlier in the Empire? What I find most intriguing, however, is Augustine's disquiet at the prospect of blurring distinctions between slave and free: "Who resists when these people everywhere and from every side, carried off by violence and ensnared by deception, are led away into the hands of those who bid for them? Who will resist in the name of Roman freedom—I shall not say, the common freedom but their very own?"[3] Augustine's examples typify the chaos of his own world, but the apprehension he expressed over the confusion of the categories of free and slave crystallizes a fundamental anxiety in the ancient world over the stability of the slave body.

The smooth functioning of the Roman system of slavery relied on the ideological positioning of slaves as bodies. As Pliny wrote, "We walk with the feet of others, we recognize our acquaintances with the eyes of others, rely on others' memory to make our salutations."[4] That slaves were more than bodies, that they possessed the attributes of personhood (individual volition, for example, will and desire distinct from the will and desire of the free slaveholder) was an internal inconsistency in the ideology of slavery. Yet these attributes of personhood—in Pliny's scheme, the ability to remember and to communicate—were essential to the value of human chattel. Not surprisingly, then, the instability of the slave body attracted attention throughout antiquity. How to account for the fact that under some circumstances—say, in the aftermath of war—free persons could be enslaved, or that in other circumstances a formerly enslaved body could walk free? Particular circumstances, such as the sale of slaves, the flight of slaves, and the freeing of slaves, forced attention to these borderline cases, instances where the demarcation was blurred between the well-defended bodies of free persons and the defenseless bodies of slaves. If the boundaries of the slave body were unstable, not only could enslaved bodies metamorphose into free persons, but free persons could be thrust into a nightmare condition of servitude.[5] On this view—the view of Augustine and perhaps the universal view of the Roman world—the horror was not slavery. This was not the expression of abolitionist nor antislavery sentiment. The horror was that free persons would not be able to protect the boundaries of their own bodies and that they would be treated as surrogate bodies for others to use as they chose, with no legal or culturally sanctioned means of self-protection.

The conditions that distressed Augustine may have been unique to the provincial situation of late antiquity. I am arguing, however, that the apprehension he expressed over slippage between slave and free states was more broadly typical of Roman thought from the early Empire to the waning years of Roman presence in the Mediterranean. Slaves are most likely to come to our attention at liminal moments: at times of enslavement, sale, escape, or manumission. This is certainly true in the documentary evidence. Such transactions and actions were more likely than others to require some official documentation. People who purchased slaves required legal records of the transactions in order to protect themselves from future claimants. When a slave ran away, a slaveholder posted a notice for return of the slave. Slaveholders who freed their household slaves on their deaths left legal records in wills. Just as documentary records focus attention on these threshold moments, literary and theological sources also direct twenty-first-century readers to the liminal experiences of slavery. Augustine is certainly not the only Christian writer to call our attention to the fragile membrane that distinguished free bodies from enslaved bodies. In a wide variety of ways, early Christian writings participated in the broader cultural anxiety about the maintenance of decent boundaries between the statuses of slave and free.

In this chapter I examine the thresholds of slavery in the early centuries of Christianity, the border instances where free bodies were not able to maintain their integrity and the open windows in the Roman slave system: enslavement, sale, escape, and manumission. The majority of slaves spent most of their lives not in these liminal states but in the closed condition of continuing enslavement. The frequent attention that these liminal states attracts in both ancient sources and modern scholarship attests to their importance as lightning rods for the anxiety produced by the internal inconsistencies of slavery. Finally, I trace the rhetorical effects of uneasiness over the inherent fragility of the boundary between slave and free in the body language of enslavement, sale, and liberation, which permeates early Christian theological discourse.

Em-bodiment: Sources of Slaves

All in the Family: Slaves Born to Enslaved Women

In his *Annals*, Tacitus recorded the events surrounding the murder of the city prefect, L. Pedanius Secundus, by one of his own slaves. In accordance with established practice, the punishment for the murder was the execution of all of the household slaves. The plebeian population of Rome expressed outrage at the extreme response of executing all four hundred slaves who lived under his roof. In response to the plebeian protest the Senate debated and affirmed the extreme punitive measure. In the course of that debate, the jurist Gaius Cassius Longinus defended the punishment as necessary. Tacitus recorded a version of Gaius Cassius's speech: "To our ancestors the temper of their slaves was always suspect, even when they were born on the same estate or under the same roof, and drew in affection for their owners with their earliest breath. But now that our households comprise nations—with customs the reverse of our own, with foreign cults or none, you will never coerce such a medley of humanity except by terror."[6] Gaius Cassius's words draw attention to a basic divide in slave populations: some slaves were born into a household, other slaves the household acquired. Of these latter slaves, some were born slaves in other households, and others had been reduced to slavery through a variety of events, including such violent means as war or kidnapping.

Gaius Cassius expressed standard sentimentality toward houseborn slaves, who (in his view) developed in infancy an intimate fondness for their owners. As with so many other aspects of Roman slavery, we lack the corresponding documentation that would allow us to discern whether slaves born and raised within the same household actually felt such warmth toward their owners or whether their owners projected these sentiments onto them.[7] The majority of documentary references to slaves born within the household are mundane. The information that a slave was houseborn could function as an identifying marker. Wills describe inheritances consisting of one or two named female slaves and their offspring: "my female slave Ilarous and her children" or "Apollonous also called Demetria and her daughter Diogenis."[8] The information that a slave was houseborn could also function as necessary evidence of the history of a slave at sale or manumission in order to forestall other claims on the slave (that the slave belonged to someone else or had been illegally reduced to the status of a slave). At least in Egypt, before a slave was sold for the first time a legal procedure called an *anacrisis* would establish the slaveholder's legitimate ownership of a previously undocumented slave. One Aurelia Senosiris wrote that she wished "to sell my own female slave Isidora also called Lamprotyche, being this year 12 years old, home-bred, her mother being my slave Alexandra, white-skinned, with long straight hair."[9] Many bills of sale recorded without sentimentality the alienation of slaves born within households, bequeathing us glimpses of otherwise undocumented houseborn slaves—from a female slave named Tereus with her male nursling child to "the male house-born slave . . . called Epagathus, aged about 19, with a slight squint and a scar on his forehead, his mother being the slave Isidora."[10] Whatever claims of affection bound slaveholders and their houseborn slaves, those ties did not interfere with the sale of slaves when it suited the interests of the owners. Moreover, slaveholders made their awareness of the reproductive value of female slaves explicit when they composed wills and dowries. As we have seen, in deeding a female slave to an heir or to a daughter given in marriage, a slaveholder would often specify that he or she also bequeathed ownership of the future offspring of the female slave.[11]

By the first century C.E., birth to a slave mother was the most common mode by which a person became enslaved, became em-bodied as a slave.[12] The phenomenon of slaves born to slaves raises few immediate problems for the internal consistency of the slave system, since it seems to maintain a clear-cut distinction between free persons and slaves. Further interrogation of this mode of enslavement, however, shows that it was ultimately inseparable from more violent means of reduction to bondage. Dio Chrysostom recognized this intrinsic ambivalence in a dialogue on slavery between two men, one a free man and one a slave. As a preface to the dialogue, Dio explained that the slave had bested the free man in an argument and that the free man had retorted by taunting his debating partner with his slave status. The two men parried: "A. 'But how can you say that? Is it possible, my good friend, to know who is a slave, or who is free?' B. 'Yes, it certainly is,' replied the other. 'I know at any rate that I myself am free . . . but that you have no lot or share in freedom.'"[13] After a lengthy debate concerning the nature of slavery, the enslaved orator detailed three means by which slaveholders acquired slaves. First, slaveholders obtained slaves through gifts, inheritance, or purchase. Second, slaveholders added slaves when their female slaves gave birth to infants who were themselves slaves. The final method of acquiring slaves, said the orator, was the most ancient of all, but the least legitimate: "A third means of acquiring possession is when a man takes a prisoner in war or even in brigandage . . . the oldest method of all, I presume. For it is not likely that the first men to become slaves were born of slaves in the first place, but that they were overpowered in brigandage or war and thus compelled to be slaves to their captors. So we see that this earliest method, upon which all others depend, is exceedingly vulnerable and has no validity at all."[14] According to Dio's enslaved orator, if one traced the genealogy of a slave through a sufficient number of generations, one would eventually reach the moment in which a free person had been illegitimately reduced to the status of slave, most likely by an act of violence. Thus, even birth to a slave, which was universally accepted as a legitimate basis for enslavement, rested on an illegitimate moment, a boundary crossed between the protected status of a free person and the defenseless status of a slave. Dio's orator concluded, "For if being captured makes a man a slave, the men who themselves were captured deserve that appellation more than their descendants do; and if it is having been born of slaves that makes men so, it is clear that by virtue of being sprung from those who were captive and were consequently freeborn, their descendants would not be slaves."[15]

Little Bodies on the Dungheap: Exposure of Infants

The Christian prophet Hermas began the work known as the *Shepherd of Hermas*: "He who raised me [*ho threpsas me*] sold me to a certain Rhoda at Rome."[16] With this introduction, Hermas identified himself as one of the many slaves who began their lives as exposed infants. Many, perhaps most, exposed infants were technically freeborn but then raised as slaves. That is, when a married woman gave birth, her husband decided whether to acknowledge and raise the child. If he did not acknowledge the child, the infant was exposed, left in the open air. Residents of a village or city knew the places where people abandoned their infants. In Egypt, that location was ordinarily the town dungheap. Slave dealers and householders who wanted to increase their stock of slaves would check the site and rescue healthy infants, who they could legally raise as slaves. Documentary evidence from Egypt features a constellation of names beginning with *kopr-*, a root meaning "excrement" in Greek (the most common language of the papyri). Although these names eventually came to be more widely used, they were first used by slaveholders for the little bodies (*ta sōmatia*) they picked up from dungheaps.[17]

What difference would the fact of free birth make to a slave rescued from the dungheap? Probably none. Even a provincial governor could be confused regarding the status of an adult slave who could prove that he or she had been born to a free family before being exposed and raised as a slave. In an exchange of letters, the governor Pliny informed Trajan that he could not find any clear answer to this legal question that would pertain to the provinces. Trajan replied that an exposed and enslaved person who could establish the fact of free birth should not have to purchase his or her liberty but should be declared free. That Pliny himself did not know the answer to this question suggests that uncertainty regarding this point would certainly have prevailed at the popular level. Apart from ignorance about the details of the law on a basic question of bondage and freedom, establishing the fact of free birth for slaves who had been exposed as infants would typically have posed overwhelming difficulties to adult slaves who wanted to establish that they had been freeborn.[18]

Only rarely did slaves attempt to establish the fact of free birth preceding exposure and rescue. However, the phenomenon in question—the exposure of freeborn infants, who were raised as slaves by those who rescued them—was quite common. Pliny even commented on the frequency of the practice. Exposed infants probably constituted the second most numerically significant source of slaves in the Empire, after children born to enslaved mothers.[19] The option of exposing one's children was so widespread that the widely circulated oracular manual known as the *Predictions of Astrampsychos* included the possibility that a husband would choose to expose his child as a response to the standard question "Is my wife going to give birth?" Moreover, "Am I to raise the child that has been conceived?" appeared as a distinct category in the manual. Possible answers to this question included all permutations of whether the child would live and, if the child lived, whether the husband would choose to raise it.[20] A disproportionate number of exposed babies were female. Perhaps nowhere is the preference for male babies more starkly expressed than in the widely quoted letter from an affectionate husband to his wife, written in the late first century B.C.E. Hilarion began his letter to Alis with standard elements of ancient letters: references to travel plans and to financial transactions. He continued, "If among the many things that are possible, you do bear a child and if it is a male, let it be, but if it is a female, cast it out. You have told Aphrodisias, 'Do not forget me'; but how can I forget you? I ask you, then, not to worry."[21]

Because of the widespread practice of child exposure, numerous technically freeborn persons throughout the Empire would have spent virtually their entire lives as slaves. A newborn infant, particularly a girl, could be a financial liability to her family of origin but an asset as a slave to another family. A fourth-century papyrus recording the sale of a girl gives us the necessary information to piece together such a biography. The sellers are a married couple, Psais, son of Pekysis, and Tatoup. The contract specifies that Psais and Tatoup had picked up a female infant and that Tatoup had fed the infant with her own milk.[22] Tithoes, the buyer, may well have been a Christian.[23] Adult slaves who continued to serve the households in which they were raised might *hope* for some loyalty from their owners or trade on the owners' belief that the slaves must have "breathed in affection" in infancy. The slave Palas referred to himself as "house-reared" (*threptos*) in a letter to Abinnaeus, his owner, in which he asked for sheep for his wife. Palas may have played up his special role as a house-reared slave in order to counteract a more recent association Abinnaeus had with him. Palas also wrote, "I am your slave and don't secede from you, as at the first," suggesting that he had earlier attempted flight from the household.[24] As so often with the documentary evidence, our sources do not give us any insight into Abinnaeus's response to the special pleading of the slave he had rescued as an infant and reared as a bondsman.

Few early Christian sources explicitly condemn child exposure. (One exception is the Jewish-Christian work known as the *Sibylline Oracles*, which condemns the exposure of children along with abortion and illicit sexual relations.[25]) No New Testament texts allude to the practice, although both the *Didache* and the *Epistle of Barnabas* forbid abortion and infanticide, with injunctions against killing what was in the womb or what had been born.[26] Modern scholars have construed both documents to condemn the practice of infant exposure.[27] This reading, however, rests on a modern conflation of infanticide and child exposure. Although exposure increased an infant's (already high) chance of death, exposed children frequently survived.[28] That an injunction against infanticide encompassed a ban on infant exposure is a claim that should be supported rather than merely asserted. Justin Martyr and Clement of Alexandria, for example, supply evidence that incidentally supports the contention that exposed children were expected to survive. As I noted in the introduction, both Justin and Clement claimed that those who frequented prostitutes risked the possibility of committing incest inadvertently, since the prostitute could be a child that the customer had exposed, who a pimp rescued and raised as an (enslaved) prostitute. Clement was vitriolic regarding what he saw as sexual excesses—frequenting male or female prostitutes—but he did not condemn the practice of infant exposure itself.[29] Justin did condemn infant exposure. He claimed that, by raising children from the dungheap, unscrupulous persons raised herds of prostitutes: "But as for us, lest we should do any injustice or impiety, we have been taught that to expose newly born infants is the work of wicked people; firstly because we see that almost all those exposed, not only the girls but also the boys, are growing up to prostitution. . . . And anyone who makes use of these . . . may by chance be consorting with his own child."[30] We cannot ascertain the accuracy of Justin's claim that the majority of enslaved infants grew up to be prostitutes. However, the basis for his denunciation of child exposure was clearly not an equation between exposure and infanticide but precisely the opposite: the fear that the exposed child would survive, albeit as an enslaved prostitute.

Although a free man could choose to expose his own child, who would likely be raised as a slave, Roman law forbade the selling of free persons, including infants and

children, into slavery. Technically, in Roman law a citizen who exposed his child nonetheless retained *potestas*, or power, over that child. He could reassert his rights to his
child later in life if he chose to do so and could somehow prove his paternity. Despite
the insistence of Roman law on the sanctity of free status, we may speculate that free
men in dire financial straits sometimes saw their infants as possible sources of revenue.
If an exposed child were to live as a slave, an impoverished free man might reason, why
not sell the infant instead and reap a profit? Such a situation seems to have prevailed,
in some confusion, in late antiquity. Constantine issued a decree, and then rescinded
it, that permitted free men to sell their children into slavery. Augustine's letters expressed
concern over the limits of bondage into which fathers could sell children, implying that
many free men committed their offspring to de facto and possibly de jure slavery. In a
fifth-century letter a man recounted to his wife the pitiful tale of his imprisonment by a
creditor. He instructed her to sell their *paidion*, Artemidorus, and to send him the proceeds in order to free himself.[31] Was the *paidion* their son or their slave? Either translation is plausible.

These examples, however, date from late antiquity, when in many situations the line
between free and slave had blurred, not so much because of the betterment of the situation of slaves but because of the worsening conditioning of the free poor. Even in the
first century, however, indigent provincial free men may not have seen the sense in a
law that permitted them to expose their children but prevented them from reducing
their infants (over whom they otherwise had absolute power) to slavery. For example, a
free man who had children with a slave concubine could sell his progeny as slaves.
Would he necessarily have understood, or cared, that the law forbade him from selling
those same infants if he had manumitted the mother during her pregnancy? Men would
have no motivation to document illegal transactions. Indeed, they would be well-
advised to disguise the true nature of such transactions. That some fathers during the
peak of the Empire sold children into slavery seems likely. However, any attempt to
estimate the numbers of children reduced to slavery in this manner would be speculation based on arguments from silence.[32]

Booty: Bodies Taken in War

The two most important sources of slaves in the early centuries of Christianity, then,
were the offspring of slaves and exposed infants. Most adult slaves had lived as slaves
their entire lives, since infancy. In contrast to those who were raised as slaves, men and
women who were kidnapped or captured in war experienced the shock of moving from
free to slave status, perhaps the ultimate fear of free persons pertaining to slavery. Rome's
great wars of expansion had slowed down by the first century, when Christianity appeared. Nonetheless, occasional wars throughout the provinces and at the edges of the
Empire meant a continuing, if episodic, supply of captives as slaves. The first-century
Jewish historian Josephus supplied a speech for Eleazar during the siege of Masada,
which emphasized the horror that slavery posed for war captives:

> I would that we had all been dead ere ever we saw that holy city razed by an enemy's
> hands. . . . But seeing that we have been beguiled by a not ignoble hope, that we might
> perchance find means of avenging her of her foes, and now that hope has vanished and
> left us alone in our distress, let us hasten to die honorably; let us have pity on ourselves,

our children, and our wives, while it is still in our power to find pity from ourselves. For we were born for death, we and those whom we have begotten; and this even the fortunate cannot escape. But outrage and slavery [*douleia*] and the sight of our wives being led to shame with their children—these are no necessary evils imposed by nature on mankind, but befall, through their own cowardice, those who, having the chance of forestalling them by death, refuse to take it. . . . Wretched will be the young whose vigorous frames [bodies, *sōmatōn*] can sustain many tortures, wretched the more advanced in years whose age is incapable of bearing such calamities. Is a man to see his wife led off to violation, to hear the voice of his child crying "Father!" when his own hands are bound? No, while these hands are free and grasp the sword, let them render an honorable service. Unenslaved [*adoulōtoi*] by the foe let us die, as free men with our children and wives to quit this life together![33]

War was an occasion when freeborn men and women, who had understood their liberty as inalienable, lost their ability to protect their bodies. Captives of war could not appeal to government authorities to establish their rightful status. In Eleazar's view, a man should prefer death to reduction to slavery and would do his wife or child a favor by killing them before they could be subject to slavery. Implicit in Eleazar's words is the repugnance that a free man would feel at the threat to his honor posed by a wife's conscription to slavery and its concomitant sexual vulnerabilities.

Centuries after that devastating defeat, rabbinic commentators remembered with horror the sale of freeborn Jewish men and women into slavery. In *Lamentations Rabbah*, the rabbis gloss the scriptural line "For these things I weep" by evoking the image of Jews faced with the horror of enslavement as prostitutes: "Vespasian—may his bones be pulverized!—filled three ships with men and women of the nobility of Jerusalem, planning to place them in the brothels of Rome."[34] In the telling of *Lamentations Rabbah*, the men throw themselves into the sea to avoid the corporeal violations to which they would be subject as slaves.

Indeed, after the Jewish War, captives flooded the slave markets of the Empire. We may surmise that at least a small number of these slaves were members of the emergent Christian cult. Military personnel would have purchased many of these slaves and taken them to urban centers throughout the Empire. The newly enslaved Jews and Christians would soon have mingled with the slave population at Rome itself. Roman slaveholders now found themselves with new slaves, who were members of foreign cults or who were perhaps recognized as practicing no religion at all. Prospective buyers of the newly and unhappily enslaved Jews and Christians might well have been uneasy about the religious practices of these bodies taken in war. We have read, in Tacitus's version of Gaius Cassius's speech, a Roman slaveholder's statement of suspicion about slaves who were devotees of foreign cults. Ulpian later held that a slavemonger had to announce the nationality of the merchandise on sale. Jurists debated the question of whether "a slave who, from time to time, associates with religious fanatics and joins in their utterances is, nonetheless, to be regarded as healthy."[35] They concluded that a slave who had a minor history of consorting with "Bacchanalian revelers" but no longer engaged in such activity was not a risk, but a slave still deeply involved with strange shrines and rituals should be reckoned a risky buy. Both Tacitus and the jurists create the impression that Romans worried that their slaves' cultic practices would affect their performance. Purchasers of Jewish and Christian slaves in the aftermath of the Jewish War thus had cause to monitor their activities and alliances both inside and outside the household. The influx of slaves from Judea followed closely on the great fire, which Nero blamed on the Christians, intensifying the likelihood that newly marketed Christians were objects of suspicion in the households in which they suddenly found themselves living.[36] A puzzle: what impact did the distrust of slaveholders have on the abilities of recently enslaved and displaced Christians to identify and associate with other Christian slaves in Rome and the unfamiliar cities in which they found themselves?

Body Snatching

Throughout antiquity, the abduction of free persons persisted as a source of slaves, although kidnapping was not as numerically significant a source of slaves as birth to a slave mother or infant exposure. Kidnapping, however, tapped into a primal fear harbored by free persons: violent reduction to the status of a slave, whose body belonged to another. The seizure and sale of free persons was a standard plot element in ancient novels, in which the typical victims were radiant young men and women likely to fetch high prices in the marketplace unless their beauty betrayed their free and noble births. In *The Golden Ass*, Charite escapes a gruesome death when her captors remember the gains they will realize from the sale of a beautiful virgin to a brothel owner.[37] In *An Ephesian Tale*, Habrocomes and Anthia ask that pirates spare their lives and agree to submit to slavery if they may only live. Such fantastic tales crystallized elite anxiety over falling into slavery. In actual practice victims of kidnapping were far more likely to be indigent people, who could not substantiate their free origins. In a document dating from 307 C.E., the petitioner begged for the return of his wife and children. They had been, in his view, abducted. He claimed that his wife was freeborn and mentioned as corroborating evidence that her brothers and parents were also free. Were they? The couple in possession of the wife and children seems to have claimed that the woman and her children were slaves to whom they had legal title.[38] Such victims of kidnapping, like the faceless numbers that Augustine claimed were regularly carried away from North Africa, lived obscure and largely undocumented lives, rendering them vulnerable to unscrupulous persons who profited from the theft of persons, body snatching. Slave traders also raided beyond the borders of the Empire, importing slaves for sale from Scotland to the Sudan.

During the same era in which Augustine wrote anxiously about the extensive raiding of free persons for the slave trade in North Africa, a former slave who had become a bishop in a land just outside the boundaries of the Empire wrote a letter excoriating a local ruler for stealing and selling massive numbers of Christians into slavery to pagan owners. Patrick, bishop of Ireland in the early fifth century, was born into a Christian family in Roman Britain. His father was a slaveholder with a large estate. At sixteen, Patrick was kidnapped and sold as a slave in Ireland, where he labored as a shepherd for six years before he made his escape. Years later, in a letter to a British king, Coroticus, he described himself as "free-born according to the flesh . . . a slave in Christ to a foreign people." Coroticus had ordered raids of the Irish coast, which stole (according to Patrick) thousands of people, some of whom were murdered and others sold into slavery to the pagan Picts, who lived in the territory that today is known as Scotland. Patrick claimed to know of a custom among the Roman Christians in Gaul of redeeming Christians from enslavement to pagans: "They send suitable holy men to the Franks and other peoples, with so many thousand solidi to ransom baptized captives; whereas you kill them or sell them to a foreign people which does not know God; you commit the members of Christ as though to a brothel."[39]

Patrick's letter holds special interest as a rare document from a former slave commenting on the evils of slavery, but he did not condemn the institution of slavery itself. Several casual references to his father's slaves, both in his *Confession* and in the letter to Coroticus, reveal his fundamental acceptance of the institution of slavery. What offended Patrick was what disturbed other freeborn persons of the era: the reduction of freeborn men and women to the status of slaves. "Freeborn men have been sold," complained Patrick.[40] Was he especially sympathetic to their plight because, in his youth, it had been his own? Exacerbating Patrick's concern for the situation was that another boundary had been crossed. Not only had freeborn folk been sold as slaves, but baptized Christians had been enslaved to pagans, "the utterly iniquitous, evil and apostate Picts."[41] Patrick mentioned several times that those who have been stolen included baptized women. The kidnappers had not respected the chastity of these women but had distributed their bodies as prizes. The theft and sale of freeborn women into a slavery that put them at sexual risk struck at the heart of ancient anxiety over the distinctions between free and slave. Slavery itself was not questioned or condemned. Freeborn, enslaved, escaped, Patrick reserved his outrage for actions that threatened the protected status of the free body.

Abduction had continuing importance as a source of slaves. In all periods of the Roman Empire, pirates and other kidnappers contributed some portion of slaves to the market. The significance of kidnapping as a source of slaves does not lie in the total number or percentage of slaves represented by this category. More important, ancient anxiety over the maintenance of the boundary between freedom and bondage crystallized in fear of kidnappers, even beyond the actual threat that kidnappers represented to freeborn people in securely established and respectable households.

Choosing Slavery: The Question of Self-sale

New Testament scholars are familiar with the thesis that self-sale was a major source of slaves in the first and second centuries. Bartchy popularized this view in his influential work, *First-Century Slavery and 1 Corinthians 7:21*. He claimed that during the first centuries of the Empire, "increasing numbers" of Roman citizens chose to enslave themselves and that this was even a route to social improvement: "There are also cases of self-improvement in order to secure a position of *servus actor*, the chief accountant of a large private household. With normal luck this man could later become a freedman in the same post, finishing his life as a rich citizen with free-born children."[42] Bartchy has continued to reiterate this claim over the course of several decades. For example, his entry on slavery in the Greco-Roman era for the 1992 *Anchor Bible Dictionary* states, "For many, self-sale into slavery with anticipation of manumission was regarded as the most direct means to be integrated into Greek and Roman society. For many this was the quickest way to climb socially and financially."[43]

Bartchy's certainty that self-sale constituted a significant source of slaves is not shared by most classicists.[44] Iza Biezunska-Malowist notes that in Roman-era documentation from Egypt, instances of self-sale are negligible.[45] Keith Bradley does not even consider self-sale in his chapter on the Roman slave supply in *Slavery and Society at Rome*. Walter Scheidel's systematic attempt to quantify sources of slaves includes natural reproduction, child exposure, warfare, and the slave trade (with an emphasis on the cross-border slave trade). Like Bradley, he ignores self-sale entirely. On the other hand, W. V. Harris has encouraged classicists to revisit the possibility that self-sale may have constituted a noteworthy source of slaves in the Empire.[46] Whether self-sale constituted an important source of slaves in the first and second centuries may ultimately be a question where lack of evidence limits our ability to deliver a decisive answer. However, the stakes of the argument are substantial. First, the debate is important because New Testament scholars frequently cite the option of self-sale as evidence that slavery in the first century was not a particularly harsh system. (By contrast, Harris explicitly disassociates himself from the view that evidence for self-sale would in any way mitigate what we know about the severity of slavery in the Roman Empire. Noting that "there is a long and tiresome tradition among classicists of softening the realities of the Roman slave system," Harris writes, "I contend that to assimilate the Roman system to any relatively mild system is a serious error of historical perspective."[47]) Second, the debate underscores the significance of the divide between slave and free in the Roman Empire by underscoring the anxiety of free persons at the potential erasure of that divide. Given the larger implications of the debate, we will consider the evidence and arguments related to self-sale in some depth.

Harris relies on a 1981 article by Paul Veyne and Jacques Ramin, which argues that self-sale has been underestimated as a source for slaves. Ancient sources yield few references to the practice of self-sale, and those references are typically obscure. However, Harris posits, we would expect the ancient sources to downplay the importance of self-sale because "self-sale offended one of the cardinal principles in Roman law, the inalienability of freedom."[48] On this view, the paucity of references to self-sale is due not to the infrequency of this practice but to the reluctance of freeborn persons in the Roman Empire to admit that free men or free women might willingly embrace the status of a slave. So fundamental was ancient belief in the importance of liberty that Ulpian supposed that a free person who was treated as a de facto slave would only reject assistance from his or her family in remedying that situation if "he wished to inflict a kind of outrage on himself and his line."[49] Even so, says Ulpian, the de facto slave's family had a right to bring a suit on his behalf, even without the nominal slave's permission, because the indignity of bondage touched not only a slave but also his or her family members.

Ulpian nevertheless provided the clearest reference to the legitimacy of the practice of self-sale. He wrote that a will was no longer valid if the testator had lost his citizenship. As an example of how that might happen, he suggested that the testator could have willingly reduced himself to the status of a slave "if, being more than twenty years old, he has allowed himself to be sold with a view to performing an act [*ad actum gerendum*] or sharing in the price [*pretium participandum*]."[50] Thus, it would seem to be at least a theoretical possibility that a free person, even a citizen, could alienate what was typically taken to be inalienable: his liberty. Along with stating a minimum age at which one would be able to bind oneself in slavery, Ulpian also set forth what he saw as the two motivations that free persons would have for self-sale. Ramin and Veyne suggest that these two motivations imply that two distinct groups of free persons were likely to sell themselves into slavery. First, since wealthy Romans preferred to have slaves manage their estates, a person who desired such a post, that is, who wanted to "perform an act," could choose slavery in order to gain an administrative post, which might eventually bring some measure of wealth. Second, utterly destitute and desperate free persons might sell themselves into slavery, possibly for the benefit of family members who would otherwise have no means of support.[51] Ramin and Veyne concede that outside of these references to the practice of self-sale by the jurists, references to self-sale in Roman literature are few and obscure. They also concede that the jurists may be treating "an academic question rarely encountered in reality," as they often did. However, they offer an alternate hypothesis to account for what they agree is a meager literary record: free persons frequently sold themselves into slavery, but discussion of self-sale was taboo.[52]

Outside the jurists, the two clearest ancient references to self-sale propose wildly different motivations for the practice. In the view of the Christian author of 1 Clement, self-sale was a noble act, intended self-sacrificially for the benefit of others: "We know that many among ourselves have given themselves to bondage that they might ransom others. Many have delivered themselves to slavery, and provided food for others with the price they received for themselves."[53] Is this text evidence that self-sale was a familiar occurrence? In order to answer that question we should consider the full context of 1 Clement's allusion to self-sale: "Many kings and rulers, when a time of pestilence has set in, have followed the counsel of oracles, and given themselves up to death, that they might rescue their subjects through their own blood. Many have gone away from their own cities, that sedition might have an end. We know that many among ourselves have given themselves to bondage that they might ransom others. Many have delivered themselves to slavery, and provided food for others with the price they received for themselves. Many women have received power through the grace of God and have performed many deeds of manly valor."[54] The letter proceeds to specify the exact referents of "many women": Judith and Esther. Taken out of context, 1 Clement's reference to self-sale leaves the impression that the author was personally familiar with multitudes whose altruism led them to reduce themselves to slavery. Taken in the context of the "many" rulers who preferred their own death to the destruction of their people or the "many" women imbued by God's grace with manly virtues, the reference to "many among ourselves" who deliberately reduced themselves to the status of slaves rings of hyperbole. Moreover, 1 Clement in no way minimizes the difficulties of slavery but rather praises those who were said to be willing to endure slavery for the benefit of others, in much the same way as it praises kings and valiant women who endured hardship and even death for selfless causes.

At the other extreme, Petronius's outrageous freedman, Trimalchio, in the *Satyricon* explains that he chose to become a slave with the eventual goal of achieving Roman citizenship and hence avoiding the taxes that Rome levied on provincials.[55] Since Petronius's satirical humor derives from the excessiveness of his portrayal of the flamboyant freedman, to describe Trimalchio's career as following a typical trajectory is tendentious. Moreover, the effectiveness of the satire depends on readers' recognition that Trimalchio violated a sacred tenet of honor by reducing himself from the status of a free man to the status of a slave.

The works 1 Clement and the *Satyricon* illustrate the two types of free persons that Ramin and Veyne suggest would be willing to sell themselves into slavery. The author of 1 Clement claimed to know of free persons who were so desperate that they would sell themselves into slavery because self-sale was the only way they could provide food for others. Trimalchio sold himself as a slave *actor* or manager, caring little for his honor and much for wealth. The interpretive question remains. Are these two literary references the tip of an iceberg, clues that self-sale was a widespread practice so shameful it was rarely mentioned aloud or in writing? Or should we construe these two examples as unusual and therefore noteworthy instances of a rare practice?

These are the two clearest literary references to self-sale that we have. Other references to self-sale that may be adduced complicate rather than clarify the picture. Dio Chrysostom wrote that "great numbers of men, we may suppose, who are free-born sell themselves, so that they are slaves by contract [*kata syggraphein*], sometimes on no easy terms but the most severe imaginable."[56] However, Dio was probably not referring to chattel slavery but to a contractually limited indentured servitude.[57] Seneca wrote that we only speak of a "benefit" when the doer of the deed reaps no benefit himself or herself: "The trader renders service to cities, the physician to the sick, the slavemonger to those he sells; but all these, because they arrive at the good of others through seeking their own, do not leave those whom they serve under any obligation."[58] How can Seneca claim that the slavemonger delivers a good to the one who is sold? Ramin and Veyne argue that Seneca must refer to a widespread practice of self-sale. The slave would benefit in receiving at least a portion of the price of the sale.

I find Seneca's meaning far from clear. The humor of Petronius's Trimalchio, for example, hinges on the disgraceful fact that he cares less about his own honor than he does about material advancement. Even if slaves received a portion of the proceeds of their sale or gained desirable posts, they sacrificed personal and family honor. In such a case, had a slave trader truly advanced "the good" of the newly created slave? Another plausible reading of the passage is that Seneca referred to a swindle in which slave dealers colluded with free persons to represent themselves as slaves. The slave dealer and the putative slave shared in the proceeds of the fraudulent sale. Soon afterward, the "slave" produced evidence of his or her free status and claimed false imprisonment. With luck, he or she profited from the sale and then walked away as a free person. Again, we do not know how often this actually happened, but the practice is more familiar from ancient sources, both legal and literary, than the relatively rare instance of the free person who in fact embraced the condition of enslavement.[59] I propose that Seneca may have had this tactic in mind when he referred to the slave dealer performing a benefit for his human merchandise.

A saying from the Gnostic anthology known as the *Gospel of Philip* is equally equivocal as evidence for the practice of self-sale: "He who is a slave against his will will be able to become free. He who has become free by the favor of his master and has sold himself into slavery will no longer be able to be free."[60] In context, the saying certainly refers to spiritual rather than physical slavery. Does the saying, however, assume acquaintance with an established practice of self-sale? The assertion that those who are unwilling slaves can become free is at variance with the realities confronted by slaves in the Roman Empire, most of whom could never realize their dreams of freedom. How literally, then, should we take the reference to freedpersons who then sell themselves back into slavery? If we could say with certainty that self-sale was widely practiced during the years that the sayings collected in the *Gospel of Philip* circulated, we could interpret this saying in that context. In the absence of such certainty, however, the saying suggests instead that many slaves and former slaves drifted into and out of relationships of obligation with owners and former owners from which they never wrested themselves entirely free.

Some scholars have suggested that Paul warned the Corinthian Christians against self-sale in 1 Corinthians: "For whoever was called in the Lord as a slave is a freed person belonging to the Lord, just as whoever was free when called is a slave of Christ. You were bought with a price; do not become slaves of human masters. In whatever condition you were called, brothers and sisters, there remain with God."[61] The Corinthians were "bought" by their new master, Christ. Commentators agree that when Paul urged the Corinthians to avoid enslavement to human masters he was urging them to avoid entanglements with those who would ensnare them in immoral practices and was thus encouraging a "spiritual" freedom. Some commentators suggest that with this counsel Paul may also have intended to warn the Corinthian Christians against the actual practice of self-sale. How tenable one finds this hypothesis is, again, contingent on whether one supports the hypothesis that self-sale was a common practice.

Among New Testament scholars, acceptance of this hypothesis is often linked to a relatively benign view of slavery in the first century. Raymond Collins, who thinks that Paul's warning against enslavement to human masters is at once figurative and literal (that is, an injunction against self-sale), makes the connection explicitly: "The slavery of the Greco-Roman world was different from slavery in nineteenth-century America. . . . Slaves sometimes rose to positions of prestige and power. There are even some recorded instances of people entering slavery in order to gain such privileges."[62] Richard Hays, who suggests that Paul's instruction to avoid enslavement to human masters may be a ban on self-sale, also downplays the severity of ancient slavery: "First, slavery in the ancient Greco-Roman world was a pervasive institution, but it was not invariably perceived as oppressive. American readers instinctively think of slavery as it was practiced in the ante-bellum South, but the ancient reality was more complicated. Dale Martin's book *Slavery as Salvation* has shown that slavery provided for many people not only economic security, but also upward social mobility."[63] Collins and Hays, like many other New Testament scholars, stress differences between Roman and American slavery, implying that to be a slave was more tolerable in the first century than the nineteenth century. In their view, that some free persons might willingly accept the condition of slavery contributes to this conclusion. In contrast, in the same article in which he invites classicists to revisit the question of self-sale, Harris contends that North American and Caribbean slaveholders evinced more care for slaves than did Roman slaveholders. In particular, he argues that the conditions of slavery in the Roman Empire—including a high mortality rate—would have prevented the slave population of the Empire from reproducing itself naturally, as occurred in the American South.[64] Like Collins and Hays, Harris stresses the differences between Roman and American systems of slavery. However, in his estimation, the conditions of Roman slavery were harsher.

Where does this leave us? Evidence supports the claim that self-sale into slavery was known and at least occasionally practiced in the Roman Empire. I do not think we have sufficient evidence to support the stronger claim that the practice was common. Unqualified assertions to the contrary imply a certainty at odds with the precarious nature of the literary, legal, and documentary sources. Perhaps self-sale was practiced widely, and our sources are merely silent on the issue. At best, though, the hypothesis that self-sale was a common occurrence rests on arguments based on historical silence. Ramin, Veyne, and Harris argue that the silence of the sources is due to the controversial nature of self-sale.

Nonetheless, if Ramin, Veyne, and Harris are right (and I reiterate that their arguments are tenuous), then the practice of self-sale underscores rather than deconstructs the divide between slave and free. Their thesis presupposes that free persons in the Roman Empire treasured their status. Honor was an all-important concept, and a man's honor was inseparable from his status as a free man. A male slave, for example, was not in the position to protect either his bodily integrity or to protect the honor of his offspring. To be a slave was to be the body of another. Self-sale, however rarely or frequently practiced, offended against all sense of propriety and decency. A free man or free woman who voluntarily embraced the state of slavery exposed the fragility and artificiality of the border between slavery and freedom.[65]

A final piece of evidence illustrates just how serious such boundary crossings could be. The *Digest* warns, "Certain offenses, which bring no penalty, or a relatively light one, on a civilian [are visited] more heavily on a soldier. For Menander writes that if a soldier takes part in stage plays or permits himself to be sold into slavery, he should suffer capital punishment."[66] The "offense" of selling oneself into slavery could plausibly refer either to self-sale or to the fraudulent practice of a slaveholder and a free person deceiving and ultimately defrauding a would-be buyer. This behavior, objectionable in a civilian, represented a threat to the security of the state when performed by a soldier. A soldier who did not have the self-respect to maintain the integrity of his own body would surely suffer in his commitment to protect the integrity of the civic body. A Roman legal metaphor described the diminution of personal status in terms of *deminutio capitis*, or "lessening of the head." In the most extreme case of *deminutio capitis*, a citizen was reduced to the status of a slave. Amy Richlin notes, "It is not that slaves don't *have* heads, but they don't count, as Paulus opines . . . 'a slave's head has no rights and cannot be reduced.'"[67] In the case of military personnel, a free man who did not treat his body as his own literally lost his head.

Body Shop: Slaves for Sale

When great Babylon falls, writes John of Patmos in the Book of Revelation, all the rich merchants of the earth will mourn it. Their grief will emanate from their loss of trade. With the destruction of Babylon, no one will buy their cargoes. John details the luxury wares that made traders wealthy: from gold to linen, from purple to ivory, from cinnamon to myrrh, from olive oil to sheep—to the bodies and souls of human beings. The list thus culminates with a reference to the human merchandise from which traders throughout the Roman Empire profited. By emphasizing that not only bodies but also souls were for sale, John implicitly condemned the practice of trading in human flesh. The slave trade disrupted human lives. Today, attention to this inevitable aspect of the slave system lays bare the pretense of seeing slaves as "a part of the family" and slavery as a humane system. Like other ancient sources, early Christian writings do not challenge the system of slavery itself. Nonetheless, like many other ancient sources, several

New Testament texts recognize the evils of the slave trade. The buying and selling of slaves, however, were not peripheral to the institution but were necessary for the smooth functioning of the slave system.

Brute perception of slaves as bodies prevailed in the rhetoric of sale. Roman law reflected the buyer's obsession with the bodies of slaves who were under consideration for purchase. The law required the vendor to publicize the physical liabilities of the slave. "Those who sell slaves are to apprise purchasers of any disease or defect in their wares and whether a given slave is a runaway, [or] a loiterer on errands," declared Ulpian.[68] Many bills of sale among the Egyptian papyri duly recorded that the slaves sold were free from physical defect. The jurists held that left-handedness, bed wetting, and bad breath were not defects in themselves, although they could qualify as defects if they stemmed from organic causes. Ulpian concluded that bed wetting was a defect if caused by incontinence, for example, but not if precipitated by laziness or excess consumption of alcohol.[69] The niceties of Roman law may have differed from the actual practices of selling slaves in the marketplace. I mention these instances of possible defects to give a flavor of the kinds of discussions between buyers and sellers, which slaves on the block might overhear. Slaves for sale were without honor, unable to screen their bodies from even the most intimate and humiliating scrutiny.

Despite the guarantees of vendors, buyers had an obligation to inspect the bodies they were purchasing. The requirement that merchants reveal the weaknesses of their merchandise only pertained to defects or diseases that were not perceptible.[70] Seneca compared the inspection of a horse being sold to the inspection of a slave. Just as you would insist that the blanket be stripped from the horse, you would insist that the garments be removed from slaves advertised for sale, "so that no bodily flaws may escape your notice."[71] Lucian's second-century satire *Philosophies for Sale* pictures a would-be buyer startled when his examination of Pythagoras yields a mark of semidivinity, a golden thigh.[72] The humor resides in the discrepancy between a familiar rite of purchase, uncovering the body of a slave, and the revelation of the putative slave's elevated origins. How did slaves respond to these corporal inspections? In particular, how did young slaves feel when potential owners undressed them, prodded them, or joked about their sexual potential?

Bills of sale and other documentary evidence from the slave trade cannot help us understand the emotions of slaves on the auction block. While we should be wary of projecting emotions onto the slaves whose bodies were exposed for sale, we should be equally wary of the trap of assuming slaves had no emotions. In a declamation of the elder Seneca, speakers debated the question of whether a respectable virgin captured by pirates and sold to a brothel owner could, after reclaiming her freedom, receive the distinction of a priesthood. The woman maintained that, despite her time as an enslaved prostitute, she had maintained her chastity. The words of one orator in the declamation, Publius Vinicus, offer us insight into the experiences of an attractive female slave on the block: "She stood naked on the shore to meet the buyer's sneers; every part of her body was inspected—and handled." Although he evinced pity for her ordeal, he declared her an entirely unsuitable candidate for a priesthood.[73]

Bradley draws attention to what he sees as the inevitable effects of the slave trade on those sold: "Personal degradation and humiliation, cultural disorientation, material deprivation, severance of familial bonds, emotional and psychological trauma."[74] In the absence of a slave literature from antiquity that would attest to the emotions of slaves, how legitimate is it to draw such conclusions? Bradley sketches the journey that a captive from rural Britain would undergo on his or her way to the crowded, noisy, and thoroughly urban Roman slave market. Over the course of the journey, the newly captured slave would no longer hear his or her native tongue spoken and would very likely not be able to understand the language in which orders were now given. Moreover, conditions of transport were appalling.[75] Documentary evidence affords glimpses into the histories of slaves sold far from their homelands. In a third-century document from Oxyrhynchus a slaveholder officially registered the purchase of a slave. Balsamea was a seventeen-year-old Mesopotamian female, sold in Phoenicia and transported across the sea to Egypt.[76] In another third-century record a slaveholder in Oxyrhynchus recorded her purchase of a slave in Arabia. The slave, originally houseborn, had been sold a total of three times. Such disruptions occurred not only in adulthood. A second-century petition from Oxyrhynchus recorded for posterity the purchase of a seven-year-old boy, Epaphroditus, who had already been sold by at least two previous owners.[77] Athenaeus's *Deipnosophists* depicted slaves as regional commodities purveyed along Mediterranean trade routes. Egypt provided papyrus to the markets. Sicily provided fish, and Aegion provided (enslaved) "flute-girls." Syracusans provided hogs and Libya, ivory. Phyrgia supplied slaves, as did Pagasae. By noting that the slaves of Pagasae were often tattooed or branded (*hai Pagasai doulous kai stigmatias parechousi*), the text implicitly draws attention to the many slaves who resisted enslavement and the practices of somatic marking, which enforced their corporal bondage.[78]

Harrill has outlined the reasons for the inclusion of slave trading in a vice list in 1 Timothy, emphasizing that, by kidnapping free persons, slaveholders violated the boundaries of legitimate families. The NRSV translation reads, "The law is laid down not for the innocent but for the lawless and disobedient, for the godless and sinful, for the unholy and profane, for those who kill their father or mother, for murderers, fornicators, sodomites, slave traders, liars, perjurers, and whatever else is contrary to the sound teaching."[79] Harrill shows that the author of 1 Timothy relied on stereotypic attitudes toward slave dealers to imply that his opponents engaged "in obviously evil behavior at every stage of their operation."[80] In Greco-Roman society, slave dealers were shady characters who sometimes acquired and often marketed their merchandise in dishonest ways.[81] Moreover, in selling attractive female slaves and young male slaves for sexual purposes, slave traders allied themselves with pimps and other disreputable characters. We have already seen that the line between pimps and slave traders was a thin one, when it existed at all.

One question that Harrill does not consider is whether the widespread disapproval of slave dealers emanated from concern for the slaves, concern for the purchasers, or both. If a free person sold into slavery could establish that he or she had been falsely identified as a slave, for example, he or she would go free, and the purchaser would be likely to suffer loss. In instances of sexual subterfuge, such as the use of cosmetics and other enhancements of the servile body, ancient authors seem concerned that buyers would be deceived into paying excessive sums for their purchases. Some ancient authors did evince concern for the young boys who were castrated to increase their value on the marketplace. Perhaps as important, however, these authors censured the celebration of what they viewed as mutilated bodies and artificial beauty. Harrill compares the reputations of slave dealers in antiquity and used-car sellers today: "although the used-car seller functions as a standard example of an untrustworthy and unsavory person, users of the example do not mean to condemn the selling of used cars in general or even to suggest that *all* used-car sellers are so bad."[82] To extend Harrill's analogy, the caricature of the used-car seller, like that of the slave dealer, invites caution on the part of purchasers without connoting any particular concern for the good of the commodities sold, regardless of whether used cars or slaves constitute the merchandise in question.

We know more about the buying and selling of slaves in antiquity from the perspective of the buyers and sellers than from the perspective of those bought and sold. Pliny mentioned casually in a letter, "I think the slaves you advised me to buy look all right, but it remains to be seen if they are honest; and here one can't go by a slave's looks, but rather by what one hears of him."[83] Slaves, too, must have been anxious to learn about the character and temperament of those who purchased them, but they left no record of their anxieties. In a scene from *The Golden Ass*, Apuleius portrays a bailiff and other residents of a country estate trying to escape when they hear of the death of their master. They fear what effect the change of ownership will have on their lives. Even the kindest master or mistress might die without manumitting all the household slaves. Well-meaning and compassionate heirs might have to sell the household chattel to even their shares of the inheritance or to satisfy creditors. Slaves put on the auction block had no control over who looked at them, prodded them, or purchased them. Whatever claims affection might make on masters or slaves, the moment at which a slave was sold was a time when the sheer brutality of the system was evident. We cannot convince ourselves that a slave for sale was a valued member of the family, under the ultimate care of a benevolent patriarch. A slave for sale was a body stripped for examination. Although John of Patmos did not expand on his condemnation of the slave trade, his reference to those who dealt in bodies and souls sounds the climactic note in his description of the merchants of the earth, a note that would have resonated with those who had stood on the auction block or watched helplessly as prospective buyers undressed and jabbed their mothers, fathers, children, or lovers.

Bodies in Motion: Fugitive Slaves

Thick metal collars inscribed with mottos marking the wearer as a slave wont to run away are among the most startling artifacts surviving from the ancient world. Most slave collars we have are post-Constantinian. The archdeacon Felix was hardly alone among Christian slaveholders in forcing slaves to wear such paraphernalia. Many slave collars bear Christian iconography, such as the alpha and the omega or the chi-rho figure. So discomforting are these objects that nineteenth-century scholars described them as dog collars rather than acknowledge that ancient Christians regularly bound other persons in such a crude manner. David Thurmond has suggested that most known slave collars are probably from Christian owners. Thurmond describes the collars as "mute reminders of the brutality of ancient slavery." Nonetheless, he argues that slave collars "ironically may have originated as an effort to humanize somewhat one of the most inhumane aspects of the institution," that is, the practice of tattooing or branding runaway slaves on the face, which Constantine forbade.[84]

Metal collars, fetters, tattoos, or brands—why would slaves run away and thus risk such punishments? Many slaves apparently felt that the prospect of freedom outweighed even the precarious conditions of life as a fugitive and the near-certainty of severe punishment if caught. One second-century census declaration listed five adult slaves as property in a household. The three adult slaves without children were all fugitives.[85] Epictetus gave us snippets of insight into the lives of slaves on the lam: "Don't they steal just a little bit to last them for the first few days, and then afterwards drift along over land or sea, contriving one scheme after another to keep themselves fed?"[86] Above all, said Epictetus, the anxiety of capture clouded all activities of runaway slaves: "I too am acting like a runaway slave. . . . I bathe, I drink, I sing, but I do it all in fear and misery."[87] Even though he was a former slave, Epictetus perpetuated stereotypes of runaway slaves, which reflected the contempt of slaveholders for their human property. All evidence suggests that many slaves reckoned flight to be a good risk. Epictetus described fugitive slaves as cowardly since their behaviors were designed to escape detection. We could just as easily, however, construe their willingness to risk the wrath and revenge of their owners and the hardships of flight as evidence of courage.

Slaveholders invested considerable energy in deterring the flight of slaves. By running from their masters or mistresses, slaves belied their identification as mere bodies. Once captured, somatic constraints (branding or tattooing, collars or fetters) reinscribed their bodies as possessions of their owners. Roman law required vendors to declare the history of flight of the slaves they sold. Even slaves who had not previously attempted to escape could not be guaranteed to remain content with their status. Therefore, vendors typically warranted that the slave in question was free of every defect except flight. When slaves did escape, their owners invested still more effort into effecting the return of their property. They posted runaway notices with detailed descriptions of missing slaves. They assigned representatives to travel as agents to recover fugitive slaves and accorded them the right of corporal control and discipline over recovered slaves. A third-century papyrus is particularly interesting in what it reveals about the different evaluations that a slaveholder and a slave might have about the situation of the bondsperson. Aurelia Sarapias sought assistance from a governor in effecting the return of the fugitive Sarapion. She wrote that Sarapion "was part of my inheritance and had been entrusted by me with our household. [Nevertheless] he, I know not how, at the instigation of certain folk, disdaining the honor afforded him by me and the provision of necessities for life," had chosen to run away.[88] Aurelia Sarapias believed that Sarapion had every reason to be content and even grateful to serve as her slave. Sarapion's flight implied that he was profoundly dissatisfied with that position and status.

David Daube has argued that the Roman legal code reveals traces of a long-standing practice in which professional slave catchers worked with fugitive slaves to separate them from their owners. The swindle worked like this. A fugitive slave contacted a slave catcher, who in turn approached the slaveholder. The slave catcher offered to buy the slave for a low price. The slaveholder was aware that if the slave did not return, he or she had lost everything. Even if the slave were found, future returns on a runaway slave were low. Therefore, the slaveholder accepted the low price offered by the slave catcher. The slave catcher then claimed to find the slave and offered him or her manumission at a reasonable price, or perhaps the slave catcher sold the slave to a prearranged buyer more acceptable as an owner to the slave.[89] From the perspective of slaveholders and therefore of the law, this was a gross form of fraud. For the slaves who attempted this gambit, it probably seemed like evening the score.

Roman law outlawed the harboring of fugitive slaves, a demand at odds with the requirement of the Torah to give shelter to fugitive slaves: "Slaves who have escaped to you from their owners shall not be given back to them. They shall reside with you, in your midst, in any place they choose. . . . you shall not oppress them."[90] Odd bits of evidence from late antiquity suggest that in some outposts Christian communities tolerated and even supported fugitive slaves. However, the documents of the orthodox church serve as the filter for these nuggets. We are left only with terse condemnations of the practice with no sympathetic presentations of the theology that might inform such an ethic. If some Christians, on principle, provided refuge for runaway slaves, they left no record of whether the ancient command of the Torah affected the development of that practice. A text of Basil of Caesarea, which may date to the fourth century, urged, "As for those slaves who are under the yoke and flee to religious communities, it is necessary to admonish and improve them and send them back to their masters."[91] The Council of Chalcedon (451 C.E.) forbade monasteries from accepting slaves as postulants without the explicit permission of their owners (canon 4). Had monasteries served as refuges for slaves seeking separation from their owners? If so, had the monasteries accepted the slaves as equal members of the community, or had they exploited the vulnerable position of the fugitive slaves to gain servants for the community? We do not know what the monks thought they were doing when they sheltered runaways. We only have direct knowledge of the official edicts. The institutional context of body-negating asceticism in late antique monasticism reinforced rather than dissolved the division between those whose legal status allowed them to control their own bodies and those whose legal status defined them as bodies belonging to others.

Perhaps even more obscure is the position of the mid–fourth-century Council of Gangra. The council condemned the otherwise unknown "partisans of Eustathius." Council documents specifically condemned the partisans' rejection of marriage; the strange apparel of females in the group, who were said to shear their hair and wear men's clothing; their vegetarian inclinations and their fasting on Sundays; and "slaves also leaving their masters, and, on account of their own strange apparel, acting insolently towards their masters."[92] The council formally condemned anyone who encouraged slaves to leave their owners, singling out those who alleged pious motivations for such encouragement. What is clear is that the orthodox church sided with slaveholders against the desires of slaves for their liberty. We are on less certain ground as we try to understand the attitudes and practices of the partisans of Eustathius and other marginal Christian groups. Were there, indeed, cohorts of Christians in antiquity whose faith led them to hold antislavery attitudes and to promote antislavery practices?

It is reasonable to infer, based on the precise references to the followers of Eustathius in the conciliar writings, that the Council of Gangra's condemnation of support for fugitive slaves was a reaction against the actual practices of some Christians, who aided and abetted (or were rumored to aid and abet) runaway slaves on principle. We cannot assume that all Christians who urged compliance with Roman fugitive slave laws framed their exhortations in such a context. For example, although John Chrysostom explicitly called on Christians to ensure that slaves remained with their legal owners, the context of his words does not imply that a group of Christians had taken a principled stance

against the return of fugitive slaves. In his first homily on Philemon, he drew this conclusion: "We ought not to withdraw slaves from the service of their masters. For if Paul
. . . was unwilling to detain Onesimus, so useful and serviceable to minister to himself,
without the consent of his master, much less ought we to act. For if the servant is so
excellent, he ought by all means to continue in that service, and to acknowledge the
authority of his master, that he may be the occasion of benefit to all in that house."[93]
Chrysostom urged Christians to return slaves to their legal owners even when they might
personally benefit from the services of the fugitive slave—hardly a principled motivation
for sheltering runaway slaves. Nonetheless, Chrysostom stands firmly with the mainstream of the ancient church in enforcing the broader cultural insistence on the control
of bodies in motion.

The most famous slave of early Christianity was, at least according to tradition, a
fugitive. Paul sends a letter to the slaveholder Philemon in the hands of Philemon's
slave Onesimus.[94] Onesimus had been with Paul in prison, and Paul had baptized him
there. Paul encourages Philemon to receive Onesimus warmly. Moreover, he promises
to repay Philemon whatever Onesimus might owe him. The received tradition of the
letter is that the slave Onesimus had run away and encountered Paul in prison and that
in this letter Paul asks Philemon for mercy for Onesimus—and perhaps even for manumission. More recently, scholars have suggested alternative scenarios. Sara Winter, for
example, proposes the following state of affairs. The church sends Onesimus to Paul in
prison to help him. What Paul asks is that Onesimus be freed from his responsibilities
at home so that he can continue to serve Paul. Moreover, on Winter's view, he urges
that Onesimus no longer be treated as a slave and, separately, hints that he should be
legally manumitted.[95] John Knox's words, first published in the mid-1930s, remain an
accurate and even eloquent summary of the exegetical difficulties of the letter:

> Since the letter contains at least two hints that Onesimus is not in favor with his master—
> he is said to have been "useless" or "unprofitable" to him, and there is a strong indica-
> tion that he has caused his master some loss—it is not unnatural that his presence with
> Paul should always have been explained by the hypothesis that he was a runaway slave. . . .
> This account of Onesimus' being with Paul may or may not be true. As a tentative theory,
> it will serve as well as any of the several others which might be constructed on the meager
> facts we have. Still, it should be realized that it rests upon no explicit statement of the
> letter itself.[96]

Ultimately, this brief letter does not permit us to deliver a final verdict on the question
of whether Onesimus had his owner's permission to be with Paul in prison or whether
Onesimus had left his owner's home without permission. As Knox acknowledges, either story is plausible. I continue to find the traditional interpretation, that Onesimus
was a runaway slave, somewhat more convincing than the proposal that the church or
the slaveholder sent Onesimus to Paul in prison.[97]

One reason that the debate continues to be so heated is that commentators often
demand that this slim letter convey, at least inchoately, Paul's view on slavery or, minimally, his view on runaway slaves. In the course of Allen Callahan's treatment of the
letter, for example, he highlights the important role the letter played in nineteenth-century American debates over slavery.[98] Some antislavery activists argued that Onesimus
was not a runaway slave. But why should this slender letter bear such a weight? Paul

knew Philemon personally. He was familiar with the church that met in Philemon's house. He was close to Onesimus. He sought to improve the relations among these Christians. Perhaps he sought continued assistance from Onesimus. He was writing about a particular situation, in which he was personally embroiled. He may well have sought personal gain in the resolution of the matter, that is, the return of Onesimus to help him in prison. He was not giving advice to all slaves or to all slaveholders nor commending a course of action to be followed by other slaveholders with runaway slaves. To transform this personal intervention into a systematic statement on fugitive slaves violates the tenor of the letter. To take this ambiguous letter as a starting point for discovering early Christian attitudes toward runaway slaves or slavery more broadly is a futile enterprise. Interpreting the letter depends on reconstruction of a background narrative, which we are only able to recreate from clues in the letter itself. Those who insist that only a single sequence of events is a viable match for the clues in the letter are reading the letter in the context of another story, usually the history of exegetical disputes over this text in modern debates over slavery.

Slaves who fled their owners used their bodies to defy their relegation to the status of bodies for others. The Torah demanded that the ancient Israelites shelter runaway slaves rather than return them to their owners. Writings of the mainstream church occasionally serve as palimpsests in which we can pick out murky references to obscure groups of Christians who provided oases to slaves seeking refuge from their owners. Paul's letter to Philemon, from which commentators often attempt to infer the earliest Christian attitudes toward slaves and especially fugitive slaves, is both too ambiguous and too personal to provide such information. On the whole, the Torah's insistence that runaway slaves deserve protection does not seem to have permeated early Christian sensibilities or customs.

Turning Bodies Around: Manumission of Slaves

In a mid-fourth-century papyrus from Kellis, Aurelius Valerius manumitted his female slave Hilaria. He wrote, "Aurelius Valerius son of Sarapion . . . to my own Hilaria, greetings. I acknowledge that I have set you free because of my exceptional Christianity [*hyperbolēn christianotētos*], under Zeus, Earth and Sun, together also with your peculium, and [because of] your loyalty towards me, in order that from hereonwards you shall have your freedom."[99] Aurelius Valerius supplied several reasons for the manumission, including the fact that Hilaria had been loyal to him. Moreover, he noted that he was motivated by his exceptional Christianity—although he still invoked the triumvirate of Zeus, Earth, and Sun, a formula traditional in deeds of manumission. Specification of a reason for manumission was not customary in such documents and citation of the slaveholder's "exceptional Christianity" as motivation is unique in the published documentation. "The most reverend father Psekes," who may or may not have been a priest, was a witness to the manumission. The form of the manumission is sui generis, corresponding not to the form of a Constantian ecclesial manumission (which would have required appearance before a body of Christian clerics) nor to the other legally recognized forms of manumission.

Slaves dreamed of a day when they would be free, the most precious of hopes. In the fourth- or fifth-century rabbinic commentary known as *Lamentations Rabbah*, a midrashist focuses on the worth of manumission to a slave: during a palace fire, while others plunder precious metals, the slave plunders his own title deed.[100] For many slaves, dreams of liberty eventually came true. For more slaves, those dreams never came true. By offering several interpretations for a single dream image, Artemidorus captures the self-doubt of a slave trying to discern the intentions of his owner regarding manumission. When a slave dreams that he is decapitated, Artemidorus opines, the imagery could be either auspicious or inauspicious. If a slave in a position of responsibility dreams that he is beheaded, he will lose the confidence of his master. "But to other slaves," Artemidorus says, "the dream signifies freedom. For the head is the master of the body, and when it is cut off, it signifies that the slave is separated from his master and will be free. But many others who have had this dream have simply been sold."[101] Slaves who were hopeful that manumission was imminent would analyze their owners' deeds and words for clues about their intentions, always aware of alternate, and less hopeful, explanations for the owners' behavior and language.

In the *Annals*, Tacitus noted that the motivation for the murder of L. Pedanius Secundus remained ambiguous. Perhaps the motivation was resistance to sexual overtures. As an alternate explanation, Tacitus held out the possibility that a disagreement over manumission motivated the murderer. He speculated that Pedanius Secundus agreed with a slave on the price to be paid for purchase out of slavery, but then reneged on that agreement.[102] That Tacitus could propose this solution as plausible underscores the tension in Roman thought over the boundary between freedom and slavery. Although manumission was relatively common for Roman slaves, the ultimate decision whether to release a slave from bondage rested with the slaveholder rather than the slave. No slave could be certain of effecting his or her own emancipation. Moreover, liberty was a prize so valued that a slave might kill for it. The slaveholding elite of Rome was sufficiently aware of the potential explosiveness of the situation to go to extreme measures, including the slaughter of even the innocent slaves in the household (the total number of slaves in the household of Pedanius Secundus was four hundred), in order to proclaim a cautionary message to slaves in other households who contemplated violence as a means to express their anger at ongoing bondage.

The slave body was subject to insult, abuse, and penetration. Still more, the slave *was* a body, available for the slaveholder's use as a surrogate. Free persons wanted to imagine their own bodies as impervious to such affronts. For this to be absolutely the case, however, the distinction between free persons and slaves had to be both clear and constant on both a practical and a theoretical level. A slave could only be a slave, and a free person could only be a free person. The presence of vast numbers of freedmen and freedwomen throughout the Empire, however, was itself a reminder that the boundary between slave and free could be, and often was, crossed. Moreover, a small percentage of former slaves became extremely wealthy. Brothers who were freedman built the elaborately decorated House of the Vetti in Pompeii, for example. (Frescoes in one room depict putti engaged in household and agricultural labors typically associated with menial slaves. What these irenic illustrations of labor meant to the former slaves who commissioned them we do not know.) Only a few of the luckiest freedmen and freedwomen could hope to achieve this level of material comfort. For freeborn persons in the ancient world, however, the visible success of wealthy former slaves, frequently interpreted by freeborn elites as inappropriate ostentation, would have been a constant reminder of the permeability of the membrane dividing free bodies from enslaved bodies.

Although in crosscultural perspective "outsider" status is intrinsic to the situation of the slave, slave systems vary in the degree of fluidity in the status of slaves. For example, in many parts of Africa, but not in Asia, slavery is a transitional status, a mode of incorporation of outsiders into kinship groups.[103] Social systems in which slaves move to kinship status upon manumission, which is thus seen as part of the natural cycle of slaves' lives, are considered to be open slave systems. Social systems that discourage manumission, in which even freed slaves lack any social recognition or status and thus remain permanent outsiders, are considered to be closed slave systems.[104] Frequent manumission is therefore a common but not a universal component of some slave systems. Far from undermining slavery, regular manumission can reinforce a slave system, particularly in instances in which slaves compensate their owners for their liberty and continue to serve them after manumission, as happened in Roman slavery.

Roman slavery was somewhere on the continuum between an open and a closed slave system. The Roman slave system featured manumission for many slaves but not for a majority of slaves.[105] Many former slaves became citizens, but again, the majority of freedpersons probably were not citizens. Bartchy exaggerates the openness of the Roman system when he writes, "In stark contrast to New World slavery, Greco-Roman slavery functioned as a process rather than a permanent condition, as a temporary phase of life by means of which an outsider obtained a place within a society."[106] With this formulation Bartchy generalizes from the experience of a minority of slaves to the experience of the entire slave population, the majority of whom were born as slaves, and the majority of whom died still in the condition of slavery. Moreover, life expectancy was much lower in antiquity than it is in modern industrialized societies. Many slaves only enjoyed a few brief years of freedom between the date of manumission and what we would perceive as a premature death.

Paul Weaver phrases the relevant question with precision. The Romans were "not known for soft-hearted generosity." Therefore, "in what form, under what conditions, and for what reasons did the Romans manumit slaves?"[107] He argues that historians have underestimated the number of Junian Latins among freedmen and freedwomen. Informally freed, Junian Latins were not citizens. Moreover, when they died their property reverted to their former owners. The law stipulated preconditions for Junian Latins to convert their status to that of citizens. However, such conversion to the status of a citizen required an appearance before a magistrate, which was both financially and logistically a difficult condition to meet. Weaver concludes, "Even in the context of Italian municipal society in the first century A.D., as compared with that of the provinces where Roman citizens were much less concentrated, citizenship was by no means to be taken for granted by those released from slavery."[108] Therefore, historians should not assume that a former slave is a citizen without positive evidence regarding the status of the freedperson. For example, Weaver argues that the *tria nomina* (a person's use of three names), often adduced as evidence of citizenship, establishes only that one who uses the name is a free man or free woman.

What are the implications of Weaver's work for classifying the Roman slave system as closed or open? Many slaves in the Roman Empire were manumitted at some point in their lives. Still, most were not. Moreover, manumission was not the direct route to Roman citizenship that is sometimes portrayed. Harrill, for example, asserts that "the Romans regularly granted citizenship to freedmen/women who had been formally manumitted by a citizen master."[109] The slippery term in Harrill's formulation is "regularly." The statement is true, as far as it goes, but glosses over the difficulties that slaves would have encountered in achieving citizenship status. Citizenship was not automatic or even semiautomatic for freedpersons. Rather, most freed slaves were Junian Latins, still outsiders to the dominant society. This was even more true in the provinces, where a lower density of citizens required fewer magistrates. Junian Latins would thus find it even more difficult and expensive to gain an audience before a magistrate in order to establish themselves as citizens. The children of Junian Latins were freeborn but not citizens. Moreover, the estate of a Junian Latin reverted to the former owner, so the offspring of Junian Latins had no rights of inheritance from their parents.[110] Thus, although the regularity of manumission in Roman practice promoted some incorporation of outsiders into the society, that process was by no means inevitable and was certainly not swift, more likely to occur over the span of several generations than within a single lifetime.

Nonetheless, many slaves were fortunate enough to spend at least a few final years of their lives not only as freedpersons but also as citizens. Along with Junian Latins who satisfied the conditions for recognition as citizens, formally manumitted slaves were automatically granted citizenship. A slaveholder could formally manumit a slave in three ways. First, a will could include a formal grant of manumission. Second, a slaveholder could, during a census, declare a slave free before a censor. Third, a slaveholder could arrange to bring a slave and a witness before a magistrate or provincial official. When the slaveholder stood silent, the magistrate would announce that the slave was in fact free. By relying on the fiction that a slave was in fact a free person, Roman law upheld the division between free bodies and enslaved bodies. In the eyes of the law, the process was not a process of transformation of a slave into a free person but rather the recognition of the free identity of the person formerly identified as a slave. As part of the manumission ceremony, the slaveholder turned the slave around. Epictetus claimed that this turning of the servile body accomplished nothing worth mentioning: "When, therefore, in the presence of the praetor a man turns his own slave about, has he done nothing?—He has done something.—What?—He has turned his slave about in the presence of the praetor.—Nothing more?—Yes, he is bound to pay a tax of five percent of the slave's value.—What then? Has not the man to whom this has been done become free?— He has no more become free than he has acquired peace of mind."[111] I expect that most slaves turned about in a Roman court believed something worth celebrating had taken place. Nonetheless, Epictetus lends ironic support to the Roman legal fiction that such an appearance was not a manumission but a restoration of free status. The introduction of new forms of manumission under Constantine stemmed not from some special Christian belief in the importance of manumitting slaves but rather from the reorganization of Roman life around the new institution of the church.[112]

Despite Aurelius Valerius's declaration that "exceptional Christianity" motivated his freeing of a slave, Christians seem to have had neither a special affinity for nor antipathy toward the manumission of slaves. In chapter two I argued that in 1 Corinthians 7:21, Paul encourages slaves to embrace opportunities for manumission. This was not groundbreaking advice in a society where manumission was an unremarkable feature of everyday life. In his letter to Polycarp, Ignatius admonished Christians not to use common funds to manumit slaves.[113] As with references forbidding the harboring of slaves, which we considered, Ignatius's text is a tantalizing palimpsest. Between the lines of his letter we may discern clues concerning what may or may not have been a well-known practice in his community: drawing on church funds to secure the liberty of church members.[114] Several centuries later, in his letter to Coroticus, Patrick asserted that some Christians ransomed slaves from captivity. However, Patrick identified the motivation as the protection of Christians from pagans as much as the protection of those falsely enslaved from slaveholders. Melania's fabled manumission of 8,000 slaves when she joined a monastery appears as evidence of her shedding of extraordinary creature comforts rather than as a challenge to other Christian slaveholders to let all their human property walk free.[115]

Just as former imperial slaves rose to positions of power, former slaves had opportunities for advancement in the developing church. In 217 C.E., the freedman Callistus became pope. Unfortunately, virtually all we know about this former slave derives from the writings of his archnemesis, Hippolytus. One of Hippolytus's particular complaints about Callistus arose from the former slave's willingness to recognize the legitimacy of marriages between free women and enslaved men. Hippolytus himself tolerated unions between enslaved women and free men. However, he viewed the easiness of the freedman pope regarding sexual unions between free women and enslaved men as an instance of moral lassitude. What the Christian Hippolytus found outrageous was equally outrageous to other freeborn denizens of the Empire. They imagined a slave body penetrating, possessing, and mastering a free body. By recognizing the legitimacy of sexual couplings between enslaved men and free women, Callistus threatened to erase the clearly drawn boundary of the free body.

Body Language: Metaphors of Enslavement, Sale, and Liberation in Christian Theological Discourse

The *Acts of Thomas*, likely composed in the early third century, opens with a scene that spins a central Christian metaphor—enslavement to Christ—into a narrative. All the apostles are together in Jerusalem. They are dividing the known world into missionary territories. To Judas Thomas comes the call to India, which he refuses. Jesus appears to him and implores him to embrace the challenge, but Judas Thomas is disobedient: "Send me where you will—but somewhere else!" Jesus, identified as the Lord/Master, spies in the marketplace an Indian merchant named Abban. Jesus asks Abban, who has come to Jerusalem to buy an enslaved carpenter, whether he wants to purchase a slave. Jesus declares, "I have a slave who is a carpenter, and wish to sell him." When Abban agrees, Jesus writes out a bill of sale: "I Jesus the son of Joseph the carpenter confirm that I have sold my slave, Judas by name, to you Abban, a merchant." Abban and Jesus approach Judas Thomas in the marketplace, and Abban asks the apostle whether Jesus is his master. Judas Thomas affirms that yes, Jesus is his master. Abban announces that he has purchased Judas Thomas from his master, Jesus. Judas Thomas is silent. His prayer changes, and he no longer rebels against Jesus' intentions. "Your will be done," Judas prays. As Judas prepares to leave with Abban, Jesus hands him the price of his redemption from slavery and instructs him to carry with him always the price of liberation, which Jesus has paid for him.[116] Although the *Acts of Thomas* does not specify what price Jesus paid, the Christian reader recognizes that the price Jesus has paid is his own life—with his own death.

The figure of the Christian as a slave of Christ or of God is inchoate in a number of Jesus' parables and familiar from the writings of Paul. Christian discourse figuratively plays on moments of reduction to and release from bondage. The twenty-first-century reader can easily lose sight of the context in which these metaphors emerged. By expanding a metaphor into a narrative, the *Acts of Thomas* exposes the debt of Christian theological language to ancient social realities. When Christians living in the Roman Empire called Jesus of Nazareth *kyrios*, lord or master, and referred to themselves as slaves, they relied on imagery rooted in the social relations of their age. Even in antiquity, however, countless repetitions of "Lord Jesus" would have deadened those who employed such language to the metaphoric dimension of the title. The story that opens the *Acts of Thomas* both relies on and revivifies the metaphor. When Judas Thomas acknowledges Jesus as his Lord, he is not thinking of himself as a literal slave of Jesus. As Master Jesus writes out a bill of sale for his slave Judas Thomas, the reader recalls with a shock of recognition the material realities that shaped Christian theological discourse.

Embedded in the *Acts of Thomas* is a Gnostic hymn, which predates the narrative in which it is preserved. The Hymn of the Pearl presents a fable of a young man from the East whose parents send him to Egypt to recover a great pearl. While in Egypt, the young man loses sight of his noble origins and serves the king as a slave. After he receives a letter from his parents he recalls and reasserts his aristocratic identity.[117] The hymn follows the rhythm of Hellenistic novels in which young people of royal lineage find themselves enslaved in foreign lands until the climactic restoration of their identity as freeborn persons of distinguished households. A Gnostic fable of spiritual humans mired in the world of the ordinary until they remember their divine origins and so capture "the pearl," the Hymn of the Pearl plays rhetorically on the anxiety of freeborn persons to maintain their status, the protected boundaries of their bodies, against the humiliations and violations of servitude.

Both the story of Jesus' sale of his slave Judas Thomas and the Hymn of the Pearl elaborate tropes that typically appear in more cryptic form in Christian writings: the Lord/Master Jesus, the Christian as the slave of Christ, and the enslavement of humanity by forces of sin and error. Moreover, both textual units rely on the dramatic reduction of free persons to the status of slaves. Both textual units promise or realize restoration of free status. In the story of the sale of Judas Thomas, Jesus provides Judas with the price of his redemption and instructs him to carry it always with him. In the Hymn of the Pearl, the noble young man remembers who he is and again acts as a freeborn aristocrat. Both texts thus stress transitional or liminal moments of slavery: the process of becoming a slave and the process of release from slavery.

In the *Acts of Thomas*, ancient recognition of and fears about the realities of slave life are more apparent than in briefer metaphorical invocations of slavery. Even passing references to the sale of slaves or enslaving powers, however, open a window onto an entire world of social relations. In Romans 6:15–23, for example, Paul draws a contrast between those who are slaves to sin and those who are slaves to righteousness. Of this extract Elizabeth Castelli has written, "This passage is not *about slaves*. Instead, it is about a theological idea that Paul finds congenial to describe in terms of slavery. . . . While this passage is clearly not *about* slavery (neither for it nor against it), it depends on the reality of slavery to convey its meanings and . . . [therefore] reinscribes the relations of slavery."[118] Castelli points out that the implications of the slavery metaphor in Romans 6, with its stress on servile submissiveness, are disturbing. Her words also apply to the use of the trope of slavery in the opening scene of *Acts of Thomas*. This text is not *about* slavery. However, the sale of Judas Thomas depends on the realities of ancient slavery to convey its theological message.

I have argued that the threshold moments of slavery received especial attention in ancient sources because freeborn men and women focused on inconsistencies and gaps in the slave system, which revealed its intrinsic instability and hence the vulnerabilities of supposedly inviolate free bodies to the indignities of slavery. Freeborn persons lived with constant reminders that the division between slave and free was not absolute. Apertures in the theoretically closed body of the free person permitted metamorphosis from one status to another. This awareness shaped the tropes of Christian rhetoric. Not only did Christians rely on the figure of the slave, but they emphasized the moments of transition that revealed the fragility of the membrane that separated slave from free. As Castelli has noted, such metaphors are not, at base, *about* slavery, but they do depend on and ultimately reinscribe the ancient social relations of a slave system, including the apprehension of free persons that a change of fortune could expose them to the indignities of slavery.

One Christian document that relies heavily on the trope of slavery and particularly the movement into and out of slavery is a Gnostic collection of sayings about ritual and sacrament, the *Gospel of Philip*. (The manuscript of the *Gospel of Philip* excavated at Nag Hammadi dates from the middle of the fourth century. The sayings recorded therein are of earlier origin.) Theological metaphors in the document draw on the material realities of slavery. One saying, for example, recognizes that slaves consumed a distinctive and cruder diet than free persons. Encouraging disciples to recognize with whom they are dealing, the saying refers to a wise estate owner, who knew which food to allocate to every group on his farm: children, slaves, cattle, dogs, and pigs, a dehumanizing formulation that associates enslaved farm laborers with livestock.[119] The *Gospel of Philip* stresses the holiness of a sacrament to which it refers as the bridal chamber, which seems to be an initiation into some form of mystical union. A substratum of material reality lies beneath the language of mystery associated with the bridal chamber: "Animals have no bridal chamber, nor do slaves or defiled women. Rather, free men and virgins have one."[120] Slaves did not enjoy legal recognition of their unions nor did the architectural structures of ancient homes allow them conjugal solitude. Slaves were regarded as bodies with no more privacy rights than animals. In concrete ways, then, the *Gospel of Philip* provides evidence of familiarity with ancient slavery and its privations.

A number of the slave sayings in the *Gospel of Philip* draw on threshold moments of slavery: the free person's fear of enslavement and the slave's hope of liberation. The story of Christ's relationship with fallen humanity is narrated precisely as a story of false enslavement and release from slavery: "The world fell into the hands of robbers and was taken captive," that is, enslaved, "but he [Christ] saved it."[121] We have seen the horror with which Augustine and Patrick viewed the seizure and sale of free persons into slavery. This saying from the *Gospel of Philip* evokes the terror of kidnapping to illustrate the dire condition of humanity apart from Christ's redemptive action. Other sayings also rely on the same implicit story. The deceptive rulers of the world, for example, want to "take the free man and make him a slave to them forever."[122] The root of evil "masters us. We are its slaves. It takes us captive, to make us do what we do [not] want; and what we do want we do [not] do."[123] Neither Augustine nor Patrick protested the ongoing bondage of those born to slavery, only the transgression of the boundary between slave and free. In a similar way these sayings concern themselves not with those who are seen as intrinsically slaves but with those intended for freedom yet consigned to servitude.

Along with their warnings against enslaving powers, the sayings in the *Gospel of Philip* also draw on the well-known hopes of slaves for freedom: "The slave seeks only to be free, but does not hope to acquire the estate of his master."[124] Christ's saving action is described in terms of purchase, ransom, and redemption.[125] Those ransomed or redeemed have ongoing obligations to the one who saved them, as a freedperson would have continuing obligations to a former owner. A number of sayings that allude to the reduction of free persons to slavery culminate in references to their eventual release from that condition, not so much a manumission as a recognition of and resumption of an original status of freedom. Ultimately, however, the promise of initiation into the sacraments encompasses liberation for all: "Then the slaves will be free [and] the captives ransomed."[126] The *Gospel of Philip* includes some sayings that rely on a static contrast between slavery and freedom: "Ignorance is a slave. Knowledge is freedom."[127] Nonetheless, the descending and ascending dramas of enslavement and liberation deepen the impact of sacramental rhetoric in this document. These sayings are *about* the rituals of a Gnostic community. While they are not *about* slavery, they do reinscribe common ancient attitudes about bondage and the prerogatives of the freeborn.

Paul, in his letters to various Christian communities, relies on tropes of slavery and freedom. He refers to himself, for example, as a slave of Christ. A number of Paul's slave metaphors participate in overarching narratives of enslavement, sale, and manumission, but not all Paul's figurative uses of slavery and freedom are commensurate with one another. "For freedom Christ has set us free," he writes to the Galatians.[128] Here Paul describes Christ as one who has secured the manumission of the formerly enslaved. Elsewhere, however, it is less clear whether Christ has secured the freedom of those for whom he has paid or whether he has become their new owner: "You were bought with a price; do not become slaves of human masters."[129] Paul's invocation of transitional moments in the life of a slave echoes the concerns and attitudes of others in his world. He suggests that death is a kind of manumission for slaves, a correlation that also appears in Artemidorus. Paul writes, "For whoever has died is freed from sin."[130] In Artemidorus's dream logic, death and manumission are fungible: "To dream that one is dead, that one is being carried out for burial, or that one is buried foretells freedom for a slave. . . . For a dead man has no master and is free from toil and service."[131] Artemidorus repeats this observation regarding a number of specific forms of death, including crucifixion and being consumed by wild beasts.[132] Paul is able, according to this same logic, to treat dying as the functional equivalent of being freed from sin.

In Paul's letters, most metaphoric permutations of enslavement, sale, and liberation position Christians as slaves or freedpersons of Christ, or else they present human persons as slaves to negative powers. In Philippians, however, Paul tells the story of Jesus himself as a saga of reduction to and release from bondage. Scholars agree that Paul is quoting a hymn already familiar among Christians. The hymn praises the anointed one, Jesus,

> who, though he was in the form of God
>> did not regard equality with God
>> as something to be exploited,
> but emptied himself,
>> taking the form of a slave,
>> being born in human likeness.
> And being found in human form,
>> he humbled himself
>> and become obedient to the point of death—
>> even death on a cross.
> Therefore God also highly exalted him
>> and gave him the name
>> that is above every name,
> so that at the name of Jesus
>> every knee should bend,
>> in heaven and on earth and under the earth,
> and every tongue should confess
>> that Jesus Christ is Lord.[133]

In assigning Jesus the role of slave, the hymn emphasizes his obedience to God and his death on the cross. Ancient writers, as we will explore more fully in chapter five, treated obedience as the most desirable virtue for slaves. Crucifixion, which was not only a cruel but also a humiliating and shameful mode of death, was not reserved for slaves. Nonetheless, crucifixion was reserved for persons of low social status and was particularly associated with the execution of slaves. Jesus is thus like a slave in his obedience and in his death.[134] The hymn configures Jesus' life to conform to the by-now familiar movement downward into slavery and upward out of slavery. Jesus, who is in the form of God (*en morphē theou*), assumes instead the form of a slave (*morphēn doulou labōn*); God vindicates Jesus and confers on him the highest of names, *kyrios*, lord or master.

Winsome Munro has interpreted the Philippians Christ hymn as evidence that the historical Jesus of Nazareth was born into slavery and lived as a slave.[135] I disagree with her inference. Greco-Roman literature and inscriptions provide evidence that the metaphor "slave of god" was familiar in pagan circles.[136] The Philippians hymn links Jesus' assumption of the form of a slave to his birth in human likeness. In a status-conscious society, the legal and cultural distinctions between freeborn persons and slaves mapped onto the imaginative terrain of immortal gods and mortal human beings. Apuleius, in his fanciful telling of the myth of Cupid and Psyche in *The Golden Ass*, teases out the implications of this metaphoric plotting. Psyche, a well-born and beautiful woman, finds herself in trouble with the gods, particularly Venus, when she becomes Cupid's wife. In the eyes of the immortal gods, the aristocratic Psyche is a mere mortal and thus no more than a slave. When Psyche seeks shelter with Juno, the goddess turns her away by explaining that the law against sheltering slaves prevents her from extending hospitality. When Psyche finally meets Venus, Venus orders her attendants Trouble and Sadness to whip the human female, as slaveholders routinely inflicted corporal abuse on their slaves (the beatings were often delivered by other slaves). Finally, when Jupiter recognizes the union between Psyche and Cupid as a legitimate marriage, he refers to the Roman laws that bar marriage between those of unequal social orders. He then provides Psyche with a cup of nectar. When Psyche imbibes the nectar she joins the ranks of the immortals, and her union with Cupid is recognized as a valid marriage.[137] Apuleius's representation of the division between immortal gods and mortal human beings in terms of the demarcation between free persons and slaves is fanciful and playful, while the representation of the boundary between the immortal God and the mortal Jesus in the Philippians hymn is entirely serious. Nonetheless, I point to Apuleius's rendition of the fable of Cupid and Psyche to illustrate the naturalness of this metaphor in a society thoroughly mired in the distinctions between slave and free. In such a context, an allusion to Jesus' acceptance of the "form of a slave" is better explained as a reference to his participation in the mortal human condition than as an oblique clue that he was born and raised as a slave.

Sheila Briggs has written of the Christ hymn in Philippians, "One is confronted with the fact that the material reality of that social relationship [slavery] has been transformed into metaphor, that the cultural, including the religious, imagination of the Greco-Roman world is bounded by the mentality of a slave society."[138] That is, the hymn is not about slavery, but it depends on and reinscribes the social relations of slavery.[139] The impact of the hymn depends on boundary crossing. One possessing a high status (in the form of God) assumes a low status (in the form of a slave) until the ultimate restoration of his elite status (the name of Lord/Master). Noting that custom and law in the Roman Empire forbade the reduction of free persons into slavery, Briggs concludes that Jesus' "degradation is heightened by the assertion that it is a divine being who has become a slave."[140] We have seen that Roman jurists proposed that Roman soldiers who accepted reduction to the status of slavery (even temporarily) should be liable to decapitation. Voluntary lowering of status was regarded with horror, and involuntary lowering of status was regarded with fear. What was most threatening to the imagination of free persons was not slavery itself. Rather, what free persons found threatening was the chance that they would not be able to protect the integrity of their own bodies and would be forcibly reduced to the vulnerable position of slaves. The Christ hymn depends on recognition of the shocking humiliation and definitive vindication of one who originally and ultimately bore a God likeness.

4

Parabolic Bodies

The Figure of the Slave in the Sayings of Jesus

A central chapter in Harriet Jacobs's autobiographical *Incidents in the Life of a Slave Girl* addresses the collusion between various churches and the nineteenth-century American slave system. She describes the spiritual leadership in a Methodist class meeting she once attended: "The class leader was the town constable—a man who bought and sold slaves, who whipped his brethren and sisters of the church at the public whipping post, in jail or out of jail. He was ready to perform that Christian office anywhere for fifty cents."[1] The irony of the passage relies on the reader's acknowledgment that the teacher's service as a torturer of slaves is anything but a Christian vocation. Before we brand the Christian constable an oxymoron or anomaly, however, we need to come to terms with some other disciplinarians lurking at the edges of Christian memory and imagination.

In the ancient Mediterranean world, slave owners could also hire a local public official to beat their slaves. An inscription from the Italian city of Puteoli details the job description of a *manceps*, which includes the task of torturing and even executing slaves on demand. Private citizens could hire the *manceps* to conduct the desired torture of their slaves. The *manceps* would supply the necessary equipment, sparing slave owners the burden of stockpiling such hardware themselves.[2] Would a first-century Jew from a Galilean village, living at the other end of the Empire, have been aware that such an apparatus of terror supported the slave system? In the Gospel of Matthew, Jesus tells the parable of the unmerciful slave to emphasize to his hearers the harsh treatment they may expect from their heavenly father if they fail to extend forgiveness to others (Matt 18:23–35). As in other parables, Jesus relies on familiar elements of Mediterranean life: mustard seeds, shepherds, slaves, and their disciplinarians. In the parable's denouement, the master turns the unmerciful slave over to the torturers (*tois basanistais*) until he repays the funds he owes his master (Matt. 18:34). Jesus does not specify whether these torturers are public officials or part of the master's retinue.[3] Since the master is himself a king, perhaps they are both. In either case, the Matthean Jesus assumes that those who hear him are familiar with the idea that slaveholders who want to punish their slaves can call on the services of torturers, like the *manceps* of Puteoli or the Methodist constable of Jacobs's vignette. Jesus thus represents the enactment of divine vengeance via the widespread ancient trope of corporal punishment of slaves.

Allusions to slaves and masters are common in the parables and other sayings of Jesus. Nonetheless, discussions of slavery and the New Testament often overlook the Gospels in their emphasis on epistolary materials. For example, in a monograph on the metaphor of slavery in early Christian writings, I. A. H. Combes devotes less than two pages to the synoptic Gospels, less than four pages to the Gospel of John, and sixteen pages to the Pauline epistles.[4] Peter Garnsey's survey of attitudes toward slavery "from Aristotle to Augustine" restricts its inquiry into New Testament materials to the epistles.[5] The parables "introduce servitude only as an incidental subject or a point of reference," but this is equally true of many passages Garnsey culls from ancient philosophical literature.[6] Even asides on slavery can yield valuable insights.[7] Slavery in the parables typically functions metaphorically, representing the Christian's relationship to God.[8] Perhaps because of this theological displacement, New Testament scholars have been slow to interrogate the ideology of slavery in the parables.[9] Indeed, classicists preceded biblical scholars in widespread recognition that the servants of the parables are in fact slaves and that parabolic constructions of slaves and slavery supply evidence about first-century attitudes on chattel slavery.[10]

New Testament scholars sometimes find it useful to distinguish between the parables *of the Gospels* and the parables *of Jesus.*[11] This distinction derives from the scholarly quest for the historical Jesus and the attempt to reconstruct Jesus' actual words and deeds as opposed to received representations of those words and deeds. Efforts to reconstruct Jesus' words, however, must begin with the versions of those sayings preserved in canonical writings as well as in selected extracanonical texts, particularly the *Gospel of Thomas.* The majority of parables that feature slaves as actors, major or minor, appear in either the Gospel of Luke, the Gospel of Matthew, or both. This concentration of slave-related sayings in Luke and Matthew may imply that slaves figured prominently in the lost sayings source presumably used by Matthew and Luke, which scholars have labeled "Q." I consider briefly slaves in the parables and other sayings of Jesus in the Gospels of Mark, Thomas, and John. I next survey Jesus' reliance on slaves in the sayings material in Luke and then concentrate on slaves in the Matthean parables, where the body of the slave most prominently figures. Finally, I consider the attempts of New Testament scholars to recover the "originating structures" of Jesus' slave parables. The moral complications posed by a set of parables that reinscribe ancient assumptions about slavery exacerbate the familiar pitfalls that scholars confront in reconstructing Jesus' sayings. In the parables of Jesus, the bodies of slaves are vulnerable to abuse. Beaten, stoned, and executed, the figure of the parabolic slave is repeatedly the locus of corporal discipline and other bodily violations. New Testament critics, however, have been reluctant to acknowledge the violence implicit in the parables' representations of slave bodies. Averting their gaze from the bloodied bodies of slaves, New Testament critics have found it easier to focus on other facets of the parabolic representation of slaves, such as the wealth and influence exercised by some of these slaves. Indeed, because some parabolic slaves command funds and influence, many New Testament critics continue to deny that the *douloi* of the parables are slaves. Nonetheless, the parabolic representation of slaves, especially their managerial responsibilities and their vulnerability to corporal punishment, is consistent with other representations of slaves in Roman society.[12] Attending to the representation of slaves in the parables requires that critics take body as seriously as soul.

Keith Bradley has written, "The fact remains, however, that slavery caused no one in antiquity a crisis of conscience or an agony of the soul as it did abolitionists in later history, and as it still does some modern historians today. For a thousand years and more slavery was not a problem in classical culture."[13] Was Jesus an exception to this general rule? Did he express disapproval of the institution of slavery when he taught in parables? In order to answer that question, we should begin with an examination of the parables themselves and not with generalizations or unexamined presuppositions about the imagery of those parables. Indeed, we have already encountered an uncanny resemblance between Jacobs's Methodist constable, available for a fee to whip his enslaved brothers and sisters in Christ, and the torturers who stand by in the parable of the unmerciful slave, ready to impress a message of divine vengeance on the body of a slave.

Figure of the Slave in Jesus' Discourse in Mark, Thomas, and John

In the Gospel of Mark, Jesus signals the importance of parabolic discourse when he says to the twelve, "To you has been given the secret of the kingdom of God, but for those outside, everything comes in parables" (4:11). Parables are central to Jesus' teaching in Mark, but slaves are not central to those parables. As in other trajectories of the Jesus' sayings tradition, slaves do appear, but they are not so ubiquitous as they are in Luke and Matthew. In Mark's version of the parable of the tenants (12:1–11), the owner of the vineyard sends successive rounds of slaves to try to obtain the rent from the recalcitrant tenants. The tenants beat the first slave. The second slave they insult and beat over the head, highlighting his status as a person outside the game of honor. The third slave they kill. And so on with other slaves, either beaten or killed. Finally, the owner of the vineyard decides to send his son. He expects that the tenants will accord him the respect they have denied the slaves. "They will respect my son," he says, knowing that the freeborn heir has a claim on honor that slaves cannot have. Not until the tenants murder the son does the vineyard owner retaliate, destroying the disrespectful tenants and deeding the vineyard to new tenants. Mark's Jesus thus exhibits awareness of the conditions in which slaves lived—in a permanent state of dishonor, which left them vulnerable to bodily abuse.

A parable from the extracanonical apocalypse known as the *Shepherd of Hermas* (first or second century) provides a useful comparison to the slave imagery in the Markan parable of the tenants and its canonical parallels. A man who owned a field and many slaves planted a vineyard on part of the field. He assigned a trustworthy slave to build a fence for the vineyard. He promised the slave that if he followed these orders he would receive manumission. The estate owner then went abroad. The slave, after constructing a fence, realized the vineyard was choked with weeds. He turned over the soil of the vineyard to rid it of the weeds. As a result, yields from the vineyard were high. When the man who was master of both field and slave returned, he was even more pleased with the work of the slave than he had anticipated. In a gathering with his friends, the master announced the slave's manumission. Moreover, as a reward for the slave's extra labors, he named his slave as joint heir with his son. The master's son agreed with the plan to share his inheritance with the slave. The master then held a feast and sent the slave/heir food from the feast. The slave kept only what he needed and shared the food with his fellow slaves. When the master heard of the slave's generosity he was so delighted that he reported the slave's generosity to his friends and his son, who also re-

joiced.[14] So, promises the shepherd, those who not only adhere to God's commandments but do still more than God commands will receive rich rewards.

The Markan vineyard parable, like its canonical parallels, relies on the contrast between the dishonored bodies of slaves and the honorable body of the son. Although
the tenants murder the son, the impact of the parable depends on the reader responding with outrage when the tenants treat the body of a freeborn heir in the same con-
temptuous way they treat the bodies of slaves. The murder of his son excites the wrath
of the vineyard owner as the abuse and murder of slaves did not. The vineyard parable
from the *Shepherd of Hermas* also juxtaposes a son/heir with a slave. However, by nam-
ing the slave as co-heir, the slaveholder minimizes the gap between slave and son. This
parable, too, depends on recognition of the divide between slave and free in order to
enhance the reader's appreciation for the magnitude of the master's gift and the son's
graciousness. Nonetheless, while the Markan parable reinscribes stereotypic relations
between slaveholders and slaves, the parable from the *Shepherd of Hermas* achieves its
effect by overturning those relations.

Two other instances in which the Markan Jesus relies on the figure of the slave require the reader to adopt the vantage point of the slave. Mark's version of the parable
of the doorkeeper is short. Culminating his apocalyptic discourse in chapter 13, Jesus
warns his hearers to remain alert because they do not know when the final hour will
be: "It is like a man going on a journey, when he leaves home and puts his slaves in
charge, each with his work, and commands the doorkeeper to be on the watch" (13:34).
Jesus then charges his hearers to respond as though they are slaves assigned to the task
of doorkeeper. "Keep awake," he says, "Or else he [the absent slaveholder] may find
you asleep when he comes suddenly" (13:35a, 36). Like a slave whose body is unable to
rest at night, the follower of Jesus is obliged to remain ever vigilant. This comparison,
as in a number of Jesus' parables in other Gospels, represents the faithful as slaves and
God as a slaveholder. In the midst of a slaveholding culture, reliance on this metaphor
is hardly surprising or even innovative. Rabbinic parables, for example, also configure
God as master, the faithful as slaves.[15] Moreover, the devotees of a number of pagan
gods refer to themselves, in inscriptions, as "slave of [the god]."

More distinctive, then, is Jesus' instruction to his followers to be slaves *to one another*: "You know that among the Gentiles those whom they recognize as their rulers
lord it over them, and their greatest ones are tyrants over them. But it is not so among
you; but whoever wishes to become great among you must be your servant [*diakonos*],
and whoever wishes to be first among you must be slave [*doulos*] of all. For the Son of
Man came not to be served [*diakonēthēnai*] but to serve [*diakonēsai*], and to give his life
as a ransom for many" (Mark 10:42–45). Matthew accepts this formulation with minimal redaction (Matt. 20:26–28). In Luke's version of the saying, however, Jesus does
not command his followers to adopt the posture of slave. "But not so among you," says
the Lukan Jesus. "Rather the greatest among you must become like the youngest, and
the leader like one who serves. For who is greater, the one who sits at the table or the
one who serves? Is it not the one at the table? But I am among you as one who serves"
(Luke 22:24–27). Ian Sloan notes, "Luke's distinction between greater and lesser depends on the distinction between benefactor and client. . . . Where Mark's distinction
of socioeconomic issues is oriented by status (free or slave), Luke's is oriented by rank

(greatest or youngest)."[16] Luke's modification implies that the Markan formulation is potentially offensive to hearers. Later generations of Christians, however, normalize this language of reciprocal slavery. Christian letters preserved among the Egyptian papyri, for example, feature Christians who sign themselves as slaves of one another. David Seeley has argued that Jesus shares with Cynic and Stoic authors an understanding that rulers *serve*. However, the examples that he provides from pagan philosophers are not conclusive. He quotes Dio: "What can give greater pleasure than a gentle and kindly ruler who desires to serve all and has it in his power to do so?" Seeley translates the Greek phrase *eu poieō*, to do good, as "to serve."[17] Dio's saying is better translated, "What can give greater pleasure than a gentle and kindly ruler who desires to do good to all and has it in his power to do so?" Jesus' interpretation of leadership as service and the leader as a slave is an innovation that shapes Christian tradition, even if its effects are more pervasive at the rhetorical level than at the level of practice or power relations.

The *Gospel of Thomas* is important both as a source for previously unknown sayings of Jesus and as an independent witness to sayings familiar from the canonical Gospels. The *Gospel of Thomas* makes a key contribution to our ability to assess the extent to which Jesus himself relied on the figure of the slave in his teachings. That is, if the figure of the slave were absent from *Thomas*, one might wonder whether the canonical evangelists had written slaves into the parable tradition. For example, although Matthew's version of the parable of the weeds and wheat features slaves, Thomas's version does not (Matt. 13:24–30; G. *Thom*. 57). Slaves do appear, however, in several of Jesus' parables and sayings as preserved in *Thomas*. As in the synoptic tradition, in Thomas's version of the parable of the tenants, the slaves of the vineyard owner are the targets of the tenants' violent actions (G. *Thom*. 65). In *Thomas*, as in Luke and Matthew, slaves serve as messengers inviting guests to dinner in the parable of the dinner party (G. *Thom*. 64). *Thomas* also preserves a version of Jesus' saying about a slave trying to serve two masters. In Thomas's version, the slave cannot serve two masters, because he will "honor one and treat the other with contempt" (G. *Thom*. 47). Although slaves are not ubiquitous in the *Gospel of Thomas*, the document does offer independent corroboration that Jesus relied on the figure of the slave in his discourse.

Finally, slaves also figure metaphorically in John's rendition of Jesus' discourse. In the Johannine farewell discourse, Jesus twice tells his followers that "the slave is not above the master," a saying preserved in another context in Matthew (John 13:16, 15:20; Matt. 10:25; cf. Luke 6:40). The Johannine Jesus first says that slaves are not greater than their master after he has washed their feet and instructed them that they are to wash one anothers' feet. Washing feet was one of the tasks consistently associated with slaves. This context thus enforces the sentiment known from Mark: the disciples are to be slaves to one another. Jesus refers back to this saying when he warns his followers that even as the world has hated and persecuted him, the world will hate and persecute his followers. Repetition of the logion is at odds with the saying that immediately precedes it: "I do not call you slaves any longer, because the slave does not know what the master is doing; but I have called you friends, because I have made known to you everything that I have heard from the father" (15:15). That is, after telling his followers that he will no longer call them slaves but friends, Jesus employs the slave-master rubric to describe their relationship. Here as elsewhere in the farewell discourse, John's logic falters. Nonetheless, these sayings reconfirm in a distinctive context the impression that Jesus

routinely drew on the imagery of slaves and slaveholders to describe the relationship between his followers and himself or perhaps between his followers and a divine master.

In a different appropriation of the imagery of slavery, the Johannine Jesus promises
the Jews who believe in him that they will be free if they persist as his disciples. They
are, however, offended. Descendants of Abraham, they claim they are already free. Jesus
responds, "Everyone who commits sin is a slave to sin. The slave does not have a permanent place in the household; the son has a place there forever. So if the Son makes
you free, you will be free indeed" (8:34b–36). Although the metaphor of one who sins
as a "slave to sin" is common elsewhere in early Christian tradition, beginning with the
letters of Paul, the twist of this saying is unique among the extant sayings of Jesus.[18] Its
preservation in John raises (but by no means establishes) the possibility that Paul derived some of his variations of the trope of slavery from lost sayings of Jesus.

The most important ancient sources purporting to pass along Jesus' sayings thus
witness to his regular use of the trope of slavery. To some degree these traditions over-
lap. Nonetheless, independent witnesses to the Jesus tradition preserve disparate sayings in which slaves figure. No trajectory of the Jesus tradition lacks slave sayings. We
may offer varying assessments of the import of the figure of the slave in the sayings of
Jesus, but the distribution of slave-related parables and other sayings throughout the
trajectories of the Jesus tradition leaves no doubt that he routinely deployed the trope of
slavery. After examining the figure of the slave in Jesus' sayings in Luke and Matthew,
I return to the implications of Jesus' metaphoric reliance on slaves and slaveholders for
attempts to reconstruct earlier versions of his parables.

Figure of the Slave in Jesus' Discourse in Luke

C. H. Dodd began his definition of parables by noting that, most simply, a parable is
a "metaphor or simile drawn from nature or common life."[19] Following his cue, commentators have noted the everydayness of the images Jesus uses in his parables: fish-
nets, leaven, weeds. As with these other metaphoric fields, the language of slavery in
the parables participates in the everydayness of life in the first century. In Luke as in
Matthew, slaves figure more prominently in the sayings of Jesus than they do in the
narrative of Jesus' ministry (that is, in the stories of Jesus' healings, exorcisms, travels,
and encounters with men and women). Because so many of Jesus' sayings preserved in
Luke and Matthew feature the figure of the slave, they create the impression that Jesus'
audience was as familiar with the world of slaveholding and enslavement as with the
worlds of farming and fishing.

"No slave," says Jesus, "can serve two masters; for a slave will either hate the one
and love the other, or be devoted to the one and despise the other. You cannot serve
God and wealth" (Luke 16:13; cf. Matt. 6:24 and G. *Thom.* 47). So proverbial has this
saying become that we have lost sight of the difficult reality to which it refers, the double
bind experienced by slaves who did in fact have two or more owners. We come across
slaves with multiple owners in the documentary evidence from Egypt, where we also
encounter some of the problems of multiple ownership. The documents, however, record
the problems that owners have as they contest rights in slaves. They only indirectly attest to the conflicts of slaves as they try to satisfy the demands of owners with differing

interests. For example, a slave with multiple owners would encounter additional ob-stacles to manumission: what would happen if one owner was willing to manumit the slave, but the other owner(s) opposed manumission? There is some evidence in Roman law that, if a partial owner manumitted his or her share in a slave, the remaining owner(s) of the slave could simply assert rights to the manumitted share of the slave.[20] Docu-ments from Egypt, however, suggest that, in some regions of the Empire, local law and custom allowed a slaveholder with partial rights in a slave to manumit his or her share. The slave would then be one-half or one-third free. In the late second century, for ex-ample, the guardian of three minors auctioned a two-thirds interest in a slave named Sarapion, "aged about 30 years, the remaining third share of whom, belonging to Diogenes their brother on the father's side, has been set free by him."[21] Though Sarapion was one-third free, he was two-thirds slave, and he remained, presumably, under the total control of his owners.

A series of documents produced over a series of six years in the late second century limns a more dramatic story over conflicting rights in the body of a slave.[22] Three brothers inherited from their mother shares in a slave named Martilla. Two of the brothers filed a legal petition complaining that two men seized Martilla "while she was at work, and having kidnapped her by violence without intervention of the strategus, kept her with themselves and keep her even up to now on pretense of a claim which they allege to have against our other brother Philantinoos." Six months later the two brothers filed a new complaint. The charge was no longer directed against the alleged kidnappers but against Philantinoos: "Philantinoos, our other brother, outrageously pledged to a credi-tor . . . our female slave . . . without our cognizance and to our prejudice, wrongfully diverting the money to his own uses only." The aggrieved brothers sought recovery of their lawful shares in Martilla. The matter had still not been resolved six years later when Philantinoos filed papers promising to produce written evidence to show that he had pledged only his own share in Martilla. The written evidence thus documents the problems that joint ownership could create for those who shared property rights. How the tense and protracted conflict affected Martilla, however, we can only infer. The ini-tial document refers to a violent kidnapping. One wonders how many shouting and shoving matches occurred over the years with Martilla caught in the middle—ordered to stay with the men who claimed to be her new owners, ordered to depart with her origi-nal owners, unsure who her legal owners were, certain only that she was subject to violence from all of these men. No slave, it seems, would want to serve two masters. Considered in the context of ancient slavery, Jesus' warning against serving two masters no longer sounds vague and metaphorical but resonates with the actual tensions im-plicit in the not uncommon occasion of a slave caught between the demands of two or more masters.

Slaves appear as either major or minor actors in seven or, arguably, eight Lukan parables. Mary Ann Beavis has argued that the unjust steward of the Lukan parable (16:1–8) is a slave and that the representation of this figure in the parable relies on familiarity with the figure of the rascally, wily slave, which we find in authors such as Plautus and Aesop.[23] The steward, knowing himself to be in disfavor with his owner, curries favors with his master's debtors by forgiving their debts in the hopes that they will shelter him when the master lets him go. In her insistence that New Testament scholars take seriously the identity of parabolic slaves as slaves, Beavis makes an essential contribution to parable studies. Nonetheless, I disagree with many of her specific conclusions, including the identification of the unjust steward as a slave.[24] As Beavis points out, many stewards were slaves. However, many others were freedmen, and some were even freeborn men. The parable does rely on the steward's underhanded cleverness, a standard twist in the representation of slaves in the literature of the time. Freedmen and other figures in subordinate positions would also be represented in a similar light. More important, Beavis acknowledges but underplays the steward's expectation that he will be dismissed and have to find his own employment and lodging.[25] A slave whose master believed that he had wasted household property would more likely fear corporal punishment, imprisonment, demotion within the household to menial tasks, or sale into a harsher slavery or away from loved ones—threats we will encounter in the Matthean parable of the unmerciful slave. I think it likely that ancient audiences would have understood the wily steward to be a freedman but not a slave. By highlighting the resemblance between the parabolic steward and the canny slaves of ancient literature, we run the risk of exaggerating the differences between representations of slaves and representations of other marginalized or lower-status persons. I therefore do not number the parable of the steward among the Lukan slave parables.

Slaves do appear in the Lukan parables, clearly, and they perform a variety of jobs. Their masters reward them, punish them, or accept their labor as a matter of course, without comment. In one Lukan parable the slaves stay awake to welcome their master home from a wedding banquet. Unexpectedly, he invites them to sit down to eat and serves them himself: "Be like those who are waiting for their master to return from the wedding banquet, so that they may open the door for him as soon as he comes and knocks. Blessed are those slaves whom the master finds alert when he comes; truly, I tell you, he will fasten his belt and have them sit down to eat, and he will come and serve them" (12:35–37). Jesus goes on to heap special praise on those slaves who are even awake in the early hours of dawn. While the reader of Luke understands that Jesus is encouraging the faithful to prepare for the return of the resurrected Lord, the parable itself relies on the recognition that slaves are expected to be available to their owners not only by day but also by night. In a second-century apprenticeship contract, a man who hired out his female slave as an apprentice weaver specified that she was nonetheless to be available to serve him in the middle of the night when he needed someone to bake bread.[26] Jesus' expectation that trustworthy slaves are waiting by the door for the master's return is thus entirely within the parameters of mandated servile labor.

The depiction of the rewards of the doorkeeping slaves contrasts sharply with the treatment of slaves in another Lukan parable, which Jesus addresses explicitly to slaveholders: "Who among you would say to your slave who has just come in from plowing or tending sheep in the field, 'Come here at once and take your place at the table'? Would you not rather say to him, 'Prepare supper for me, put on your apron and serve me while I eat and drink; later you may eat and drink'?" (17:7–8). Beavis rightly objects to Bernard Brandon Scott's assertion that this parable challenges the mores of the hierarchical Roman Empire: "On the contrary, this parable is rather conservative in that it casually assumes that the listener is a slave owner who treats his/her slaves without undue consideration."[27] That is, the hardworking slave in this parable receives neither reward nor arbitrary punishment. The slaveholder continues to extract the slave's labor so long as it benefits him. Perhaps more important, Jesus' lead-in to the parable anticipates that slaveholders will agree that slaves who have worked hard in the field still have labor to complete before they can think about resting. In several Lukan parables, then, conditions of slave labor militate against adequate rest for the bodies of slaves.

What determines the difference between treatment of slaves in these two Lukan parables is not the conduct of the slaves, which in both cases conforms to the behavior demanded of countless menial slaves in the ancient world. What determines the difference between the treatment of slaves in the two parables is rather the whim of the slaveholder. Indeed, the temperament of the slaveholder played an inevitable role in the good or poor treatment of slaves, a factor over which slaves themselves had no control. Finley points out that the judgment of a nineteenth-century student of American slave laws is equally relevant for understanding the position of ancient slaves: "I speak of the case of slaves *generally*. Their condition will, no doubt, in a greater degree, take its complexion from the peculiar disposition of their respective masters,—a consideration which operates as much *against* as in *favor* of the slave."[28] While Luke leaves no doubt that slaveholders would not customarily act as waiters for weary slaves, the structure of these parables rests on the recognition that the welfare of chattel slaves depends on the caprice of the slaveholder and not on the intrinsic merits of the slave.

In Lukan parables, slaves in small households perform multiple mundane tasks. In the Markan version of the parable of the doorkeeper, each slave has his own work, and only one slave serves as doorkeeper. In the Lukan version of the same parable, slaves who presumably have a variety of diurnal tasks are expected to serve as nocturnal doorkeepers. The slave who works in the fields is expected to come in and prepare the owner's meal. Luke represents slaves engaged in both menial tasks and managerial tasks. In the parable generally known as the prodigal son, for example, the owner sends for his slaves to serve as body attendants for the estranged son. The slaves are instructed to dress the son in a robe and to put a ring on his finger and sandals on his feet (15:11–24). Alicia Batten has argued that the parable disrupts on several levels the prevailing cultural code of honor and shame. The prodigal son has dishonored not only father but also family. In running to greet the errant son, the father, too, exhibits a lack of concern for dignity and honor. In challenging his father, the elder son reveals a deficiency of respect.[29] Batten's arguments are valid, as far as they go, but the parable ultimately returns the prodigal son to a position of respect within the family: honorably garbed and honorably shod. The presence of the family's slaves reinforces the dignity and uniqueness of the position of the son. The slaves, kneeling at the son's feet to fasten his sandals, are represented as bodies outside the game of honor.

In the first chapter, we saw that Ulpian distinguished between slaves with baser jobs, such as washing guests' feet or disposing of household waste, and slaves with relatively dignified work, such as handling household accounts. Along with portraying slaves engaged in menial tasks, Luke also portrays slaves handling high-level business for their owners. In several Lukan parables, slaves serve as personal or business emissaries for their owners. The master sends slaves to collect rent in the parable of the tenants (20:9–18). In the parable of the dinner party, the master orders his slaves to invite guests to a dinner (14:16–24). When the first guests decline the invitation, the master asks his slaves to deliver invitations to the poor, the disabled, and the shabby folks in roads and lanes. Still, the master does not ask the slaves to join the party, reinforcing the status division between slaves and even the most destitute of freeborn persons.

Slaves play important roles in managing the owner's estate in two Lukan parables. In the parable of the pounds, a king distributes ten pounds to ten slaves as he prepares for a journey (19:12–27). He instructs the slaves to use the pounds to engage in business in his absence. When he returns he demands an accounting from three of the slaves. The king expresses approval for the slaves who have successfully engaged in business and assigns them additional responsibility and authority within the kingdom. The king expresses displeasure with the slave who has buried his single pound. The identification of the slaveholder as a king invites us to think of the extensive influence wielded by imperial slaves. Many members of the familia Caesaris, or family of Caesar, exercised considerable influence and controlled massive sums of money. Luke's version of the parable of the pounds/talents resonates with the actual opportunities enjoyed by slaves owned by the emperor or other members of his household, including well-placed imperial slaves.[30] To the parabolic slaves whose business acumen has pleased him, the master/king gives control over many cities. To a twenty-first-century reader this may seem peculiar. The king does not separate his personal and public funds. However, this is exactly the way imperial finances worked. According to P. R. C. Weaver, "The emperor's *patrimonium* . . . held an ambivalent position as more than personal and less than state property attached to the Imperial title."[31] Slaves who managed the emperor's funds were thus instrumental in handling the finances of the Empire. We cannot easily disentangle the parabolic king's personal staff from the administrative team upon which he relied. Within the context of imperial slavery in the first century, the demands and responses of the king to his enslaved managers in the parable of the pounds are routine. Some commentators seize on the managerial role of the *douloi* to imply that they are not actually slaves. Joseph Fitzmyer, for example, refers to the *douloi* as "agents empowered to trade in his [the king's] name."[32] This statement is true but potentially misleading. What may well be overlooked in such a formulation is the extent to which ancient elites relied on slaves as financial agents.

In the parable of the overseer, the owner entrusts one slave to manage the estate in his absence (12:42–48). Greater responsibility is in store if the overseer is faithful; punishment awaits a feckless overseer. The presence of a slave manager was typical of Roman household structure.[33] Even in this parable, however, the majority of slaves are in more menial positions, subordinated to management by the slave overseer. The authority of the enslaved overseer extends to corporal control over the other household slaves. These slaves have their very food ration controlled by a figure who is their fellow slave. In the absence of the owner, he eats, he drinks to excess, and he beats the other slaves. This is the only canonical parable that features female slaves: the overseer beats both male slaves and female slaves (*typtein tous paidas kai tas paidiskas*), underscoring that the female as well as the male slave body was subject to violence. The parable of the overseer ends with a scene of gruesome corporal abuse, as the angry slaveholder cuts his overseer in pieces. Luke is less consistent than Matthew in representing the slave body as vulnerable to physical violations. However, Luke's conclusion to the parable of the overseer offers a sober assessment of the prospects of slaves for corporal punishment: "The slave who knew what his master wanted, but did not prepare himself or do what was wanted, will receive a severe beating. But the one who did not know and did what deserved a beating will receive a light beating" (12:47–48a). What seems inevitable is that the body of the slave will be battered. Let us turn, then, to Matthew, where this theme figures most prominently.

Parabolic Slaves in Matthew

In keeping with their laconic style, the parables supply few details about the slaves they represent. The reader may nonetheless make some inferences about the nature of their work. The slaves who approach the master in the parable of the weeds and wheat to tell him that tares are growing amidst the grain are agricultural slaves (13:24–30). In the parables of the wicked tenants and the wedding banquet, slaves serve as messengers or emissaries, collecting rent or inviting guests to the banquet (21:33–41, 22:1–14). Since the master expects the slaves in the parable of the wicked tenants to return with the rent, he must trust them with handling his funds. In the parable of the unmerciful slave, the slaveholder initially forgives the unmerciful slave the enormous debt of ten thousand talents. However, when the slaveholder learns that the unmerciful slave has ordered the imprisonment of another slave who owes a much smaller debt, he turns the unmerciful slave over to the torturers (18:23–35). Although there are no clear indications regarding the work of the unmerciful slave (nor the slave he abuses), the magnitude of his debt to his owner suggests that he is deeply involved in household financial affairs. To lesser but still significant degrees the slaves in the parable of the talents (25:14–36) serve as their master's financial agents. Finally, the master in the parable of the overseer entrusts the enslaved overseer with managing an important part of his property: his other slaves (24:45–51). The assortment of work performed by these parabolic slaves is heavily skewed toward managerial tasks. While it was not uncommon for slaves to fill such roles, the majority of slaves in the early Empire labored at more onerous tasks, ranging from mining to attending to their owners' bodily needs. Nonetheless, those we are labeling as managerial slaves constituted the most visible sector of slaves in Greco-Roman society. That is, managerial slaves were more likely than other groups of slaves to attract the attention of various authors, to erect memorials, and to engage in the kinds of transactions that created a documentary trail.

Managerial slaves often worked in close proximity to their owners, who were thus acutely aware of the quality of their work. Not surprisingly, the theme of the faithful slave emerges in several of the parables, notably the parables of the overseer and the talents. Both parables contrast the exemplary work of the faithful slave with the flawed work of the wicked slave.

Despite the relatively prestigious work of these slaves, the parables stress that they are subject to corporal punishment. The master of the unmerciful slave hands him over to torturers, the wicked overseer is cut in half, and the slave entrusted with a single talent is expelled into the outer darkness. The punishments of the overseer and the slave entrusted with a single talent fuse the theme of corporal punishment of the slave with the Matthean leitmotiv of punishment at the time of judgment, "weeping and gnashing of teeth." All three parables are predicated on the widespread trope of the slave as a body awaiting discipline, even, or perhaps especially, when that slave has been a trusted manager. Other slaves in the Matthean parables are also subject to corporal mistreatment. The unmerciful slave seizes his fellow slave and imprisons him; the wicked overseer beats his master's other slaves. Even the enslaved emissaries in the parables of the wicked tenants and the wedding banquet meet physical violation to the point of death, although the agents of that treatment are not their owners but their owners' tenants and associates. The slave's body as the locus of abuse is thus pervasive in the Matthean parables, constituting the most prominent dimension of Matthew's representation of slavery.

Table 4.1 offers an overview of the principal themes of Matthew's parabolic representation of slaves, which we consider in greater detail in the next sections.

Managerial Slaves

How does the parabolic representation of managerial slaves affect our understanding of the practice and ideology of slavery in the first century? We may read several of the Matthean parables as vignettes sketching the route that slaves often took to increasing responsibility and influence. The parable of the overseer and the parable of the talents feature slaves who, through their competent or exceptional discharge of managerial responsibilities, acquire enhanced roles in the management of their masters' households. The parable of the unmerciful slave gestures toward the heights that elite slaves could reach: the unmerciful slave has access to his royal master's resources to the extent that he eventually amasses indebtedness to his owner totaling ten thousand talents.

Modern readers sometimes find these details of ancient slavery startling. In fact, commentators have insisted that the slaves (*douloi*) in these parables are not really slaves. Joachim Jeremias suggests that the *doulos* in the parable of the unmerciful slave is a "satrap."[34] Jeremias notes that *syndouloi* refers to high-placed Palestinian officials in 2 Esdras 4–6. He does not, however, cite other uses of *doulos* to justify his assumption that the term could refer to free court officials rather than to slaves. J. D. M. Derrett asserts that the unmerciful servant is a "minister" of the king: "*douloi* means ministers."[35] Bernard Brandon Scott, who perceived the indebted servant to be heavily involved in tax farming, took for granted that Derrett was correct in his explication of details of this parable.[36] Commentators still rely on Derrett's monumental volume on law in the New Testament. Although Derrett treated slavery in the context of specific parables, slavery as a category did not merit an entry in his index. Throughout his research, Derrett drew on later Jewish and Islamic law and even referred to the practices

Table 4.1 Matthew's Representation of Slaves

Parable	Managerial slave	Faithful slave/ wicked slave	Slave body as site of abuse/discipline
Weeds and wheat (13:24–30)			
Unmerciful slave (18:23–35)	X		X
Wicked tenants (21:33–41)	X		X
Wedding banquet (22:1–10)			X
Overseer (24:45–51)	X	X	X
Talents (25:14–30)	X	X	X

of India. He did not, however, consider the practices and ideology of slavery in the early Roman Empire, nor did he draw on Roman law regarding slaves and slavery.

Matthew, however, clearly uses the language of slavery. Moreover, in no way does he indicate that these slaves are atypical. Rather, his parabolic slaves personify first-century stereotypes of managerial slaves.

Do these parables tell slave success stories, offering evidence that slavery could serve as a positive route to advancement in the ancient world? In one sense we may respond affirmatively. The Matthean parables depict slaves who enhance their own positions by diligently pursuing their owners' interests. At the same time, however, every Matthean parable that features a managerial slave also highlights the vulnerability of such slaves to physical abuse. An elite slave may have sufficient access to his owner's estate to accrue an enormous debt of ten thousand talents, but this slave still knows that his master has absolute rights over his body, rights that include the prerogatives of torturing him or selling him and his family into a harsher slavery, which could include the sale of family members to geographically scattered households. Parabolic masters displeased with the work of their managerial slaves enacted their displeasure via a range of bodily punishments ranging from dismemberment to banishment (which first-century readers might associate with the familiar exiles of slavery, including imprisonment or sale into distant slavery). The master in the parable of the wicked tenants assumes that his tenants would not dare to treat his son in the bloody manner that they have treated the enslaved agents who function as his legal surrogates; the master's assumption creates the impression that managerial slaves worked in a climate of disrespect, even contempt, for their very humanity.

In Orlando Patterson's sweeping survey of slavery around the world and through the ages, he considered the familia Caesaris in the context of other categories of slaves who test the limits of what it means to be a slave: "What could an important slave *dispensatores* or freedman *procurator* possibly have in common with a rural slave or freedman?"[37] Well-placed slaves could accrue personal fortunes; because of their access to power they could develop extensive spheres of influence. Patterson argued that despite these advantages, elite slaves, including the enslaved members of the familia Caesaris and other Roman managerial slaves, still fell within the limits of his definition of slavery: "*slavery is the permanent, violent domination of natally alienated and generally dishonored persons.*"[38] In support of this contention Patterson emphasized that regardless of the influence and personal wealth an elite slave achieved, he (or, sometimes, she) was still answerable with his body: "We should be careful not to forget the most obvious advantage of using slaves: the fact that they could be literally whipped into shape. We are likely to neglect this in considering the elite slaves, since it is true that they did not have drivers behind them as they worked. Nonetheless, naked force did apply. The slave or freedman could not only be moved about and used without any regard to his feelings on the matter, but in the event that he was inefficient and corrupt, he could be punished in the most degrading and painful manner possible."[39] As evidence for the first-century practice and ideology of slavery, the Matthean parables corroborate Patterson's analysis of the paradoxes of elite slavery. Matthew does not depict slaves in the mines or the mills or even cleaning up their owners' wastes, onerous tasks common among first-century slaves.[40] Nonetheless, his household stewards and financial agents embody what may be the most basic and pervasive reality of ancient slavery: the slave's absolute corporal vulnerability.

A number of New Testament scholars (including John Dominic Crossan, Bruce Malina, and Bernard Brandon Scott) treat slavery predominantly or exclusively as a subset of patron-client relations. The Matthean representation of the slave as a body to be used and abused serves as counterevidence to the categorization of master-slave relationships within the patron-client rubric. In a later section of this chapter, "Toward the Parables of Jesus," I offer an extensive critique of this paradigm. Here, let us note how the Matthean parables challenge the identification of masters and patrons, slaves and clients. In the parable of the talents, for example, the faithful slaves may be proud to advance their owner's interests, but they should certainly be fearful of the punishment that awaits them should they fail to do so. In the parable of the unmerciful slave, the king seems to have placed the slave in a position where he can accumulate a personal fortune. Still, the king does not function as a patron but as a man with the power to hand his slave over to torturers. The analogy between slavery and the patron-client network breaks down at the consideration of the slave as a body, in particular a body to be disciplined, which indeed is the most consistent element in ancient representations of slaves, including the Matthean parables.[41]

Ideal of the Faithful Slave

How does the parabolic theme of the faithful slave affect our understanding of the practice and ideology of slavery in the first century? Jesus begins the parable of the overseer with a related question: "Who then is the faithful and wise slave, whom the master put in charge of his household, to give them their food at the appropriate time?" (24:45). From the outset, the faithful slave has his owner's trust.[42] The slave merits praise as faithful simply by completing his duties, working diligently in his master's absence. Other slaves appear in the parable, receiving their rations from the overseer and later suffering abuse from the wicked slave. Although the parable does not suggest that they are negligent in their duties, their master does not single them out for faithfulness. In the parable of the talents, the master acknowledges two of his slaves with the phrase "Well done, good and faithful slave" (25:21, 23). As in the parable of the overseer, the master entrusts them with property in his absence. In fact, the master entrusts them with considerable property, the respective sums of five talents and two talents. Their accomplishments are greater than that of the faithful overseer, since they go beyond safeguarding their master's property to double the sums with which they are entrusted. Both parables seem to assume that a faithful slave is one who occupies a managerial position and has moreover internalized the master's interests to the extent that he will work unsupervised when his master is away. Slave morality is inextricably identified with the master's interests. In return for their labors, these faithful slaves receive additional responsibility. The faithful overseer will have oversight of his master's entire estate (24:47); the first two slaves in the parable of the talents will have care of many of their master's affairs (25:21, 23). Even their rewards forward their master's concerns.

We might equally ask, who is the wicked slave? In the parable of the overseer, the wicked slave abuses the property with which he has been entrusted. He beats his fellow slaves. It seems he opens his master's stores of food and drink to his gluttonous friends (24:49). In the parable of the talents, however, the wicked slave does not abuse his master's property but neither does he work assiduously for his master. Rather, he stores the goods with which he has been entrusted, the single talent (still a considerable sum). Jesus does not consider the possibility that the slave's moral options are separable from the master's interests. In both parables, physical abuse is the punishment for harming, or even failing to increase, the master's property. The wicked overseer is dismembered, and the luckless slave with a single talent is banished to a place of torment.

Consideration of the motif of the wicked slave leads to a further insight concerning the ideal of the faithful slave. The third slave in the parable of the talents explains to his owner that he has buried his single talent because his master is a harsh man, who he fears. Although the faithful slaves do not identify fear as a motivation, surely they are aware that vulnerability to physical abuse is inherent in the situation of the slave. In the parable of the overseer, the wicked slave is vicious, abusing his fellow slaves for no stated reason. In the parable of the talents, the third slave is called wicked on the basis not of viciousness but of indolence.[43] The slave and his owner offer different assessments of his inaction. The slave focuses on the harshness of the master, citing fear as the reason for his paralysis (verse 25). According to the master, however, the slave's inaction proves that he is both lazy and wicked.[44] On the other hand, both master and slave acknowledge that the master exacts difficult standards, reaping where he does not sow and gathering where he does not scatter. The master does not explicitly repeat the slave's description of him as harsh, but neither does the parable challenge this verdict.[45] Modern sensibilities are likely to shrink from an endorsement of the master's grasping and punitive nature.[46]

In the words of Richard Saller, "The lot of bad slaves was to be beaten and that of good slaves was to internalize the constant threat of a beating."[47] Joseph Vogt noted that in several plays, Plautus wrote speeches for faithful slaves in which they discussed both the attributes of a good slave and their motivation for fidelity, notably fear of punishment.[48] By concluding with examples of wicked slaves enduring corporal punishment, the parables allude to what was probably the strongest incentive slaves had for loyalty to their owners, that is, the fear of disciplinary retribution.

Vogt cited the parables as the culmination of his discussion of the ideal of the faithful slave: "This transformation of the faithful slave into one who does nothing particularly heroic, but merely performs his duties with devotion, belongs not to pagan literature but to the writings of the early Christians. . . . I refer to the *doulos agathos kai pistos* [good and faithful slave]."[49] For Vogt, the parabolic enunciation of the ideal of the faithful slave is wholly positive: "All that matters here is to recognize how slaves have been ennobled merely by becoming the symbols of man's place in the Kingdom of God."[50] Finley offered a critique of Vogt's romantic distortion of the faithful slave: "Not everyone will rank the creation of honorable and decent servants as one of the higher goals of humanity, or accommodation to enslavement as a moral virtue."[51] Vogt and Finley both acknowledged that the parabolic ideal of the faithful slave was significant for understanding the ideology of slavery in the early Empire. Vogt, however, construed the parabolic elevation of servile fidelity as confirmation of a noble ideal, whereas Finley insisted that such a construal cloaked the exploitative nature of exchanges between master and slave.

Beavis asserts that "the parables are distinctive in that the reward offered to faithful slaves is not manumission but more trust and responsibility."[52] However, many slave owners did increase the responsibilities of faithful slaves, long before manumitting them. Most well known, though highly atypical, were the slaves of the family of Caesar, whose increasing responsibilities also brought them increasing social influence.[53] Furthermore, Augustan reforms restricted the formal manumission of slaves before the age of thirty. Numerous acts of faithful service necessarily preceded the typical act of manumission. Ancient audiences would thus have realized that not every dutiful act (for example, safe-guarding a master's property in his absence) merited instantaneous manumission. Moreover, as we saw in chapter three, not all faithful slaves realized their hopes for manumission before dying.

While ancient literature includes many allusions to the manumission of faithful slaves, not every literary report of servile fidelity culminates in the slave's manumission. Holt Parker draws attention to the centrality of the trope of the faithful slave in Roman *exemplum* literature: "Although images of faithful slaves and faithful wives appear in a wide range of genres—comedy, history, elegy, letters—these comfortable words form their own sub-group within the extraordinarily popular genre of *exemplum* literature. The *exemplum* is a self-contained short story, illustrating a particular cultural rule."[54] Parker notes that in the *exempla*, loyal slaves "may be given freedom itself, as are, *on equally infrequent occa-sions*, the clever slaves of Roman comedy" (emphasis added). *Pace* Beavis, the parables are not distinctive in depicting faithful slaves who are not rewarded with manumission. For example, Seneca's *De Beneficiis* offers an extended treatment of the exchange of favors between masters and slaves.[55] Although Seneca relates many stories of servile loyalty, only two conclude with the manumission of the faithful slave. In one of these stories, a slave helps Rufus, his master, with a plan to appease Augustus Caesar, who he has offended. The plan is successful, and Rufus insists to Caesar that in order to convince others of his restoration to Caesar's graces, Caesar should give him a substantial gift. Caesar accedes to Rufus's request. Seneca concludes the story with the announcement of the slave's manumission: "Yet it was not a gratuitous act—Caesar had paid the price of his liberty!"[56] Valerius Maximus and Appian also compile accounts of servile loyalty (with some repetition among these accounts). However, neither mentions a single in-stance where a master accords a slave freedom for even heroic service.[57] All three au-thors feature a number of tales in which servile fidelity costs a slave his life as he pro-tects his master from death or dishonor. Valerius Maximus specifies the reward of one such faithful slave. During the time of unrest following the civil wars, a slave helped his master escape from the house and then took the master's place in bed, where soldiers killed him. His reward? A monument that his master erected in his memory.[58]

A final tale from Valerius Maximus offers a sobering perspective on the faithful slave.[59] Antius Restio had a slave, who he had punished repeatedly, keeping him in chains, even branding his forehead.[60] Nonetheless, when Antius came under the proscription of the triumvirs, the slave engineered his escape. At one point, when soldiers pursued them, the slave built a fire, found a helpless old man, and threw him on the fire. The slave told the soldiers that the burning man was his master, Antius Restio, who he had thrown on the fire on account of his cruelty. The soldiers believed the account, at least long enough for the slave to bring Antius to safety.[61] Even in the case of a harsh master, ancient au-thors admired and applauded acts of heroic loyalty by a slave. Perhaps we are not so far from the Matthean version of the parable of the talents, where a master acknowledged to be harsh praises the performance of his faithful slaves in increasing his wealth.

Both in practice and in literature many faithful slaves achieved manumission; both in practice and in literature, many faithful slaves did not achieve manumission. As we have seen, the *Shepherd of Hermas* relates a parable in which a faithful slave not only receives manumission but also joins the slaveholder's son as co-heir of the vineyard, a reward for faithful service that was both distinctive and countercultural. The reward of faithful slaves in the Matthean parables—additional responsibility rather than freedom—was neither distinctive nor countercultural. In order to ensure smooth functioning of their households, masters relied on skillful slaves. In turn, as they undertook increasing responsibility, slaves sometimes amassed personal funds and even political influence. Such rewards were a strong positive incentive to fidelity. On the other hand, ever-present threats of corporal punishment or sale into a harsher slavery were even stronger incentives, driving slaves to work diligently on behalf of their owners' interests. To a large extent, the faithful slave was a by-product of the fear of corporal punishment. Moreover, by representing the reward and punishment of faithless and feckless slaves as the natural consequences of the slaves' own actions, the parables divert attention from the masters' ultimate control over their slaves' bodies and fortunes.[62]

The Enslaved Body as the Site of Discipline

Again and again, the Matthean parables emphasize the liability of the slave, as a body, to abuse and punishment. The agricultural slaves of the parable of the weeds and wheat escape this cycle of violence. However, every other Matthean parable that features slaves in either central or supporting roles describes the physical violation of at least some of those slaves. As in the plays of Plautus, the parables of Matthew seem to define a slave as "one who gets whipped"; the trope of the beaten slave is an almost obsessive concern in Matthew as in Plautus.[63]

So pervasive is this theme that we may attempt several taxonomies of the parabolic abuse of slaves. We may first categorize the parables according to the agents of abuse. The slave owner is responsible for physical abuse in the guise of discipline in three parables (the unmerciful slave, the overseer, and the talents). Explicitly in the parable of the unmerciful slave and implicitly in the parable of the talents, the slaveholder assigns an agent or agents to enact the violence on the slave's body. Slaveholders frequently relied on surrogates to whip their slaves. The agents of such violence were often slaves themselves. In a study of the representation of slaves in Roman literature, William Fitzgerald argues, "The man of intellect distinguishes himself from the man of the body and the passions by having an intermediary act out his anger for him."[64] By depicting parabolic slaveholders employing intermediaries, Matthew preserves their dignity by distancing them from the passionate expression of anger or vengeance. In contrast, in the two parables in which slaves enact abuse against their fellow slaves, the abusers perform the acts associated with their own violent emotions. The unmerciful slave seizes and tries to choke a fellow slave, and then imprisons him; the wicked overseer beats his fellow slaves in the absence of his master.

In the two parables that feature enslaved emissaries, those outside the household are responsible for the abuse. On two occasions the wicked tenants beat and then kill the slaves sent to collect the rent. Apparently, the vineyard owner accounts for this treatment on the basis of the servile status of the emissaries, since he anticipates that the tenants will treat his son with greater respect (21:37). In the parable of the wedding banquet the invited guests treat the enslaved messengers with disrespect (*hybrisan*) and ultimately kill them (22:6). These final examples point to the general dishonor accorded to slaves in the first century. Not only were slaves vulnerable to abuse from within the household, but they had few protections against others who sought to harm them. Such a finding is consistent with other ancient literature, in which slaves are routinely subject to maltreatment from a variety of persons. Two incidents from *The Golden Ass* serve as illustrations. Lucius's enslaved lover, Fotis, recounts an incident in which her mistress sent her to a barber's shop to retrieve a man's hair to use in sorcery. When the barber saw her there, he felt free to grab her roughly and search her person for snippets of hair.[65] In a complex tale of adultery, a slaveholder named Barbarus entrusts his slave Myrmex with the protection of his wife's chastity when he leaves on a journey. Instead, Myrmex abets a man named Philesitherus in arranging a liaison with the wife. Barbarus returns from the trip to find the other man's slippers under his bed. He blames Myrmex for the breach of security. Barbarus orders the other slaves to put Myrmex in chains, and they lead him to the forum. When Philesitherus sees Myrmex there, he remembers the slippers and improvises. He approaches Myrmex and beats him, accusing him of stealing his slippers from the bath. As a result, Barbarus believes that he was mistaken to suspect adultery and releases Myrmex. What is relevant for the present discussion is that Barbarus, the slave owner, finds nothing unusual in a stranger accosting and beating his slave.[66] As in the parables of the wedding banquet and the wicked tenants, slaves seem to have little protection against anyone who accosts them. Roman law treated violence against a slave as an insult to the owner. Moreover, violence against a free person merited harsher legal penalties than violence against a slave. Ulpian even stipulated that slaves involved in the meanest tasks have no legal protection from random violence or insults.[67] One might also recall the scene of Jesus' arrest: all four canonical Gospels identify the man whose ear is cut off as a *doulos*, the slave of the high priest (Matt. 26:51; Mark 14:47; Luke 22:50; John 18:10).

A second taxonomy classifies the kinds of abuse that slaves endure in the Matthean parables. Slaves are seized (*kratēsas*, 18:28; *labontes*, 21:35; *kratēsantes*, 22:6), imprisoned (18:30), treated with dishonor (*hybrisan*, 22:6), beaten (*edeiran*, 21:35; *typtein*, 24:49), cut in pieces (*dichotomēsei*, 24:51), handed over to torturers (*paredōken auton tois basanistais*, 18:34), consigned to a place of "weeping and gnashing of teeth" (24:51, 25:30), killed (21:35, 22:6), and stoned (21:35). Although most of these instances of abuse occur as disciplinary action, in the two parables where slaves are killed (the parable of the wicked tenants and the parable of the wedding banquet), the violent encounters take place outside the master's household, as slaves perform duties required of them.[68] This list of the injuries to slaves' bodies is evidence of first-century familiarity with the travails of enslaved life. However, it does not really contribute to our knowledge of the kinds of abuse slaves anticipated. In fact, this catalog seems almost tame compared to other Greco-Roman references to the kinds of punishments routinely meted out to slaves. Erich Segal summarizes the varieties of abuse threatened against slaves in the comedies of Plautus: "Besides the countless references to the standard whipping instruments like *virgae* (rods) and *stimuli* (goads), his comedies display a vocabulary of tortures. . . . Plautus mentions an astounding number of torture devices, including iron chains, hot tar, burning clothes, restraining collars, the rack, the pillory, and the mill. The fact that his bondsmen are so frequently referred to as *verbero* (flogworthy), *mastigia* (whip-worthy), and *furcifer* (gallows bird) is an additional reminder of what retribution usually awaits a misbehaving slave."[69] Although

Plautus enumerates an unusual number of torture devices and practices, consideration of other Greco-Roman sources only increases our awareness of the disturbing array of disciplinary devices available to slave owners: spiked whips, hot irons, torture, and various means of execution.[70] Shocking to modern readers, Matthew's inventory of the abuses to which slaves were subject is easily within the mainstream of ancient literature. Members of an imperial society in which the violence of blood-sports constituted a common spectacle and wildly popular entertainment were likely to be inured in any case to accounts of everyday brutality directed against the bodies of slaves.

Fitzgerald writes: "Being beaten is one of the most important things that literary slaves do. Listing the tasks required of a maid, Demipho in Plautus' *Mercator* comes up with the following: "We have no need of a maid, except one to weave, grind, / Cut wood, do her spinning, sweep the house, be beaten."[71] One consistent difference between the representation of violence toward slaves in the plays of Plautus and the Matthean parables is the question of whether the slaves portrayed actually incur blows. The humor of Plautus's comedies revolves around slaves who narrowly but consistently avoid threatened abuse.[72] Slaves in the Matthean parables, less fortunate, rarely seem to elude punishment or other forms of brutality.

What is Matthew's attitude toward the abuse of slaves? The maltreatment of slaves has a negative valence in the parables of the wicked tenants and the wedding banquet, in which outsiders attack enslaved emissaries. In both parables, however, the insult can be construed to be primarily against the slave owner rather than the slaves. As we saw in the first chapter, slaves often served as surrogate bodies, absorbing violence intended as affront and insult to slave owners. In the parable of the wedding banquet, the murder of the slaves excites the king's anger (22:7), but Matthew does not specify whether the king is angry at the loss of human life or the affront to him. In the parable of the wicked tenants the vineyard owner reacts with anger, not to the repeated murder of his slaves, but to the murder of his son (21:41). The parables of the unmerciful slave and the overseer offer negative portrayals of the violent treatment of slaves that is committed by other slaves and unsanctioned by slaveholders. In the three slave parables where the relation of the slave owner to slaves signifies the relation of God to humans, the disciplinary action suffered by the slaves symbolizes torments of an afterlife, punishment in conjunction with ultimate judgment on one's actions in this world.[73] Matthew's appropriation of the image of the master ordering the punishment of his slaves as a metaphor for divine justice does not necessarily imply that Matthew condones customary first-century practices of disciplining slaves. Nonetheless, his inscription of this image assumes and participates in the normalcy of such terror in slaves' lives. The Matthean parables liken divine punishment to a slave owner's punishment of his (or, presumably, her) slaves. Unless we are to assume that Matthew considers divine punishment to be disproportionate to the demerits of those who suffer it, by analogy, we cannot presume Matthew supposes the punishments that slave owners commonly visit on their slaves to be excessive. As with Paul's deployment of slave metaphors, Matthew "depends on the reality of slavery to convey . . . [his] meanings and therefore reinscribes the relation[s] of slavery."[74]

In the context of Matthew 24–25, the parables of the overseer and the talents caution readers about what they may expect if they do not live up to the demands of Jesus' message. Slaves in the ancient Mediterranean world lived with the constant pressure of knowing their liability to sudden and sometimes arbitrary punishments at the whim of their owners; the punishments of the wicked overseer and the slave with a single talent (too frightened of his master's acknowledged violence to act) remind readers of their liability to divinely mandated penalties. This message is even explicit in the parable of the unmerciful slave, which concludes with a warning to the community: "Thus my heavenly father will also do to you, unless every one of you forgives your brother or sister from your hearts" (18:35). Consciousness of disciplinary realities produces the faithful slave of a divine master as of a human master.

Punishment of slaves in antiquity was typically a public affair, so that other slaves could absorb lessons with every blow to the body of the slave being disciplined. For example, the tale we have already considered from *The Golden Ass*, where Barbarus leads Myrmex to the forum, presupposes that the corporal punishment of slaves is a common public spectacle. Livy narrates a tale in which a slaveholder drives his yoke-wearing slave through the circus, scourging the slave as he goes, and bystanders find nothing amiss. Suetonius describes Augustus ordering an actor named Hylas to be publicly scourged in the atrium of his own home.[75] The indignity of being publicly beaten emphasized the slave's position outside the code of honor and respect. Matthew's rehearsal of the slave parables publicizes the tortures associated with divine wrath. They have a pedagogical function, instructing the faithful by making an example of others who were not faithful.[76] What lesson is the reader to take from these parables? Slaves' exposure to the imminence of abuse reminded them incessantly of their status as slaves, while emphasizing the power of the slave owner. The slave parables teach the reader that the status of humans in the divine economy is that of slaves.[77] They also construct an image of God that stresses divine omnipotence.[78]

Like Matthew, other Greco-Roman writers seem to accept slavery as part of the natural order of the world. So common was cruelty to slaves in the Roman world that Tacitus could pinpoint the uniqueness of the Germanic approach to slavery by noting that, among Germans, "to beat a slave and coerce him with hard labor and imprisonment is rare."[79] Unlike Matthew, however, some writers expressed abhorrence at the excesses of discipline that slaves daily endured, calling attention to the disproportion between the minor offenses of slaves and the extreme nature of the punishments they received. Seneca, for example, asks, "What right have I to make my slave atone by stripes and manacles for too loud a reply, too rebellious a look, a muttering of something that I do not quite hear?"[80] Martial comments on the disparity between infraction and penalty in an epigram: "You say that the hare is underdone, and call for a whip / You prefer, Rufus, cutting up your cook rather than your hare."[81] Juvenal expects his readers to resonate with the implied rebuke in his description of a matron who calmly dresses herself while ordering vicious floggings of her slaves for such crimes as failing to meet the expectations of the mistress for her coiffeur.[82]

In the parable of the talents, the slave with a single talent incurs his owner's wrath because of an offense related to property: he has failed to increase his owner's wealth. The punishment he receives, however, is corporal: he is thrown into a place of darkness. Although this is a Matthean image of judgment at the endtime, it also invokes the darkness of prison cells, which slave owners maintained in their repertoire of disciplinary apparatus. As Finley contended: "One fundamental distinction through much of antiquity was that corporal punishment, public or private, was restricted to slaves. Demosthenes said with a flourish (22.55) that the greatest difference between the slave

and the free man is that the former 'is answerable with his body for all offenses.'"[83]
Saller argues that, although Roman fathers had the right to inflict corporal punishment
on their children, they rarely did so, precisely because such treatment was understood
to be suitable for slaves and not for free persons: "(1) the Romans attached symbolic
meaning to whippings, (2) the whip was used to make distinctions in the public sphere
between free and subject, and (3) the distinction between free and subject carried over
into the household in the administration of corporal punishment."[84] Quintilian supported his position that free children should never be beaten with the observation that
"flogging . . . is a disgraceful form of punishment and fit only for slaves."[85] In the Greco-
Roman world, the most pervasive image associated with slavery was that of a body being
beaten; in turn, ancient readers would associate representations of beaten bodies with
slaves. Thus, as Matthew turns repeatedly to the figure of the slave at disciplinary moments, he reinforces a stereotype ubiquitous in antiquity. The evidence from the Matthean
parables underscores impressions from other Greco-Roman literature concerning the
practice and ideology of first-century slavery.

During the centuries that witnessed the beginnings of Christianity and its transformation into the religion of the Empire, "the figure of the *pater flagellans*, the father who
'whips' the son he loves," takes its place alongside the figure of the disciplinary slaveholder.[86] That is, Latin Christian authors, in emphasizing that God is both father and
master, featured God disciplining the faithful not only as slaves but also as sons. In the
third and fourth centuries, official governmental punishments became harsher. Those
previously exempt from servile punishments were subjected to them, and slaves were
subjected to still more ferocious punishments. Theodore de Bruyn, who traces the
emergent Christian image of God as father/disciplinarian, speculates that the blurring
of distinctions between slave and free bodies in the public arena (a blurring that de-
pressed the status of the free poor without a corresponding elevation in the status of the
enslaved) carried over into relations between fathers and sons, which in turn shaped
the contours of Christian imagery. Imagery of God as a father who shows his love for
his sons by whipping them, however, does not displace imagery of God as a master
who beats his undeserving slaves—imagery that is drawn directly from the words of Jesus,
at least Jesus' words as they are preserved in the Matthean parables.

Toward the Parables of Jesus

Slaves appear throughout the tradition of Jesus' sayings and play a particularly prominent role in the parables. Matthew and Luke include a distinct concentration of this
material. Some, but not all, of their material appears to derive from the sayings source,
Q. In addition, Mark, Thomas, and John all preserve sayings attributed to Jesus that
feature slaves. So far we have concentrated on the representation of slaves within particular trajectories of the sayings tradition, highlighting the representation of slaves in
the Matthean and Lukan parables. Ultimately, however, we must acknowledge that all
evidence suggests that not only early Christian theologians but also Jesus himself relied
on the figure of the slave in his teachings. This should not be surprising. Jesus drew his
metaphors from the culture in which he lived, and he lived in a slaveholding culture.
The scholar who has most clearly noted the ubiquity of slave-figures in Jesus' sayings is

Winsome Munro. In support of her hypothesis that Jesus was a slave or former slave, she proposes that the parables represent "an insider understanding of what it meant to be a slave."[87] In my discussion below, I disagree with her contention that a servile identity for Jesus (Jesus as slave or as former slave) best accounts for his consistent emphasis on slaves in the parables. Nonetheless, her insistence that scholars acknowledge the centrality of the trope of the slave in Jesus' sayings, especially his parables, is an important counterbalance to scholars who continue to ignore, diminish, or distort the representation of slavery and slaves within the sayings material.

In plotting the movement of slaves within the parables, I have mapped a terrain distinct from scholars who have worked within the domain of "servant parables," although the landscape in question necessarily overlaps. In several classic works, Crossan defined the category of servant parables.[88] "*Which* are the servant parables? The criterion . . . involves two axes: a master-servant relationship or superior-subordinate relationship and a moment of critical reckoning between them. Servant parables are those whose central story line concerns such a relationship at some instance of critical confrontation between servant and master."[89] Employing this criterion, Crossan included parables that fall outside the purview of the present study because the subordinate figures they represent are not slaves, for example, the parable of the workers in the vineyard (Matt. 20:1–16). On the other hand, Crossan omitted parables that feature slaves in merely supporting roles, such as the parable of the weeds and wheat and the parable of the wedding banquet/dinner party.

Crossan divides the servant parables into two categories. Group A includes parables that operate "within a horizon of expected order and orderly expectations."[90] This category includes, for example, the parable of the overseer and the parable of the talents/pounds. What is the horizon of normalcy? Good servants receive rewards. Punishment awaits wicked servants. Parables in Group B call into question the stable parabolic world of Group A. Crossan argues that the cluster of servant parables reenacts the movement of reversal that he discerns elsewhere within discrete parables: "The reversal within the parabolic theme of the servants represents another example of what was seen earlier in the parables of reversal themselves . . . linguistic attempts to shatter the complacency of one's world in the name of the Kingdom's advent. Here it is not a short proverb or even a long parable which is in question. It is an entire parabolic theme which is developed in one set of parables (Group A) and then reversed and overthrown in another (Group B)."[91] Crossan's treatment of the servant parables was a landmark in structuralist studies of the New Testament. However, the results of his studies are of limited interest for consideration of parabolic slavery. According to Crossan's analysis, for example, the parable of the tenants belongs to Group B because it upsets expectations when the bad servants, the tenants, reap rewards instead of punishment. Crossan does not consider the treatment of the enslaved emissaries because they are not involved in a confrontation with their master. The violent treatment the slaves receive would not have upset expectations, either of first-century readers or indeed of the vineyard owner himself, who anticipates that his son will receive more respectful treatment than his slaves received. Crossan's insights based on the structure of reversal in the parables are thus of limited relevance for investigation of slavery qua slavery in the parables.

Crossan nowhere suggests, of course, that he is attempting to analyze the ideology of slavery in his structuralist investigation of the servant parables. In his more recent work on the historical Jesus, however, he does claim to consider the institution of slavery, only to subsume it within the practice of patron-client relations. In this he is not alone. A number of New Testament scholars persist in discussing slavery primarily within the rubric of patronage networks. Such misunderstanding of slavery is an impediment to research on Jesus' social world and, more immediately, to attempts to recover Jesus' teachings via the parables. For example, in a chapter of *The Historical Jesus: The Life of a Mediterranean Jewish Peasant* entitled "Slave and Patron," Crossan jumps from a brief treatment of the plight of slaves on large agricultural estates to an extensive treatment of two slaves, one historical and one fictional. Tiro, the historical slave, moved from the status of Cicero's slave to his freedman, acting throughout as his confidant. Trimalchio, the fictional slave, is the freedman lampooned in Petronius's *Satyricon*. Crossan interprets Petronius's depiction of Trimalchio as "realistic," with no recognition of the elements of satire or exaggeration in that portrayal.[92] Did the Roman Empire include slaves like Tiro and Trimalchio? Leaving aside the exaggerated elements of Petronius's satire (itself a major omission), the answer is to some extent, yes. But in focusing his treatment of slavery on these atypical figures, Crossan leaves the false impression that they were the rule rather than the exception. In Jesus' parables we do not encounter Cato's or Varro's faceless drones on large agricultural estates, but neither do we encounter slaves who enjoy the kind of bond with their owners that Tiro seems to have enjoyed with Cicero. If we want to know what impressions of slavery a Mediterranean Jewish peasant would have had in the first century, we would do well to start with the representations of slaves and slaveholders in the words of such a person. Crossan's historical and literary allusions to anomalous slaves distract his readers from attending to the portrayal of slaves in the sayings of the very person whose world he purports to illumine. In particular, Crossan evinces no interest in the vulnerabilities of slave bodies, a recurring theme in Jesus' parables.

Bernard Brandon Scott's influential commentary has largely determined the parameters of later discussions of the slave parables. He situates parabolic master-servant relationships entirely within the anthropological rubric of patron-client relationships, which were pervasive and pivotal in the Roman world.[93] In Scott's words, a patron-client relationship was "voluntary." "Solidarity is strong, and bonds extend beyond legal to even extralegal requirements."[94] Indeed, anthropologists consider the voluntary nature of patron-client connections a core analytic characteristic of such relationships.[95] Nowhere, however, does Scott justify his inclusion of master-slave relations in the patron-client rubric. In response to Scott, Beavis rightly objects that "the translation of *doulos* as 'servant' rather than 'slave' or 'bondsperson' downplays the servile status of the parabolic actors and, in certain instances, leads to interpretations that do not fully comprehend the probable response of ancient audiences to the parables." However, she concedes to Scott that "the patron-client relation was the backbone of Greco-Roman society, and it neatly subsumes all the NT parables of inequality."[96]

Although crucial to Roman social relations, the patron-client structure is an unsuitable category for the analysis of slavery. The standard treatment of patron-client relations in the early Empire is Richard Saller's 1982 monograph, *Personal Patronage under the Early Empire*.[97] Saller acknowledges that a slave or freedperson could perform a *beneficium*, a kindness or favor, for an owner (or former owner). However, he recognizes this possibility as he catalogs instances of *beneficium* that are outside the parameters of patron-client relations. For example, Saller writes, "A new husband, having been given his wife's virginity, was said to be *beneficio obstrictus*."[98] Saller excludes from his study patronage of freedpersons "on the ground that, in being subject to legal regulation, it differed fundamentally from voluntary associations between freeborn men."[99] Still less is the rubric of patronage an appropriate basis for the investigation of involuntary, legally regulated slavery.[100] In his introduction to an edited volume on patronage in ancient societies, Andrew Wallace-Hadrill emphasizes the chasm between clients and slaves: "What is equally important to remember is that patronage in antiquity was only one of the available forms of inequality. That of master and slave . . . was far harsher, less flexible and nuanced, and was legally enforceable."[101] Despite certain similarities, including the asymmetry of power relations, a slave was not a client, and an owner was not a patron. By collapsing master-slave relations into the patron-client paradigm, Scott and other New Testament scholars distort the parabolic representation of slavery.[102]

Scott and Crossan are hardly alone among New Testament scholars in their assumption that the network of patron-client relations offers a satisfactory context for understanding slavery, especially the phenomenon of slavery among a managerial elite. In his treatment of the ideology of slavery in the Pauline epistles, Dale Martin also elides the differences between patrons and slave owners, clients and slaves. After noting a number of similarities between the upward mobility of managerial slaves and the mechanics of Roman patronage, he asserts: "These examples show that slavery, especially higher- and middle-level slavery, was part of the wider social structure of patron-client obligations and benefits. An individual's access to power and social progress depended more than anything else on her or his connections to someone higher up in the social pyramid. *In this regard, slaves were in much the same situation as free people, except that in their owner they had a built-in patron. In order to understand the dynamics of Greco-Roman slavery, therefore, we must recognize that it functioned within the dynamics of Greco-Roman patronage*" (emphasis added).[103]

Martin argues persuasively that for a small but visible sector of elite, managerial slaves, the institution of slavery could serve as a conduit for a kind of upward mobility. Nonetheless, to locate even the relationships of elite slaves with their owners in the context of patron-client networks distorts our understandings of the practice and ideology of slavery in the first century. Martin implies, for example, that patron-client networks and ideology explain "lack of revolutionary sentiment and activity among slaves." He then quotes John D'Arms: "From the emperor on down, patron-client ties had an integrating effect, promoting cohesion vertically between groups of differing rank and status, and inhibiting class consciousness and horizontal group action."[104] This quotation, however, is D'Arms's summary of what he labels Saller's "anthropological functionalism." Neither Saller nor D'Arms includes the enslaved population in this vision of cohesiveness.

In his treatment of the social world of Jesus and the Gospels, Bruce Malina's only references to the institution of slavery occur in his chapter on patrons and clients. He writes, "In the world of the New Testament, patron-client relations might be added to the legally sanctioned subordination of a slave to his or her owner. . . . Thus the slave might be protected against the risks of being sold, killed or beaten, while the slave owner obtains the trust and commitment of the slave in question."[105] Whether ancient slaves or slaveholders actually understood their relations to be akin to patron-client relations is not a topic Malina explores, nor does he adduce any evidence to support this supposition. Moreover, the parables do depict slaves who are vulnerable to physical abuse and murder; they do not depict slaves who enjoy protection from such treatment. Parabolic slaveholders seem to earn the commitment of their slaves not by shielding them from brutality but, at least in part, by the implicit or explicit threat of violence. Perhaps some slaves in the first century understood themselves as clients, although that is a case that remains to be argued. However, even if there were such slaves, we do not encounter them in the Gospels or, more narrowly, in Jesus' sayings.

How, then, did the idea that we can account for ancient master-slave relations in terms of patronage networks seize the imagination of New Testament scholars? A limited answer may lie in the seductive appeal of models drawn from social science. Reliance on social science models, including the anthropological model of patron-client relations, has an aura of objectivity attractive to scripture scholars who seek a more objective base for the discipline. While social-scientific approaches continue to prove useful in the study of ancient materials, they must always be tested against the evidence of the ancient texts themselves. When we check the model of patron-client relations against the representation of slaves in the parables of Jesus, we find that the contemporary model does not do justice to the first-century texts. A further answer may lie in the long-standing tradition of subordinating matters of the body to matters of the soul—even among those who claim to do precisely the opposite.

Perhaps, one might argue, the versions of parables preserved in the Gospels distort Jesus' original words. Parable scholars often seek to discern the ur-structures of Jesus' parables. Within these parameters, scholars have an obligation to acknowledge and assess Jesus' reliance on the figure of the slave in his patterns of discourse. William Herzog, who claims to start from the materialist dimensions of the parables, typifies a trend among parable scholars over the past decade. He writes, "What if the parables of Jesus were neither theological nor moral stories but political and economic ones. . . . What if the scenes they presented were not stories about how God works in this world but codifications about how exploitation worked in Palestine?"[106] Curiously, in considering systems of exploitation in first-century Palestine, Herzog evinces no awareness of the operations of slavery as a system of exploitation; most curiously, because slaves and their bodily vulnerabilities figure prominently in the parables about which he writes. For example, he describes the setting of the parable of the unmerciful slave as "the world of retainers," in which context he labels the unmerciful slave as a "highly placed bureaucrat" and "an important retainer": "The high retainers were the survivors of the endless court intrigues by which they sought their advancement and the advancement of their clients at the expense of their competitors. It was a cutthroat world constructed around competing pyramids of patron-client loyalties." He elaborates, "Of course, an immense distance separates even highly placed court bureaucrats from the ruler, so he is called a 'servant' (*doulos*). . . . Just as the wealth of the realm belonged, in principle, to the ruler, so all subjects of the realm were his servants."[107] Herzog thus denies the specificity of the experience of enslavement as represented in a parable that emphasizes the absolute power of an imperial master over the body of even his most highly valued slave.

In the parable of the tenants, Herzog highlights the social and economic tension between the marginalized tenant farmers and the vineyard owner. Of the slaves he writes: "Because the tenants cannot get at the protected elite, they turn their aggressive impulses on the aristocrats' bureaucratic agents. The treatment the agents receive at the hands of the tenants is simply one of the liabilities of their job."[108] He does not specify whether he sees the identification of the agents as slaves as a contribution of the parable's canonical forms or an original element of Jesus' parable. In order to argue that the tenants act as oppressed persons rising against a powerful and wealthy opponent, Herzog must ignore the inconvenient description of the owner's agents as slaves and the repeated battering of slaves' bodies by the marginalized tenant farmers. Again, what makes this reading especially problematic is Herzog's claim that he is building his readings directly on the material realities of systems of exploitation in the first century. Along with Herzog, a number of other New Testament critics who have recently attempted to locate the parables in a first-century sociopolitical context of imperialism have somehow ignored the identity of slaves *as slaves*, treated as bodies, in the parables.[109] These scholars desire to recreate the parables of Jesus apart from the theological constraints of the Gospels. At some point, those engaged in this project must come to terms with Jesus' pervasive reliance on the trope of slavery in his parables.[110]

Beavis has invited readers to consider the so-called servant parables in light of what we know about slavery in the first century. Although I disagree with a number of her specific conclusions, Beavis's work advances understandings of the function and social location of slave rhetoric in the parables. For example, she criticizes New Testament scholars who describe the dismemberment of the wicked slave in the parable of the overseer as outlandish or fantastic. She insists that critics should evaluate the parable's strong imagery in light of what we read elsewhere in first-century literature about extreme practices in the punishment of slaves. Her work stresses the importance of looking directly at the bodies of slaves as represented in Jesus' parables.

One scholar who has systematically examined the role of slaves in the parables and other sayings of Jesus is the late Winsome Munro. In *Jesus, Born of a Slave*, Munro attempted an ambitious thought experiment: how would it affect our readings of some problematic early Christian texts if we consider the hypothesis that Jesus may have been a slave or former slave, born of an enslaved woman? While I do not find Munro's hypothesis convincing, I nonetheless find her thought experiment to be provocative. In the course of her argument, Munro points out that Jesus' parables rely as much or more on the imagery of slavery as they do on any other set of images. She contends that the parables consistently give the slave's perspective and proposes that prior to the moralizing of the evangelists many of these parables offered a critique of the master's perspective. Munro asks, again and again, "Who but a slave would have spoken so extensively of the labors and punishments of slaves?" For example, when the fellow slaves of the unmerciful slave witness his harsh treatment of the slave who is his debtor, they approach the slaveholder to inform him that the unmerciful slave has behaved in this fashion (18:31). Munro insists that only a slave would have been sufficiently familiar with "slave quarter gossip about what is fair and unfair" to include this detail.[111] Is this, however, the case? Anyone who had contact with the slaves in such establishments could have been aware of the rivalries and cruelties among slaves. Perhaps only those of us who are removed from the everyday world of slavery would so romanticize solidarity among slaves as to assume that slaves would never treat each other in a petty or vindictive fashion.

Munro asserts that "in parables where a slave or slaves play a key role, it is always the slave characters and experience with which the hearer/reader is to identify."[112] One parable that defies this assertion is the parable of the slave who comes in from work in the fields to the next task, that of preparing and serving the master his dinner (Luke 17:7-10). In the only extant version of this parable, Jesus asks the hearer explicitly to identify with the slaveholder who benefits from the labor of the slave. Although Munro invites the reader to focus on parables where "a slave or slaves play a key role," perhaps the parables where slaves appear not as major players, but as incidental characters, are even more interesting in this context. For example, in the parable commonly known as the prodigal son, the father calls on his slaves to put a ring on the prodigal son's finger and sandals on his feet. Some who hear the parable may identify with the reprobate younger son and some may identify with the long-suffering elder son. Few, however, identify with the slaves, whose labors barely attract the attention of commentators. Indeed, the presence of the slaves emphasizes the chasm between the submissive bodies of the slaves and the honored body of the son.

The reason that I am ultimately unconvinced that the parables reflect what Munro calls a "slave's eye view" is that they uncritically accept the liability of the slave's body to violation by slaveholders, by other slaves, and even by outsiders to the household. Munro notes that slaves, like other subordinates, would have had incentives to learn the epistemic vantage points of their superiors, so that we should not be surprised to find some parables that reflect the perspectives of slaveholders.[113] I find no way to recount Jesus' parables, however, without repeating the violence against slave bodies that they iterate. If this is a slave's eye view, it is a perspective that has been subordinated to the dominant viewpoint of the slaveholding society to the extent that we can make no meaningful assertions about the distinguishing marks of a slave's perspective.

Although I contest Munro's hypothesis that the parables support the claim that Jesus was a slave or former slave, I think she has successfully outlined the centrality of the figure of the slave in Jesus' parables. As a New Testament scholar, I admit to a continuing hesitancy about the project of attempting to recreate the parables of Jesus in a form more "original" than we find in the Gospels, both canonical and apocryphal. I am not arguing that the Gospels give us unmediated access to original versions of Jesus' words, only that I am skeptical that we can responsibly and objectively reconstruct more primitive forms of those sayings. However, this task plays an ineluctable role in any quest for the historical Jesus. Munro has demonstrated that anyone who wants to come to terms with the material dimensions of Jesus' symbolic world has to take seriously his pervasive reliance on the trope of slavery in the parables. Like Beavis, Munro also points to the necessity of reading these texts in the context of other literature from the early Empire in which slaves figure as major or minor characters.

In reconstructing the "originating structures" of the parables, a number of scholars who attempt what they label "nontheological," "materialist" readings assume that earlier forms of the parables must have overturned first-century norms by offering critiques of imperial values. In this, they continue in the tradition of scholars who expect the parables to challenge and subvert what the structuralist Crossan labeled the "horizon of normalcy." What may ultimately be most challenging to New Testament critics is to confront the degree to which the slave parables undergird the horizon of normalcy and reinforce other evidence concerning the practice and ideology of slavery in the early Roman Empire. Perhaps the most prominent and consistent aspect of the parabolic construction of slavery is an emphasis on the vulnerability of the enslaved body to violence, notably to brutal disciplinary practices.

Body of Evidence

As we have seen, every level of the sayings tradition includes evidence that Jesus routinely evoked the figure of the slave in his teachings. Slaves emerge with startling immediacy as we comb through this material. Slaves work long hours. They labor in the fields. They fasten sandals on their masters' feet. They deliver social and business messages. They do not always get along well with one another. They take advantage of their owners' absences to eat and drink from storerooms. For modern commentators, slaves and slavery have often been, first and foremost, metaphorical. For Jesus, slaves and slavery were part of the fabric of everyday life. Jesus relied on the figure of the slave in his discourse not because the trope of slavery was part of his philosophical or rhetorical inheritance, but because slaves were ubiquitous in the world in which he lived: cooking food, harvesting grain, and absorbing blows.

In this chapter I have paid particular attention to the parables in Matthew, which have an internal coherence lacking in the overall collection of Jesus' sayings pertaining to slavery. The Matthean parables often focus on managerial slaves, an influential minority among the enslaved population. They promote the view that the moral purpose of the slave is to advance the interests of the slaveholder. While these parables depict slaves who amass considerable influence, the most prominent and consistent aspect of the parabolic construction of slavery in Matthew is an emphasis on the vulnerability of the enslaved body to violence, notably to brutal disciplinary practices. The Matthean parables thus reinforce other evidence concerning the practice of slavery in the Greco-Roman world, especially during the early Empire. They reinscribe the slaveholding ideology of that world. Like other literary productions of the era, the Matthean parables represent slaves as bodies inscribed by the whip.

Readers of the Gospels come to recognize the disciplined flesh of parabolic slaves as an antitype, a model to avoid. Curiously, however, the Gospels feature another tortured body as a model to emulate: the battered and crucified body of Jesus.[114] Jesus himself calls his followers to be willing to endure the sufferings of the cross (Mark 8:34 and parallels). In a peculiar way, the corporal punishment of disobedient slaves in the parables foreshadows the broken body of Jesus: ridiculed, beaten, executed.[115] A final, counterline of inquiry into the parabolic ideology of slavery would ask whether the crucifixion of Jesus prompts us to reconsider our interpretations of the slaves whose representations prefigure the Gospels' climactic scenes of torture.

5

Moral Bodies

Ecclesiastical Development and Slaveholding Culture

In the early second century, the younger Pliny served for several seasons as the governor of Bithynia, a territory in Asia Minor. In one of his letters to Trajan, Pliny described his efforts to obtain information about the fledgling Christian movement. He sought informants among slave women who, he claimed, played leadership roles in the new cult. To acquire information he resorted to physical torture, the standard means of interrogating slaves. In Demosthenes' words, slaves were answerable with their bodies, quite literally. "I judged it so much the more necessary to extract the real truth, with the assistance of torture, from two female slaves, who were styled deaconesses [or ministers]," Pliny writes, "but I could discover nothing more than depraved and excessive superstition."[1] Pliny's words leave the impression that early Christianity was a religion of slaves, a movement where the most likely informants were slave women who ministered to the community. Decades earlier, in correspondence with the Christian community in Corinth, Paul had also implied that persons of low status figured prominently in the early churches: "Consider your own call, brothers . . . not many of you were powerful, not many were of noble birth. . . . God chose what is weak in the world to shame the strong."[2] We do not, however, have coeval writings from enslaved Christian women and men, describing their experiences and roles in the churches of the first and second centuries.

Paul's words may seem to corroborate Pliny's suggestion that slaves dominated the earliest churches. Wayne Meeks's influential volume, *The First Urban Christians*, established the limitations of that picture of the Pauline churches. An examination of all of the evidence of the Pauline epistles supports the unsurprising claim that the Pauline churches did not attract members from the highest rungs of imperial society. At the same time, the epistles offer no evidence regarding participation of the most destitute or marginalized members of society: slaves who labored in mines, for example, or prostitutes who frequented the streets and ports. Church membership appears to have been mixed, including both wealthy persons and poor persons. Meeks argued that the Pauline churches were especially attractive to persons of inconsistent status, including freedpersons and women who controlled significant wealth.

The churches in the Pauline orbit included slaves, but we have no basis for claiming that the ratio of slaves present in those churches exceeded the percentage of slaves in the Greek-speaking cities of the Eastern Empire. "There are slaves," wrote Meeks, "although we cannot tell how many."[3] Similarly, we have no basis for claiming that the percentage of slaveholders in Pauline churches differed perceptibly (greater or lesser) from the corresponding proportion of slaveholders in cities where Pauline churches were situated. "The 'typical' Christian," Meeks continued, "the one who most often signals his presence in the letters by one or another small clue, is a free artisan or small trader. Some even in those occupational categories had houses, slaves, the ability to travel, and other signs of wealth."[4] In other words, our evidence implies that the "typical" Christian was as likely to be a slaveholder as a slave. More accurately, we are at least as likely to have evidence regarding Christian slaveholders as Christian slaves in the first century. In chapter two we considered the influence of heads of household over the religious practices of all members of the household, including slaves. We might therefore anticipate that the early churches, including churches in the Pauline orbit, would have "dominating—if minoritarian—representation of people well-placed in that society."[5]

This remained true as the Christian movement entered the second century. Even Pliny, who centered his investigation on slave women, indicated that the movement included both women and men of all ages and ranks, from the country as well as from the city. (He noted with some relief that efforts against the Christian movement had been sufficiently successful for traditional sacred festivals to resume; sales had picked up at markets for sacrificial animals.) Christianity's attractiveness to such a cross-section of people in the Eastern Empire precipitated Pliny's concern over the movement's successes. Pliny chose to torture enslaved Christian leaders not because most Christians, or most Christian leaders, were slaves. Rather, he chose to interrogate slaves because their bodies were liable to torture. Freeborn persons were exempt from such treatment. Like many others in the Roman Empire, Pliny exploited the inability of slaves to protect their own bodies in order to gain access to information he thought they might possess.

Incidental comments by Christian authors in the second century confirm the ongoing presence of slaveholders in Christian congregations. Defending the reputations of Christians, Justin Martyr wrote that, in order to fabricate evidence against Christians, wicked men had tortured the slaves of Christians, including enslaved women and children. Athenagoras wrote, "And yet we have slaves, some more and some fewer, by whom we could not help being seen; but even of these, not one has been found to invent even such things [charges of murder] against us."[6] Justin and Athenagoras thus identified Christian targets of persecution not as slaves but as slaveholders. Slaves served as surrogate bodies for their Christian owners, absorbing blows from torturers who hoped that the abuse of enslaved bodies would yield insights into slaveholding souls. Some Christian slaveholders had fewer slaves and some Christian slaveholders had more slaves, Athenagoras noted in passing, but the fact that Christians owned slaves was a matter of public record and not of contention nor controversy. The activities and cult affiliations of elite persons were more likely to attract official attention than the parallel activities and cult affiliations of persons of lesser status, including slaves. We therefore cannot determine on the basis of Justin's or Athenagoras's words whether the slaves who belonged to Christian slaveholders were themselves baptized.

In the popular imagination, the notion that the ubiquitous presence of slaves shaped the young church has prevailed over evidence regarding the active involvement and leadership of slaveholders in the earliest centuries of the church. Perhaps most influential—though for reasons he never intended—has been Nietzsche's problematic discussion of Christianity as a religion rooted in what he termed the "slave morality" of Judaism. (Although Nietzsche is culpable for the venom of his anti-Semitic discourse, he did not foresee the rise of fascism and the use of his language in fascist discourse. We do not know how he would have responded to this appropriation.) Nietzsche claimed that the slave morality of Christianity represented the devious triumph of Judaism, insinuating what he considered its servile values into the noble and aristocratic classical world view. The struggle of Rome against Judaea culminated, according to Nietzsche, in Judaea's ultimate, albeit veiled, conquest of the Empire. "This Jesus of Nazareth, the incarnate gospel of love, this 'redeemer' who brought blessedness and victory to the poor, the sick, and the sinners—was he not this seduction in its most uncanny and irresistible form, a seduction and bypath to precisely those *Jewish* values and new ideals?" wrote Nietzsche.[7] Elsewhere, he wrote:

> It is different with the second type of morality, *slave morality*. Suppose the violated, op-
> pressed, suffering unfree, who are uncertain of themselves and weary, moralize: what will
> their moral valuations have in common? . . . The slave's eye is not favorable to the virtues
> of the powerful: he is skeptical and suspicious, *subtly* suspicious, of all the "good" that is
> honored there—he would like to persuade himself that even their happiness is not genu-
> ine. Conversely, those qualities are brought out and flooded with light which serve to
> ease existence for those who suffer: here pity, the complaisant and obliging hand, the
> warm heart, patience, industry, humility, and friendliness are honored—for here these are
> the most useful qualities and almost the only means for enduring the pressure of exist-
> ence. Slave morality is essentially a morality of utility.[8]

The ultimate hallmark of slave morality, claimed Nietzsche, is a longing for freedom itself.

According to the current consensus in New Testament and patristic studies, Nietzsche's description of Christian origins as a movement of the "violated, oppressed, suffering unfree" is demographically inaccurate. Nonetheless, he makes an important contribution through his recognition of a "slave's eye" in morality, a viewpoint on ethical ques-
tions that differs from the perspective of slaveholders or those who align their moral perspective with slaveholders. Whether Nietzsche is equally insightful about the con-
tent of what he calls "slave morality" is still another question. He is clearly right about the slave's longing for freedom, manifest in antiquity not so much in slave declarations or creeds but in the actions of slaves: efforts to secure manumission, a propensity for running away from owners, and even an occasional willingness to engage in violent rebellion. I am dubious, however, about Nietzsche's broader emphasis on the slave's "patience, industry, humility, and friendliness." Were these the moral values of slaves or the moral values that slaveholders extolled for slaves?[9] The question is complicated. I expect that many slaves internalized the values and behaviors advocated by slaveholders and that many other slaves learned to behave so that their owners believed they had internalized the desired moral code. Evidence suggests, however, that many slaves resisted, implicitly or explicitly, such expectations for attitude and conduct. I revisit the content of slave(holder) morality when I examine the household codes of Colossians, Ephesians, the Pastoral epistles, 1 Peter, and extracanonical Christian writings. Rather than asking how the presence of slaves in the congregations shaped the emerging structures and ideology of Christianity, examination of the household codes leads me to ask how the presence of slave*holders* in the congregations shaped the emerging structures and ideology of Christianity.

Nietzsche was hardly the first to recognize that slaves and slaveholders had differing perspectives, moral and otherwise. As Artemidorus offers endless interpretations of dreams in the second-century *Oneirocritica*, for example, he frequently notes that one cannot infer the same meaning for a dream experienced by a free dreamer and for the identical dream experienced by an enslaved dreamer. We read, "Olive trees whose fruit has been gathered up mean good luck for all men but slaves. For slaves, they prophesy thrashings, since it is by blows that the fruit is taken down."[10] Indeed, for Artemidorus the ever-present fear of beatings and hope of manumission establish the poles of the slave's experience and the most frequent parameters for the interpretation of slaves' dreams. We may not be surprised that Artemidorus interprets a slave's dream of flying as a prediction of manumission. As he points out, birds have no one above them. Hence, they have no masters. But he likewise interprets a slave's dream of his own death as a dream of freedom, since one who is dead neither has a master nor toils for another.[11] Artemidorus insists that there is a characteristic "slave's eye" in dreaming. His insistence illustrates how firmly ancient thinkers believed that slaves and slaveholders had distinctive models of cognitive appraisal and, ultimately, of moral valuing.

In this chapter I consider the instructions to slaves and slaveholders in the Christian household codes and situate this discussion in the context of the representation of slave morality in other ancient sources. However, the household codes do not exhaust the significance of ancient slavery for the study of early Christian ethics. An important question for students of early Christianity is how the presence of slaves and slaveholders in Christian congregations affected Christian moral formations and, more broadly, how the structures of a slaveholding society influenced the ethos of the Christian movement from its origins through late antiquity.

Slave Morality versus Slaveholder Morality

A slave labored a decade or more for a slaveholder. Through the years, the slaveholder privately promised that when the slave reached the age of thirty, he could use the funds in his peculium to purchase his freedom. (The peculium consisted of resources a slave amassed and used with an owner's permission. Under law, the peculium was the property of the owner; slaves owned nothing in their own right.) The slave undertook extra jobs outside the household and eventually saved substantial funds to use toward the goal of manumission. When the slave was in his late twenties, the slaveholder died. In settling the estate, the heirs sold the hardworking slave. They did not include the slave's peculium in the sale but retained it as their own. The slave would have to begin again to save for the day of freedom, now delayed. As he left the household for his new home, he took a few choice pieces he had acquired out of his wages: a cooking pot and, perhaps, a treasured silver ornament. He thought of these items as his own. He certainly did not consider his appropriation of these items to be theft until one of the heirs appeared at the home of his purchaser and protested that the slave had stolen household goods.

My scene is hypothetical, sketched on the basis of Ulpian's verdict in the *Digest*. Ulpian noted that a slave's peculium was not included in the sale of the slave: "In consequence, if a thing, part of the *peculium*, be purloined by the slave, a *condictio* will be in respect of it, as if it had been stolen."[12] Theft was one of the most common charges leveled against slaves by owners, former owners, employers, and others, as though the servile character found perfect expression in all manners of thievery, from pilfering from the larder to the equivalent of grand larceny. In highlighting the exemplary character of the wrongly enslaved Joseph, the rabbis casually proffered the truism "All slaves are assumed to steal."[13] Generations of commentators have found it plausible that a runaway Onesimus stole an item of some value from Philemon, since Paul offered to compensate Philemon for possible losses. "If he has wronged you in any way," Paul assured Philemon, "or owes you anything, charge it to my account. I, Paul, am writing this with my own hand: I will repay it."[14] Roman jurists assumed that runaway slaves would abscond not only with their own bodies but with other household property.[15] In *The Golden Ass*, Apuleius sketches a chaotic scene that transpires when slaves on a country estate learn of their owner's death. Fearing new ownership, they decide to flee the estate. They load themselves (and Lucius the ass) with the valuables of the household, including livestock.[16] The expectation that runaway slaves would purloin household goods as a matter of course is logical. If the slave were successful in escaping the owner, the theft would also be successful. If the slave were caught, he or she was already certain to face stiff punishment. Slaves contemplating flight might well have calculated that the benefits outweighed the risks of a concomitant theft. They did not confide in posterity whether they also reckoned such contraband a payment (however inadequate) for their time in bondage.

Since ancient sources uniformly adopt a slaveholding perspective, identification of what slaves believed they were doing when they took things from their owners remains an elusive question. A slave who pilfered an extra measure of flour or oil for a hungry child was likely to understand her action differently than the enslaved steward of an estate who embezzled household funds for his own pleasure or gain. Neither of these slaves would have been likely to identify her or his motivation as rebellion against slavery. Nonetheless, their actions constituted acts of resistance, not against the institution of slavery per se, but against the particular circumstances under which they operated. Working from Roman legal sources and comparative evidence from New World slave societies, Keith Bradley has argued that theft is just one of the so-called criminal activities in which ancient slaves engaged that, from a slave's eye view, are better understood as strategies of resistance.[17]

From a practical standpoint, what would stop a slave from stealing? Slaveholders expected that slaves would be negligent in caring for household supplies and goods. Managing a household was a matter of surveillance and control of recalcitrant bodies, which could not be counted on to put the good of the household first (modern economists call this the "principal agent problem"). Slaves, however, expected to be blamed for incidents outside of their control. In *The Golden Ass*, Apuleius includes a vignette in which a wild dog steals a side of meat hanging in a kitchen. A tenant had presented the fine slab of venison to the householder. The enslaved cook, Hephaestion, panics when he realizes that the wild dog has consumed the meat. He anticipates with surety that the householder will blame him for the incident.[18] Hephaestion's owner might well have charged the slave with consuming the meat himself. Under such circumstances, why not steal? Particularly if one had a master deficient in self-control, punishment was not only inevitable but also, frequently, arbitrary. Why not take whatever one could, whenever one could? Nietzsche named subservience and hard work as the virtues of slaves. Ancient slaveholders hoped their slaves would cultivate these virtues but feared they would not. For slaves themselves, other kinds of excellence might have been more functional: canniness and courage, for example. As we read ancient condemnations of the personalities and activities of particular slaves we must ask ourselves, again and again, whose moral framework governs the criticism.

The Roman jurists declared it illegal to exert a negative influence on another person's slave, "not only for making a good slave bad, but also for making a bad slave worse."[19] We do not know how often charges of corrupting a slave were formally filed. Ulpian's list of ways to make slaves worse, however, illuminates the fears that ancient slaveholders had about the urges and actions of the bodies who animated their households: "One also makes a slave worse if one persuades him to commit an injury or theft, to run away, to incite another man's slave, to mismanage his *peculium*, to become a lover, to play truant, to practice evil arts, to spend too much time at public entertainments, or to become seditious; or if, by argument or bribe, one persuades a slave-agent to tamper with or falsify his master's accounts, or to confuse accounts entrusted to him."[20] Ulpian's catalog includes some actions that were clearly criminal and that would be criminal regardless of the identity of the agent. Theft was a crime regardless of whether the thief was a free person or a slave. Running away, however, was only a crime when the one who fled was legally bound not to run. A free person who left town permanently without notification was not, as a result of that action, a criminal. A slave was. Ulpian's catalog of undesirable servile behavior also includes actions that were not criminal, even for slaves—spending too much time at public entertainments, for example.[21]

Athenaeus's second-century epic account of banqueting, the *Deipnosophists*, preserves a vignette in which a slave's voice draws the reader's attention to one of those instances in which behavior acceptable among free persons was a sign of vice among slaves: "What is more hateful than to be summoned with Slave, Slave! [*Pai, Pai* = Boy, Boy] to where they are drinking; to serve, moreover, some beardless stripling or fetch him the chamber-pot, and to see things lying spilt before us—half-eaten milk-cakes and bits of chicken which, though left over, no slave may touch, as the women tell us. But what makes us rage is to have them call any of us who eats any of these things an impudent glutton!"[22] The text implies that an adult slave would grit his teeth when a "beardless stripling" called him "boy." The outraged slave calls attention to the implicit irony that actual gluttons would criticize hungry slaves consuming crumbs as greedy. The waste of the banquet table accompanies the shabby treatment of slaves. The vignette, however, is brief and in no way reflects the overarching voice of the *Deipnosophists*, with its endless reiteration and celebration of the excessive pleasures of the table.

Separate moral standards for free persons and slaves thus prevailed. These discrete standards were often contradictory. William Fitzgerald articulates a central paradox of servility: if it is bad to be slavish, is the concept of a "good slave" defensible? He quotes Seneca: "How vile to hate someone you should praise—and how much more vile to hate someone for something because of which he deserves to be pitied; namely because as a captive who has suddenly fallen into slavery he holds on to some remnants of his former free status and fails to hurry to perform sordid and difficult services."[23] Although noble slaves emerge from the pages of antiquity—for example, the slaves who populate the *exemplum* literature—the virtues of free men were not reckoned as virtues for slaves. Slaves who exhibited the virtues laudatory in free men ran the risk of appearing not as virtuous but as vicious. Speech honorable for a free man was likely to be considered insolence coming from the mouth of a slave, for example.

A late first-century letter from a son to his father confirms that slaves nonetheless spoke their minds and that, in turn, slaveholders found such self-expression intolerable. Neilus was away from home, studying. He wrote his father, Theon, to inform him about various problems that had arisen and also to request further subsidies. The letter is intriguing in its hints regarding the life of a student in antiquity but also frustrating in its lack of context for interpreting those hints. Neilus opened the letter, "You have released me from my present despondency by making it plain that the business about the theatre was a matter of indifference to you."[24] We never learn the nature of "the business about the theatre." A few lines later, Neilus wrote that the chariots "were smashed up, as I have already written to you, the day before yesterday." Are the smashed chariots connected to the theatre business, as the editor of the text proposes? Neilus did not make the connection, if there were a connection, explicit, arguably because his father was already familiar with the events to which he alluded. Later in the letter Neilus dropped equally tantalizing hints about a slave named Heraclas. Caught between his dependence on the slave and his fear at the harm his outspoken slave could do to him and his family, Neilus exemplified the double bind of the ancient slaveholder:

> The useful Heraclas—curse him!—used daily to contribute some obols, but now, what with his being imprisoned by Isidorus, as he deserved, he's escaped and gone back, I think, to you. Be assured that he would never hesitate to intrigue about you, for, of all things, he felt no shame at gleefully spreading reports in the city about the incident in the theatre and telling lies such as would not come even from the mouth of an accuser and that too when, so far from suffering what he deserves, he's been released and behaves in every respect like a free man. All the same, if you are not sending him back, you could at any rate hand him over to a carpenter—for I'm told that a young fellow makes two drachmas a day—or put him to some other employment at which he'll earn more money; his wages can then be collected and in due course sent to us, for you know that Diogas, too, is studying. (*P.Oxy.* 18.2190)

Neilus implied that he wanted nothing to do with the "useful" (*chrēsimos*) Heraclas and warned his father that the slave lacked proper deference. Although he accused the slave of speaking falsely, modern readers may nonetheless suspect that what Neilus really feared was that Heraclas would tell Theon the truth about various scrapes into which the student had gotten. The language that Neilus chose to diminish the slave's credibility is revealing. Heraclas's chief infraction, it seems, was that he "behaves in every respect like a free man." The most elementary expectation for servile behavior was that slaves would distinguish their attitude and speech from the affect of the freeborn. Neilus represented Heraclas as a wicked slave not because he broke laws or performed poorly, but because he did not enact the role of the deferential servant. So, the son warned the father, "he would never hesitate to intrigue about you." At the same time that Neilus insinuated that he was relieved to be rid of the vocal slave, we learn that the labors of Heraclas funded the young man's studies. Neilus hoped and schemed to perpetuate this dependency.

Slaveholders in antiquity could not imagine their households functioning without the omnipresence of enslaved bodies, waiting to do their bidding. Artemidorus opined that a householder's dream of small rodents was propitious: "A mouse signifies a household slave. For it lives in the same house as the dreamer, is nourished by the same food, and is timid. It is auspicious, therefore, to see many mice playing cheerfully about the house. For they foretell great festivity and the acquisition of more slaves."[25] At the same time, Artemidorus might have continued, the presence of mice in a household is not entirely benign, since mice eat into food stores and can damage a building structurally through gnawing. Analogously, the presence of slaves in a household was not entirely benign. Slaves often consumed more than their allocated share, like mice nibbling away in the storeroom. Slaves also caused all sorts of structural problems. A slave left in charge of a household in his owner's absence, like the parabolic overseer or Tranio in Plautus's *Mostellaria*, could disrupt the smooth functioning of the household through the mishandling of funds or the mismanagement of fellow slaves. Unlike mice, slaves were not always timid. For example, they sometimes defamed their owners by loose talk in the marketplace. (So Neilus, for instance, warned his father of Heraclas's habit of broadcasting disreputable stories about the family.)

Given ancient stereotypes about the inherent character of the slave—at best faithful, most often childlike and incompetent, at worst dangerously hostile—the harmonious and effective management of the slaveholding establishment emerges as a dangerous challenge. In chapter three we reviewed Tacitus's account of the Senate debate regarding the execution of four hundred slaves when one of their number murdered the slaveholder, L. Pedanius Secundus. The Senate's decision to proceed with the mass execution, despite the protests of the free plebeian population, rested on the senators' observation that the security of all householders was contingent on instilling a common understanding among slaves that they had an obligation to police one another. A slave who acted on his or her enmity to a slaveholder thereby threatened the well-being of other slaves (potentially including offspring, lovers, and parents) in the household.[26] Seneca quotes an ancient proverb: a householder has as many enemies as he has slaves.[27]

To maintain order among slaves and to secure the well-being of family members, slaveholders had a variety of tools at their disposal. The continuum of strategies for controlling domestic slaves ranged from the outright terror of death (as in the execution of four hundred slaves in retaliation for the death of one slaveholder), through the wide range of corporal punishments commonly or less commonly used to coerce slaves to behave appropriately, to the maintenance of a system of incentives and rewards. Bradley has argued that Seneca's advocacy of decency toward slaves derived not from a Stoic celebration of the humanity of the slave but from a strategic interest in managing the slaveholding household. Although Seneca conceded that slaveholders would have to resort to violence at one time or another to control their slaves, he urged slaveholders not to depend regularly on such means. However, Bradley argues, Seneca was not a radical reformer. A slaveholder himself, Seneca was self-interested and practical: "Seneca's problem was thus the same as any other slave owner: how were tensions between slave and free to be alleviated, how was servile compliance to the master to be achieved?"[28] Seneca accepted the ancient tenet that slaves were a problem to be managed. Concern for the security of slaveholders rather than the good of slaves themselves motivated his (relatively) clement approach to household management.

Seneca argued, for example, that gentle treatment of slaves would buy their loyalty in even the most extreme circumstances. He described a scene parallel to the one we reviewed from Athenaeus's *Deipnosophists*, in which slaves stood silently by as diners gorged themselves: "The slightest murmur is repressed by the rod; even a chance sound,—a cough, a sneeze, or a hiccup,—is visited with the lash." Seneca warned of the consequences of such disproportionate discipline for petty offenses: "The result of it all is that these slaves, who may not talk in their master's presence, talk about their master." He spoke nostalgically of an earlier time in Roman society when masters and slaves were on more familiar terms, dining and conversing together. In those days, Seneca claimed, slaves "were ready to bare their neck for their master, to bring upon their own heads any danger that threatened him; they spoke at the feast, but kept silent during torture."[29] Although Seneca exhibited some basic respect for the humanity of the slave, the presentation of his advice to slaveholders played more on their desire to minimize the threat that household slaves posed to their well-being. Responding to the ancient proverb, Seneca concluded, "They are not enemies when we acquire them; we make them enemies."[30] And, he implied, "we" could also make them allies and would be safer if we chose this latter course.

According to Nietzsche, the slave values a "warm heart, patience, industry, humility, and friendliness." For the ancient slaveholder, the question was whether to coax these qualities out of the slave or to beat them into the slave. Slave morality was understood by slaveholders as a problem. The slave character was inherently suspect and the conduct of slaves a management problem. A slave's poor performance could stem from incompetence or a will to sabotage; it mattered little. Slaves ran away. They stole. They were insolent in private, and they betrayed family secrets to outsiders. Thus slaves, without whom life was unimaginable to the well-to-do denizen of the ancient world, lurked as constant threats to the health and security of the slaveholder and the slaveholder's kin. The potential acts of slaves represented an unpredictable raft of problems in the eye of the slaveholder. Once we accept, however, that the values of a warm heart, patience, industry, humility, and friendliness do not govern the behavior of (all) slaves, we can easily imagine coherent moral frameworks based upon which many slaves may have operated. For example, Roman *exemplum* literature delights in repetitive accounts of loyal slaves. However, slaves who possessed the virtue of loyalty would not always have directed that loyalty to the slaveholder. A slave loyal to a parent, a sibling, a lover, a child, or a friend could easily come in conflict with his or her owner. A slave loyal to a parent or lover might play truant or run away in order to be with that person or otherwise compromise the owner's interests in order to promote the interests of that parent or lover. Should we consider the slave any less virtuous? Or should we additionally attribute the virtue of courage to slaves whose loyalty to loved ones led them to defy slaveholder?

In assessing the ethical codes of ancient slaves, we are at a particular loss, since the slaves of antiquity did not leave the kinds of written records that enable us to reconstruct the complex and heroic moral worlds of New World slaves. Finley concluded that the majority of slaves in Greco-Roman antiquity "somehow accommodated themselves to their condition, whether passively and sullenly or positively."[31] While sympathetic to those slaves who absorbed the values that slaveholders wanted them to embody, Finley also pointed out that accommodation to such a moral framework hardly represented the apogee of ethical achievement. In the ancient world, modesty and sexual self-control were commonly touted as the highest virtues attainable by freeborn women. Submissiveness and obedience were commonly touted as the highest virtues desirable for enslaved men and women. Freeborn women and male and female slaves who developed other virtues would have been at least as likely to appear deficient in virtue as excelling in virtue. In reviewing ancient sources today, we should be no more respectful of those persons who recorded their moral codes than of those persons who did not leave written records of their moral aims and visions.

What moral vision, for example, informed the actions of the slaves who led and participated in the great slave rebellions of Sicily and Italy between 140 B.C.E. and 70 B.C.E.? With countless other slaves of antiquity they shared a passionate desire for their own personal freedom. In his influential monograph on the slave rebellions, Bradley argued convincingly that the rebel slaves were not attempting to abolish the system of slavery but only to wrest themselves from the conditions of their own servitude.[32] Everything we know about the rebellions is filtered through the writings of men who were appalled by the violent slave uprisings. We can only infer the motivations and purposes of the slaves themselves. We have no evidence that slaves passed down through the generations stories of Spartacus and other rebel leaders. Slaveholders, however, certainly passed on these tales as a cautionary exercise; the names of Eunus and Spartacus continued to resonate for centuries in the rhetoric of Roman politicians. Occasional outbursts of violence among slaves, such as an attempted insurrection among gladiators in 64 C.E., reminded slaveholding elites of all they could lose in a slave uprising.

The great slave insurrections occurred within a relatively short time frame and were geographically restricted. As we grapple with the tension between slave morality and slaveholder morality, the significance of the slave rebellions extends beyond those narrow parameters. Bradley refers to "the permanent state of hostility that existed between slave and master in the Roman system of slavery, a state made manifest by slaveowners' perceptions of their slaves as the enemy within." Although Roman history did not witness a repetition of the era of slave rebellions, slaveholders must have always feared that a recurrence was possible: "Slaveowners' fears of their slaves, though doubtless often latent, were a natural product of slave ownership, reflecting the potential for violent resistance by slaves that lay at the core of Roman society."[33] The specter of insurrection haunted the imaginations of slaveholders in the Greco-Roman world. Although most slaveholders did not have to hide their families from the retaliatory actions of rebel slaves, they did confront on a daily level a myriad of actions that displeased them and revealed the recalcitrance of enslaved bodies. From metal collars to the obsessions of Roman law, from implements of torture to the compassionate conservatism of Seneca, we can discern the attempts of ancient slaveholders to convince their human property of the moral values of a warm heart, patience, industry, humility, and friendliness. Christianity emerges in this context. Generations of scholars have proposed that the church introduced a humane and humanizing voice in the ancient discourse on slavery. However, the household codes that proliferated in early Christian writings gave a new and subtle tool to slaveholders seeking to create compliant bodies.[34]

Household Codes: Slave Morality or Slaveholder Morality?

My discussion of conflicting moral visions in a slaveholding society has centered largely on indirect evidence culled from works as disparate as personal letters, Roman legal writings, and novels. As we turn explicitly to Christian sources, the household codes (or *haustafeln*) of both canonical and extracanonical sources explicitly spell out expectations for the attitudes and behavior of slaves and, to a lesser extent, expectations for the attitudes and behavior of slaveholders. Close attention to the dynamics of the *haustafeln* helps us recognize the stark modernity of the Kantian categorical imperative, which argues that moral laws are universal rather than rooted in particulars of class, caste, gender, or status. Like ancient legal codes, early Christian household codes distinguish between what is proper for free persons and what is proper for enslaved persons. Encountering the strangeness of the status-inflected moral grid of the household codes promotes appreciation of the innovations of the Enlightenment project, even in a postmodern era.[35]

Colossians and Ephesians

In Galatians 3:28, Paul quotes a primitive baptismal formula: for those in Christ there is neither Jew nor Greek, neither slave nor free, not male and female. Within a few decades, however, Christians articulated moral codes that specified distinctive roles for slaves and for slaveholders, for husbands and wives. Today, we perceive the baptismal formula and the household codes to be contradictory. Whether ancient Christians also sensed this opposition is unclear. Colossians 3:11 repeats a version of the baptismal formula: "There is no longer Greek and Jew, circumcised and uncircumcised, barbarian, Scythian, slave and free; but Christ is all in all!" Along with this ringing declaration of the dissolution of barriers between slave and free, Colossians also includes a household code, which devotes an unusual amount of attention to expectations for the comportment of slaves—more attention than wives, husbands, fathers, children, or indeed slaveholders receive. The letter writer urges slaves to be obedient and wholehearted in their service to their owners (3:22–25). The abolition of cultic distinctions between slaves and slaveholders proclaimed just a few verses earlier does not transform the obligations nor relations of members of the same Christian household.

Although Colossians identifies Paul along with his coworker Timothy as its author, scholars generally (but not unanimously) dispute Paul's personal authorship of the letter. Colossians is usually identified as the earliest of the deutero-Pauline epistles, letters written under the mantle of Paul's apostolic authority by his associates and/or successors. In the seven authentic Pauline letters, Paul alludes in various places to the presence of both slaves and slaveholders in the Christian congregation. He hints at how slaves and slaveholders should regard one another, particularly in his letter to Philemon. However, the letters do not establish the kind of institutionalized code of behavior that we find in the deutero-Pauline letters, which prescribe behavior appropriate for those who play particular roles within Greco-Roman households: husbands and wives, fathers and children, slaveholders and slaves.[36]

Obedience, humility, industriousness, patience, self-effacement—the behavior and virtues prescribed for slaves in the early Christian household codes easily fall within Nietzsche's rubric of slave morality. Paul himself speaks only obliquely of praiseworthy behavior for slaveholders, for example, instructing Philemon to regard Onesimus as a brother. I have argued in chapter three that Paul's highly personal relations with the two men, Philemon and Onesimus, dictated the content and style of his rhetorical intervention in the relationship between them. His words do not dictate how slaveholders' entry into the Christian community should generally affect their treatment of household slaves. Even those who attempt to draw wide-ranging conclusions from Philemon about norms for slaveholder behavior would have to concede that the letter does not comment on expectations or standards for the behavior of Christian slaveholders toward non-Christian slaves. Moreover, nowhere in the authentic letters does Paul attempt to establish norms of behavior for slaves.

Margaret MacDonald has argued that the household code in Colossians offers evidence for the increasing conservatism of Pauline groups.[37] This may be the case. However, we ultimately cannot determine whether Colossians represents a new stage of development in Christian thought regarding the relations between slaves and slaveholders or simply a more explicit and extensive articulation of normative behavior than the authentic Pauline letters preserve. When Paul met in person with Christian communities, he may have delivered instructions regarding norms for the behavior of slaves and slaveholders similar to the norms we find in Colossians or other deutero-Pauline letters. He may have given quite different instructions than we find in the later writings. We may equally well imagine that it never occurred to Paul that such instruction should be part of the kerygma, the Christian proclamation. Because the preserved body of authentic Pauline writings is so small, I believe we should be cautious in constructing arguments based on Paul's silence in those documents. Precisely what instructions does the author of Colossians outline for slaveholders and slaves? "Slaves, obey your earthly masters [*kyrioi*] according to the flesh in everything, not only while being watched and in order to please them, but wholeheartedly, fearing the Lord [*kyrios*]. Whatever your task, put yourselves into it, as done for the Lord and not for human beings, since you know that from the Lord you will receive the inheritance as your reward; you are slaves to the Lord Christ. For the wrongdoer will be paid back for whatever wrong has been done, and there is no partiality. Masters [*kyrioi*], treat your slaves justly and fairly, for you know that you also have a Master [*kyrios*] in heaven."[38] The text plays on the fact that Greek uses the same word, *kyrios*, for human slaveholders as for the heavenly Lord. Implicit in the passage is the insight that all Christians, slaveholding Christians as well as enslaved Christians, are ultimately slaves of the same *kyrios*, the Christ.[39]

Petr Pokorný argues that such subtle elision of status differences leads "in an indirect manner to the dissolution of the order of slave maintenance."[40] Whatever eschatological leveling of distinctions before the heavenly Lord that Colossians may promise, the Colossians household code clearly casts the quotidian submission of slaves to their slaveholders as a Christian obligation. In MacDonald's words, "Both slaves and masters ultimately serve the same Lord and are subject to the rewards and punishments of final judgment. But daily life for slaves is to be governed by fleshly masters."[41] Like others, MacDonald identifies the relations dictated by Colossians as "love-patriarchalism": "The negation of differences between slave and free (Col. 3:11) does not lead to the complete abolition of differences in the community. The code prescribes how the members of the unified body should interact with one another. The author takes for granted that the cohesion of the group should be preserved in the way that it was in ancient society in general—by the hierarchical structure of those who rule and those who are subordinate."[42]

Why does the author of Colossians emphasize, as he does, moral instructions to slaves? James E. Crouch has argued that the household code in Colossians highlights norms for servile behavior because the behavior of Christian slaves had emerged as a source of conflict in the church at Colossae. He contends that slaves, like women, may have interpreted the pre-Pauline baptismal formula ("neither Jew nor Greek, neither slave nor free, not male and female") as promising a dissolution of categories, which Paul had not anticipated when he quoted the formula. In 1 Corinthians, Crouch reasons, the "problem" that Paul attempts to curb is "enthusiastic" participation in worship, particularly the enthusiastic participation of women in worship.[43] The "problem" in Colossae is different. The household code in Colossians "reflects a threat to the social order. In this area, the slave question becomes the most crucial problem. It is one thing for a Christian slave to act equal in the gathering of the church. It is quite another situation, however, when the same slave asserts his equality in society."[44] (Although Crouch refers to this situation as a slave problem, we might better name the reaction of Christian slaveholders against fully acknowledging baptized slaves as brothers and sisters in Christ a slaveholder problem.)

Responding to Crouch, a number of scholars have noted that when Paul alludes to the baptismal formula in 1 Corinthians 12:13, he only refers to two antinomies, Jew-Greek and slave-free, omitting the third antinomy, male-female. Because Paul wants to control aspects of women's behavior that he finds unseemly or threatening to the community, he excludes the very language that may have inspired such behavior. Crouch argues that the baptismal formula has similarly inspired Christian slaves at Colossae and that the author of Colossians has concerns about the attitudes and actions of these slaves. But Colossians cites the very language that Crouch believes has precipitated a situation that the letter writer finds problematic (Col. 3:11). If slaves believe that the gospel promotes their claim to emancipation and equality, deliberate inclusion of the formula would appear to be incendiary and thus (in the context of Crouch's argument) counterproductive.[45]

Rather than finding anything out of the ordinary in the letter writer's concerns over the behavior of slaves, Mary Rose D'Angelo argues that the household code of Colossians relies on Greco-Roman stereotypes of slaves as moral inferiors: "These counsels reflect ancient conventions about the character of slaves: slaves attempt to ingratiate themselves (3:22, 23), to defraud (*adikein*) their masters, and to evade punishment by exploiting their masters' favoritism (v. 25)."[46] As we have seen, Greco-Roman writers were almost obsessively concerned with the theme of domestic slaves as threats to the stability and harmony of their households. What Nietzsche identified as "slave morality" (submission, obedience, respect), ancient writers presented as "slaveholder morality," the attitudes that slaveholders desired to inculcate in the enslaved bodies in their households.

The household codes articulated a strategy that Christian slaveholders could use to pacify members of their households. As I have noted, we do not know whether Paul himself urged slaves to submit to their owners. The extant authentic letters include no such instruction. Thus, as D'Angelo notes, Colossians is the first text we have that explicitly "christianizes" the subordination of women, children, and slaves.[47] Other scholars have also noted that Colossians is innovative in supplying explicit moral instructions to slaves, although they have thereby arrived at inferences quite different from D'Angelo's. Christian household codes derived their form from Jewish and other Greco-Roman *haustafeln*. The Christian *haustafeln* were distinctive in addressing themselves directly to slaves.[48] Minimally, by directly addressing slaves, the household codes provide evidence to confirm the presence of slaves in Christian congregations; the authors of these codes expected that slaves were among those who would hear their instructions.

One might interpret the inclusion of slaves in the Christian household codes as an acknowledgment of their moral agency. However, the form of the *haustafel* is inseparable from the moral content of the teaching, and the morality of the Christian *haustafeln* promotes the interests of slaveholders, not of slaves. The household codes identified submission and obedience as the highest virtues that slaves could attain. Slavery was thus perceived as a kind of moral training. The slave was the student, the slaveholder the teacher.[49] MacDonald even speculates, "One would assume that the slaves of believing masters are to turn to their masters for guidance about what teaching is to be followed, how one should relate to outsiders, and generally how to live one's life in the Lord."[50] Although I think MacDonald here goes somewhat beyond the evidence of Colossians 3:22–4:1, I agree that the content of the Colossians household code encourages moral dependency rather than moral maturity among slaves. The household code of Colossians encourages slaves to be slavish, at best an equivocal achievement, as Seneca observed.

The instructions to slaveholders are brief. Slaveholders have their own master (*kyrios*) in heaven, and so they should treat their slaves justly and fairly. Based on the assumption that most slaves in the Roman Empire were ultimately manumitted, MacDonald proposes that this injunction may implicitly instruct slaveholders to uphold their end of the bargain by granting timely manumission to their slaves.[51] I argue in chapter three that New Testament scholars slide too easily from the observation that manumission of slaves was routine in the first century to the assertion that most slaves would be manumitted within their lifetimes. We have seen in chapter three that manumission was hardly an exceptional or a revolutionary occurrence. Indeed, regular manumission was part of the smooth functioning of the Roman slave system, and hope of manumission motivated loyalty and hard work among slaves. Slave earnings typically financed a slave's liberty; the slaveholder could use those funds to purchase a younger, more vigorous slave. Nonetheless, the majority of slaves in the first century were still enslaved when they died. Regular manumission was not coextensive with universal, or near-universal, manumission. No one in the first century would have expressed surprise when a slaveholder manumitted a slave. However, slaveholders did not understand themselves to be morally obliged to promise and deliver manumission to all of their slaves, even to all of their faithful slaves. Still less would a slaveholder have felt obliged to manumit slaves whose dissatisfaction with the state of slavery contributed to poor performance and disrespectful speech. *Pace* MacDonald, the injunction in Colossians to treat slaves justly and fairly did not entail an expectation that Christian slaveholders would manumit their slaves.

How did first-century slaveholders understand instructions to treat slaves justly and fairly? Did many slaveholders in the Roman Empire perceive themselves to be unjust and unfair? Did the author of Colossians intend anything different than any other Greco-Roman moralist would intend with these words? Carolyn Osiek and David Balch argue that, although all the New Testament *haustafeln* accepted slavery as an institution, "abusive Christian owners were not acceptable."[52] Such a formulation begs the question. The range of behaviors that we would consider abusive today is wider than the range of behaviors considered abusive in the first century. For example, I would consider one person beating another to be abusive, regardless of provocation. Precisely in question is whether first- or second-century Christians would consider slaveholders abusive if they whipped slaves who had neglected their duties or performed those duties beneath a required standard. If there were distinctive, countercultural norms for the comportment of Christian slaveholders, I find it surprising that writers in the first or second generation of the church did not reinforce those norms whenever they addressed slaveholders. Roman slaveholders considered the disciplining of slave bodies a standard and even necessary dimension of household management. Did the author of Colossians consider corporal punishment within the parameters of just and fair behavior? Without specification of what he meant by "just and fair" conduct, his readers would have resorted to the codes of behavior with which they had lived all their lives.

The prevalent expectation that slaves provided a convenient sexual outlet for slaveholders raises further questions about the letter writer's instructions to both slaveholders and slaves. MacDonald notes that slaves might have a difficult choice between the obedience enjoined in the household code and preservation of their sexual purity, upon which the letter writer also insists (3:5). The identification of slaves as submissive bodies creates an undeniable moral tension for female slaves and young male slaves, who would have been the special targets of their owners' sexual interest. MacDonald aptly raises the further question of whether Christian slaveholders would respect the sexual integrity of bodies they owned: "The sexual ethics adopted by the Pauline Christians would presumably have meant that Christian slave owners would need to relinquish sexual relations with slaves. But reluctance on the part of some masters to give up past patterns (cf. 1:21–23, 2:20) might have made it especially important to warn them of their accountability before the Lord (3:25–4:1)."[53] MacDonald is honest in using the word "presumably." As I have argued in chapter two, nowhere in the New Testament epistles does Paul or any other letter writer state explicitly that the sexual use of slaves constitutes sexual immorality or sexual impurity. Since the practice of using slaves as a benign and safe sexual outlet persisted throughout antiquity, I wonder how and when Christian slaveholders would have come to understand that this behavior was inconsistent with the gospel. Perhaps the letter writers delivered such a teaching orally or in letters we no longer possess. Still, I wonder why the letter writers would not reinforce such a countercultural teaching. From the perspective of wider Greco-Roman culture, the sexual use of slaves falls easily within the parameters of "just and fair" behavior. The question is not only whether the author of Colossians would countenance such use of slaves as "just and fair." If he adopts the distinctive posture of decrying the sexual use of slaves, we must also ask how he expects his readers to grasp his position.

The household code in Ephesians is adapted from the household code in Colossians. The variation in instructions to slaves and slaveholders is minimal. Andrew Lincoln and A. J. M. Wedderburn conclude that the Ephesians household code "accommodates to and modifies the conventions of the Greco-Roman patriarchal household."[54] Specifically, they claim that the love-patriarchalism of the Christian household codes transforms the hierarchical relationships within households. Many Greco-Roman slaveholders understood the benefits of treating slaves fairly in order to maintain the stability of the household. As we have seen, for example, Seneca directed his advice to slaveholders toward the goal of stabilizing relations with household slaves through benign treatment. In turn, many Greco-Roman slaves understood that compliance with their owners' demands was a safer course of action than outright defiance. Perhaps the most striking modification of wider cultural values in the *haustafeln* is the articulation of a theological basis for the submission of slaves to slaveholders. The author of Ephesians advises, "Slaves, obey your masters with fear and trembling, in singleness of heart, as you obey Christ; not only while being watched, and in order to please them, but as slaves of Christ, doing the will of God from the heart."[55] Throughout the Empire, slaves understood that obedience and hard work might promote their own interests. With their eyes cast deferentially down, slaves hoped that their faithful execution of duties might spare them from the sting of the whip or aid them in securing their own manumission or the manumission of others they loved. Colossians and Ephesians disparage such motivation for servile cooperation, advocating instead that slaves submit their bodies and souls to their masters because such behavior is pleasing to God.

Pastoral Epistles

Scholars of early Christianity like to tell two stories about slavery, the church, and society. While not exactly contradictory, these stories follow distinct trajectories, one of ascent and one of descent. According to the first story, the rise of Christianity leads over a period of centuries to the weakening and demise of a slave society. Although the church does not directly oppose the institution of slavery, Jesus' teaching about the dignity of each person ultimately undermines centuries of the dehumanization of slaves. A Christianized Empire modifies the practices of and attitudes toward slavery and thereby decreases the significance of slaveholding as a social institution. Christianity is incompatible with the institution of slavery, but it takes centuries for Christians to come to understand this and to transform the structures of their world in accordance with this moral vision. According to the second story, the earliest years of the Christian movement are a golden age for relations between men and women, slaveholders and slaves. Although this story begins with the circle of men and women who are disciples of Jesus, those who recount the story tend not to acknowledge Jesus' reliance on the trope of slavery in his teachings. An anchor in this tale is Galatians 3:28 and the proclamation that those in Christ are divided neither by gender nor by legal status (slave or free). This second story supposes that as the decades continue, the Christian movement accommodates itself more and more to the structures of the surrounding society. In some versions of the story the adaptation is a consequence of persecution. Christians seek to become more like their neighbors to avoid the attention of authorities. The accommodation is thus not so much a compromise as an evangelical strategy, an attempt to create conditions in which preaching the gospel is likely to be successful. In some versions of the story, the acclimatization is a consequence of ambition, the desire to attract and retain wealthier and more influential members. In the first story, Christianity triumphs over the social values of the Roman Empire. In at least some versions of the second story, the Roman Empire triumphs over the social values of Christianity.

The Pastoral epistles play a signal role in the unfolding of this second narrative. Assuming the mantle of Pauline authority, the Pastor wrote to Christian communities late in the first century or early in the second century. He was preoccupied with authority within the church and attempted to dictate minimal requirements for those who sought to become ecclesial leaders. According to the Pastor, a church leader should exhibit an ability to manage his own household. Describing the qualifications for the office of bishop he wrote, "He must manage his own household well, keeping his children submissive and respectful in every way—for if someone does not know how to manage his own household, how can he take care of God's church?"[56] The leader of the house church was identified as the quintessential householder: husband, father, and presumably, slaveholder. Church management was a kind of home economics. The Pastor perceived that efficient management of a congregation drew on the same skills as efficient management of wives, children, slaves, and other dependents. The householder (free, male, slaveholding, and rich) demonstrated his concern for those in his care.[57] In turn, his dependents willingly embraced their subordinate roles within the household and within the church.[58] The acceptance by subordinates of their place in the household was ultimately the responsibility of the householder. According to ancient norms, the householder had an obligation to use corporal punishment to exact the compliance of members of the household, especially slaves. Corporal punishment denied the dignity of the person whipped (typically, a slave, but sometimes a son or a daughter) and affirmed the authority of the householder who had ordered the whipping.[59] The Pastoral epistles did not instruct householders to use physical violence to create harmony within their households, but householders who read these documents would have understood that such discipline was a standard strategy for creating the mandated order within the household. How else are we to read the Pastor's words? "He must manage his own household well, keeping his children submissive and respectful in every way—for if someone does not know how to manage his own household, how can he take care of God's church?"

Both 1 Timothy and Titus supplied advice to slaves but not to slaveholders qua slaveholders. Despite the absence of advice to slaveholders, these communities certainly included Christian slaveholders: 1 Timothy 6:2 refers to "believing masters." The Pastor, however, had no apparent concerns about the behavior of slaveholders within the communities or else his advice to slaveholders was subsumed within his advice more generally to senior men and to householders. Whatever general advice the Pastor gave householders was directed toward the preservation of order and harmony in the household and, by extension, the church. As a result, the author of the Pastoral epistles did not highlight expectations nor criticisms that Christian slaves might have had about the exercise of power by their owners, who worshiped alongside of them.[60]

Although the communities addressed by the Pastor included Christian slaveholders, they also included slaves belonging to non-Christian owners.[61] Perhaps the author's encouragement of servile submissiveness derived from a concern that Christians enslaved by pagans would be disruptive and therefore invite the disciplinary gaze of the slaveholder, not only against the offending slave but also against the entire Christian body. At least in 1 Timothy, however, the author addresses more explicitly and extensively the attitudes and actions of Christians enslaved by other Christians: "Let all who are under the yoke of slavery regard their masters as worthy of all honors, so that the name of God and the teaching may not be blasphemed. Those who have believing masters must not be disrespectful to them on the ground that they are members of the church; rather they must serve them all the more, since those who benefit by their service are believers and beloved."[62] Philip Towner justifies these instructions as necessary for the spread of the gospel. Towner expounds two basic principles, which he believes underlie regulations for Christian behavior in the Pastoral epistles: "(1) The social institutions were to be respected and participated in as they stand; and (2) that this was to be done in order to facilitate the proclamation of the gospel, which would be unhindered by unruly and revolutionary behavior."[63] What Towner does not consider is whether such accommodation to the patterns of a slaveholding society itself compromises the gospel, that is, whether the proclamation of human freedom and dignity is central to the gospel. Towner explicitly identifies the interests of the gospel with the interests of slaveholders and those sympathetic to slaveholders: "Some of the slaves referred to in v. 2 [slaves of "believing masters"] may have been owned by officers of the church, which only serves to demonstrate how directly their insubordination could have affected the ministry and witness of the community."[64] Let us consider the logic of Towner's claim that a slaveholder's headache of an "insubordinate" slave would have implications for the health of the Christian movement.

According to the Pastoral epistles, a man was eligible for consideration as a church leader if he had already demonstrated his ability to maintain discipline within his own household. Throughout the Greco-Roman world, slaves were always viewed as potential threats to household order and harmony. Management of household slaves was a basic element of home economics. Towner's analysis replicates the logic of the Pastoral epistles themselves.[65] He represents independent behavior by slaves, as by women or children, as a threat to the very survival of the church. He goes so far as to assert that "brotherhood in Christ must, within the slave-master relationship, be realized through the submission of slaves to masters."[66] On this view, the master-slave relationship is not transformed within the rubric of Christian brotherhood or sisterhood. Rather, Christian brotherhood and sisterhood are transformed within the rubric of human bondage.

The Pastoral epistles represent slaveholder morality as compatible and possibly synonymous with Christian morality. The Pastor seems completely assimilated to the values of the society in which he lived.[67] At least based on our surviving evidence, his writings may represent the end of the golden or perhaps the silver age of the Christian movement: that transitory moment in which Christians attempted to live out of a vision of unity in Christ that obliterated gender and status divisions. Nonetheless, commentators attempt to find something distinctively Christian in the Pastor's ethics. Luke Johnson, for example, claims that by enjoining slaves to perform the benefaction of according their masters respect, the author of 1 Timothy overturns ancient categories of honor and shame, since slaves were generally excluded from the category of those in a position to perform benefactions.[68] I disagree. An injunction to slaves to promote their owners' honor conforms to one of the most conspicuous characteristics of the slaveholding relationship in antiquity. As I argued in the first chapter, slaveholders used slaves as surrogate bodies to surround and buffer their own bodies and thereby safeguard their honor. A man or woman who appeared in public surrounded by a retinue of slaves promoted his own reputation and the dignity of his household. The role of slaves in promoting their owners' honor continued even after the slaveholder's death. When a will manumitted household slaves, they marched in their former owner's funeral procession as evidence of his or her largesse, reputation, and honor. Far from overturning the ancient category of honor, 1 Timothy's instructions to slaves to foster their owners' honor derives from the basic reliance of ancient slaveholders on their human property as surrogate bodies to prop up their own sense of self. By teaching slaves that honoring their owners was part of their Christian obligation, 1 Timothy sanctified slaveholder morality beyond the standard claims of the Greco-Roman ethos.

The instructions to slaves recorded in the epistle to Titus reinforce fundamental stereotypes of servile behavior: "Tell slaves to be submissive to their masters and to give satisfaction in every respect; they are not to talk back, not to pilfer, but to show complete and perfect fidelity, so that in everything they may be an ornament to the doctrine of God our Savior."[69] Do not talk back, and do not steal. The Pastor does not call slaves to contribute to the growth of the church through noble virtues. Rather, in David Verner's words, "Slaves and younger women could contribute to the life of the community by not damaging the church's reputation."[70] Verner comments on the instructions to slaves in Titus: "The slaves of Titus 2 are . . . warned against petty vices attributed to slaves according to the popular stereotypes. These warnings convey a sense of great social distance from slaves."[71] As Verner recognizes, the author of Titus identified with the moral standpoint of the slaveholder, in which the highest virtues of the slave were obedience and submission. Other commentators enter more willingly into the moral perspective of the Pastor. Johnson argues that "the specific instructions not to 'pilfer/steal' and not to 'talk back' seem . . . so rudimentary as to suggest—if we are to take these as real instructions for a real situation—a population that is need of the most basic moral formation."[72]

In this context, Bradley's assessment of the representation of troublesome slaves in Roman law seems germane: "So far I have referred to slaves' misdeeds as misdeeds or crimes, reflecting thereby the attitudes of the jurists and other writers who, by definition, were proslavery in outlook. At this stage, however, the extent of this prejudice needs to be brought out, both for its consistently moralistic tone to be fully seen, and for the underlying assumption that in committing misdeeds slaves deviated from a moral code they otherwise recognized and endorsed to be fully appreciated."[73] Throughout antiquity, slaveholders and other persons concerned with their personal honor bristled at perceived affronts by slaves who were careless of status distinctions. We have heard, for example, the complaint of the student Neilus against the slave Heraclas for telling tales out of school: "He behaves in every respect like a free man." Slaveholders who withheld from their human chattel their very liberty guarded their household goods jealously, worried lest a slave obtain more than his or her ration of flour, oil, or wine. Johnson and other commentators, however, evince more concern over the perceived moral failings of slaves (insolence and theft) than over the evident moral distortions of slaveholders.

1 Peter

The advice that 1 Peter delivers to enslaved Christians is at once more troubling and more poignant than the counsel that other New Testament epistles convey to slaves. In the Pastoral epistles, the letter writer suggests that the submission of slaves to the legitimate authority of householders/church leaders is a function of the decent and proper ordering of Christian life. The author of 1 Peter, in contrast, acknowledges that slaves may be forced to submit to excessive and disorderly authority. Although he guides slaves to submit to their owners, he does not uphold the patriarchal, slaveholding Greco-Roman household as a model for the church. Nonetheless, he encourages slaves to conform themselves to the distorted dictates of their owners: "Slaves [*oiketai*], accept the authority of your masters [*despotais*] with all deference, not only those who are kind and gentle but also those who are harsh. For it is a credit to you if, being aware of God, you endure pain while suffering unjustly. If you endure when you are beaten for doing wrong, what credit is that? But if you endure when you do right and suffer for it, you have God's approval. For to this you have been called, because Christ also suffered for you, leaving you an example so that you should follow in his steps."[74] Details of the passage underscore the divide between ancient and modern perceptions of justice. The author of 1 Peter considers a slaveholder beating a slave because he or she had "done wrong" a just dessert rather than evidence of the inherent and brutal injustice of slavery. Nonetheless, 1 Peter does not identify servile subordination with the will of God nor of Christ. Rather, 1 Peter links the bodily violations to which slaves were subject with the bodily violations of Jesus in his passion and death. The author of 1 Peter invites slaves to contemplate the wounds of Jesus in order to give them strength to endure their own wounds.

In his acknowledgment that slaves suffer excessive cruelty from their owners and in his invitation to slaves to view their own suffering in light of the suffering of Jesus, the author of 1 Peter exhibits a compassionate appreciation for the vicissitudes of life among domestic slaves. He emphasizes the physical violation of the tortured and crucified Jesus as he encourages Christian slaves to persevere: "When he was abused, he did not return abuse; when he suffered, he did not threaten; but he entrusted himself to the one who judges justly. He himself bore our sins in his body on the cross . . . by his bruises you have been healed."[75] Moreover, since the author of 1 Peter enjoins the entire community to endure suffering in a Christlike manner, enslaved Christians whose bodies absorb unwarranted abuse serve as a model for the entire Christian community to emulate.[76]

Like Epictetus, the author of 1 Peter calls on slaves to accept corporal abuse without flinching. However, the author of 1 Peter is no Stoic. For Epictetus, what happens to the body is a matter of no moral import. In 1 Peter, what happens to the body is very much a matter of moral import. Both slaves and the Christian community are to identify themselves with the sufferings of Jesus, whose bodily passion was redemptive: "by his bruises you have been healed." Epictetus counts the body among the external circumstances of a person's life. The body is a servile beast of burden. Although the person who abuses the body of another is guilty of cruelty, the person whose body is abused should find that circumstance a matter of indifference, which in no way affects his or her conduct or even volition. By contrast, the author of 1 Peter claims that through their willing acceptance of unjust physical violence, slaves earn the commendation of God. Although Epictetus and 1 Peter both urge slaves to absorb unjust blows, in 1 Peter, the body matters.

Carolyn Osiek and David Balch invite us to consider the guidance of 1 Peter in the context of options available to first-century slaves. They argue that "slaves are in the vulnerable position of having no recourse when abused. Their conformity to the suffering Christ, therefore, is meant to be comfort and encouragement in suffering that they are powerless to avoid, not a legitimation of the oppression of slavery."[77] Osiek and Balch overstate the lack of recourse that first-century slaves had to the brutality of their daily lives. We have seen the resistant behavior of slaves, which ancient moralists characterized as immoral and even criminal, including running away, appropriation of the owner's resources ("theft"), assertion of one's own dignity ("insolence"), and even outright rebellion. Each of these options would likely invite further abuse in time. Nonetheless, countless slaves adopted these approaches rather than passively accepting the conditions of their servitude.

On another level, Osiek and Balch are correct in their assessment of the lack of viable options for effecting change in the slave system. No abolition movement existed in antiquity. Slaves did not have legitimate channels for working to redress wrongs against them. As we have seen, increasingly coercive oppression was the likely consequence of slave rebellions or other obvious affronts to slaveholding authority. Furthermore, the entire community of 1 Peter seems to have been under suspicion. The advice that 1 Peter delivers to enslaved Christians parallels the advice that 1 Peter delivers to the entire congregation. For slaveholders in any historical epoch to cite this text to foster the submission of their slaves is therefore egregious, since the author implies that the slaveholders' treatment of their slaves is unjust and will ultimately be judged harshly by God.

The authors of Colossians and Ephesians urge slaves to submit themselves to their owners as they submit themselves to Christ, thereby likening the will of the slaveholder to the will of Christ. The argument of 1 Peter is distinctive. Slaves rather than slaveholders are assimilated to Christ. This identification is written on the bodies of slaves, whose bruises liken them to Jesus. The effect of the advice in the various epistles may be similar: slaves are to submit docilely to slaveholders. Nonetheless, the underlying logic of the passages is quite different. Unlike the world-affirming ethos of the deutero-Pauline letters, 1 Peter offers grounds for condemning the system of slavery by inviting comparisons between the abuse of slaves and the passion of Jesus.

The history of interpretation demonstrates that this is not a straightforward word of liberation. What may have been offered as a strategy of psychic survival to slaves who could not alter the conditions of servitude was deployed against slaves in the Americas to rebut their arguments for the elimination of the institution of slavery. What may have been a word of comfort and encouragement to enslaved Greco-Roman Christians, who were members of a marginalized and vulnerable congregation, later became a threatening word directed by slaveholders and their supporters to American slaves who protested the violent conditions of their servitude.

Still, the equation between the violated bodies of slaves and the tortured body of Jesus, which underlies the advice of 1 Peter, invites Christians to align themselves not with slaveholders but with slaves. I find scant evidence that this logic affected Christian ideology in the ancient world. The imagery was not lost, however, on nineteenth-century abolitionists, both African American and European American. Perhaps most familiar is Harriet Beecher Stowe's rendition of the martyrdom of the enslaved Tom when he would not betray his fellow slaves. Tom's knowing silence evokes the silence of Jesus on trial for his own life. When Simon Legree threatens to kill Tom, the slave offers, "Mas'r, if you was sick, or in trouble or dying, and I could save ye, I'd *give* ye my heart's blood; and if taking every drop of blood in this poor old body would save your precious soul, I'd give 'em freely, as the Lord gave his for me."[78] Stowe treats Tom's death as redemptive as it leads to the conversion of several bystanders, who tend him during the night of his death. Stowe elaborates on the isomorphism between the suffering bodies of the slave and Christ: "But of old, there was One whose suffering changed an instrument of torture, degradation, and shame, into a symbol of glory, honor, and immortal life; and where his Spirit is, neither degrading stripes, nor blood, nor insults, can make the Christian's last struggle less than glorious."[79]

In sanctifying the suffering of slaves, does 1 Peter reinforce slaveholder morality or assist those in hopeless situations to construct meaning in their lives? Does 1 Peter promote complacency or courage? The text itself is ambivalent, as is the history of interpretation. Like other ancient texts, the author of 1 Peter starts with the equation of slaves and bodies. However, unlike many ancient writers, the letter writer does not dismiss the significance of what is done to the slave body but associates Christian identity with the very violation of that body.

Extracanonical Household Codes

Extracanonical evidence attests to the popularity of the literary form of the *haustafel* among Christians. Several of these extracanonical household codes include instructions for slaves. Although these codes are generally consistent with the canonical codes in the tenor of their advice, each includes some distinctive elements.

The *Didache*, for example, moves from the injunction to share what one has with the needy to the following advice: "You will not withhold your hand from your son or your daughter, but you will teach them the fear of God from their youth up. You will not command in your bitterness your slave [*doulos*] or your slave girl [*paidiskē*], who hope in the same God, lest they cease to fear the God who is over you both; for he comes not to call men with respect of persons, but those whom the Spirit has prepared. You who are slaves are to be subject to your master [*kyrios*, Lord], as to God's representative [*hōs typō theou*], in reverence and fear."[80] For the author of the *Didache*, corporal punishment of sons and daughters is not only permitted but necessary in order to instill the requisite fear of God in young people. The *Didache* enjoins slaveholders to avoid bitterness in dealings with slaves. However, given the author's endorsement of the physical discipline of children, we must suppose that the everyday brutality directed against the bodies of slaves would not have merited his censure. The author of the *Didache* addresses slaveholders whose slaves are themselves members of the church and slaves who belong to fellow Christians. Although the *Didache* invites temperate treatment of slaves, the author mandates fearfulness as the suitable affect for the Christian slave. Presumably in the background of these instructions looms the slaveholder/parent (or possibly the slaveholder/father) as the disciplinarian of household bodies and souls.

In the context of my treatment of manumission in chapter three, I have already discussed Ignatius's letter to Polycarp. What distinguishes the household code in this text is its reference to manumission. Harrill has argued convincingly that Ignatius does not oppose manumission per se but seeks to limit or eliminate reliance on ecclesial resources to fund manumissions. Such a policy would not only rapidly consume limited funds but might offer a problematic motivation to slaves for joining the church. On the other hand, since Ignatius seeks to restrict the practice, one may conjecture that other Christians believed that their faith compelled them to ransom members of the church from slavery.[81] We have no direct record of the practices or beliefs of these Christians, only the palimpsest of Ignatius's words. Ignatius writes Polycarp, "Do not be haughty to male slaves or female slaves; yet do not let them be puffed up, but let them rather endure slavery to the glory of God, that they may obtain a better freedom from Christ. Let them not desire to be set free at the Church's expense, that they be not found the slaves of desire [*epithumia*]."[82] Have these slaves heard the baptismal formula of Galatians 3:28 as a promise of freedom? Perhaps, although Ignatius seems equally concerned with the haughtiness of slaveholders as the haughtiness of slaves (which slaveholders would represent as insolence). Ignatius subordinates the goal of corporal freedom to what he represents as the more glorious end of spiritual freedom. Like other Stoic and Christian authors, he thus subordinates the body to the soul. By enduring the enslavement of the body, slaves could hope to attain from Christ a more splendid freedom—far better, Ignatius suggests, than the mere release from physical bondage obtained in manumission. Ignatius invites slaves to embrace their somatic bondage as a positive step in their moral training.[83] We do not know how Christian slaves who heard this letter responded in Ignatius's day. Later critics, however, have been convinced by Ignatius and other ancient writers to discount the bodily costs of slavery as trivial or even to view them as assets in the movement of the soul to liberation.

Controlling Bodies

When Rome finally overpowered Spartacus's army of enslaved gladiators and other desperate men, the victors crucified six thousand defeated partisans on the road between Capua and Rome. Slavery was not an invisible institution. What effect did those crucified bodies have on all who walked down the road? What messages did passing slaves, carrying heavy burdens to market, absorb? What thoughts filled the heads of free artisans, who worked side by side in their workshops with a few slaves? Perhaps most important, what lessons did young children glean as they looked up at the once-feared army of slaves, now gasping for breath or hanging lifeless on rows of crosses? How did a young slave whose father or protector was suspended on one of the crosses interpret the sight of so many crucified men? How did the scene influence a young slave boy's emerging sense of masculinity? How did this same panorama affect the self-image of freeborn boys who passed down the road, perhaps accompanied by their slave minders?

More broadly, we should ask how the violent, coercive, dehumanizing institution of slavery affected freeborn children, who grew up in the midst of a slaveholding culture. That is, how did the ethos of slaveholding mold the children who were likely to be slaveholders themselves? How did the structures of slavery affect the relations of freeborn persons not only to slaves and freedpersons but also to other freeborn persons? to their spouses? to their own children and to their own parents? How did it affect the emotional lives of ancient slaveholders to have slaves near to hand whenever a wave of anger passed over them? How did the proximity of attractive, available slaves shape the emergent sexuality of slaveholding adolescent males?[84]

I am suggesting that the institution of slavery marked the character of the inhabitants of the Greco-Roman world in ways that will not always appear immediately to be associated with the practices of slavery. Toni Morrison raises a parallel set of questions about the impact of an enslaved Africanist population on the imagination of the young American nation. She inaugurates "a serious intellectual effort to see what racial [for the ancient world, substitute *slaveholding*] ideology does to the mind, imagination, and behavior of masters."[85] In the Gospel of Luke, a centurion says to Jesus, "I also am a man set under authority, with soldiers under me; and I say to one, 'Go,' and he goes, and to another, 'Come,' and he comes, and to my slave, 'Do this,' and the slave does it."[86] One becomes habituated to power, the centurion implies. Elite children of the Roman Empire acquired early the habit of command. Exercises copied by schoolboys relied on and reinforced the customary directives that little children gave their slaves. One version of these exercises followed the schoolboy through a typical day. Martin Bloomer gives a quick summary of the exercises: "Starting with the dawn the boy orders his slave to wash him. Clothe me. Feed me and so on." The format includes various lists for the student to practice writing: body parts that the slave is to dry, for example. Bloomer argues, "The boy was learning to command: he was rehearsing the role of slave owner, father, advocate, all the roles of the pater familias."[87]

The churches, too, grew up in the midst of a slaveholding society. Both slaveholders and slaves populated early Christian congregations. They brought with them characters and habits molded by lifetimes of command and of obedience. What effects did the institution of slavery have on the emerging structures and ideology of the early churches, even in those areas of communal and individual life that may not immediately appear to be associated with the practices of slavery or the persons of slaves?

The question of the effect of a slaveholding culture on the character of the slaveholder is an ancient one. Clement of Alexandria raises it in his treatment of Christ the Educator, *Paedagogues*. Clement does not disapprove of slaveholding but suggests that owning too many slaves softens and corrupts slaveholders by feeding their baser appetitites. A large staff of kitchen slaves "ministers to the gluttony" of slaveholders, carving meats and making honey cakes and other pastries. Women have staffs of slaves to tend to their beauty, fostering vanity with mirrors, hairnets, and combs. Clement does not concern himself with the effect of such service on the slaves, but on the availability of slaves as props for fostering the vices of slaveholders. "There are many Celts to lift and carry the litters for these women, but nowhere can one see any spinning or weaving or loom-working or, for that matter, any feminine occupations or household chores," writes Clement. Women rely on these carriers "not out of modesty, to keep from being gazed at (it would be praiseworthy if they hung up the draperies [of their litters] for such a purpose), but have themselves borne by their servants to attract attention."[88] Clement is particularly concerned that being surrounded by male slaves erodes a decent woman's sense of modesty. Women who pretend to be ashamed to undress in front of their husbands think nothing of stripping in the baths and ordering their male slaves to massage them, Clement claims. (He does not tell us how he knows what transpires among women at the baths.[89]) Clearly, some of the slaveholders characterized by Clement are pagans, since he alludes to slaves bearing their mistresses' litters to the temples to perform sacrifices or consult with oracles. His concern, however, is that the decadent effects of slaveholding will taint Christian slaveholders as well. He addresses slaveholders within the congregation when he writes, "For my part, I would advise husbands never to manifest their affection for their wives at home when slaves are present."[90] Although Clement's distaste may seem farfetched, frescos from Pompeii depict young slaves standing by with toiletries as adult couples engage in sexual relations. Both in establishments with many slaves and (differently) in households with but a few slaves, slaves were constantly present at the most intimate moments of family life. We may not fully understand how the ubiquity of slaves affected the emotional, erotic, and moral lives of slaveholders, but it would be peculiar to assume that living in a household with slaves—"like mice," Artemidorus tells us—left no traces on the personalities of the slaveholders. I believe that it is equally peculiar to assume that the structures and ideology of a slaveholding society left few discernible traces on the ethos of the churches that matured in that context.

The question, then, is how are we to recognize and trace the effects of slaveholding in ancient Christian sources and evidence. We may anticipate the shadows cast by the practice of slaveholding to be various, multiform, and frequently indistinct, but one silhouette's outline is worth filling in. Throughout this work, I have highlighted the ancient equivalence between slaves and bodies. On a basic semantic level, the term *sōma*, body, can function as a synonym for "slave," particularly when the slave is figured as object rather than subject. I have argued more broadly that the history of interpretation underemphasizes the somatic dimensions of slavery, including the sexual availability of the slave body and the vulnerability of the slave body to corporal abuse. In contrast, the connection between slaves and bodies is often explicit in ancient sources. I opened the present study with a reference to a heavy metal collar, which identified the slave who wore it as a body belonging to a Christian archdeacon. At the beginning of the first chapter, we also considered the words of Artemidorus in the *Oneirocritica*: "Slaves also indicate the bodies of their masters. The very man who dreamt that he saw his household slave sick with a fever became ill himself, as one might expect. For the household slave has the same relationship to the dreamer that the body has to the soul."[91] On an imaginary level, slaves and bodies are fungible. In tracing the impact of the slaveholding culture on the church that grew up in its midst, therefore, one might well examine the ethos of the body in the first centuries of Christianity.

Ascetic disciplines emerged early among various Christian sects and became increasingly important. Ascetic Christians simultaneously disciplined the body and guarded the integrity of the body through rejection of sexual activity. What was the significance of such practices in a culture where slaves and bodies mutated into one another at the level of rhetoric, where the slave body had no practical integrity since the slave was not in a position to resist sexual advances or other corporal violations?

Ascetic practices were more common among elite Christians than among Christians of lesser status.[92] Asceticism would not have been a viable choice for the vast majority of slaves. The privations of fasting or refusing sleep would exhaust the body. Slaves who had to work long hours would be less likely to willingly forgo sustenance than persons of leisure. Rough clothes, which chafed delicate skin, could only be considered a punishment for those accustomed to finer garments. The ascetic Melania the Younger, heir to a vast fortune, persisted in her desire to sleep on the hard ground. For many slaves, a night's sleep on the bare ground was not a choice but an inevitability. Melania wore cheap clothing. As a young wife, while still participating in the elite social circle of her birth and rearing, she was expected to wear appropriately luxurious garments. Even then, however, she wore coarse woolen clothing underneath her silk outer garments.[93] Gillian Clark notes that the practices of asceticism mimic the necessary conditions of poverty in antiquity. Along with rough clothing, she writes, "Other aspects of the ascetic life could also be interpreted as consequences of the choice of poverty: hunger, dirt, extremes of heat and cold."[94] What differentiated the hunger, filth, exhaustion, and threadbare clothes of the ascetic from that of the slave was the element of choice.

Slaves were not in a position to reject sexual liaisons, a sine qua non of asceticism in early Christian communities. Writing about Mary of Nazareth, Athanasius stated that in her youth she so eschewed the company of men that she even avoided contact with male slaves—hardly a realistic behavioral goal for female slaves.[95] In describing the practice of asceticism among Alexandrian women, David Brakke concludes, "Virgins came, then, from a variety of backgrounds: some were wealthy enough to own slaves and property; others were themselves slaves." However, the example he offers of a female slave embarking on the life of a dedicated virgin is this: "A rich woman who had no daughter could dedicate one of her female slaves to the ascetic life, but then had to remove her from normal slave duties and 'care for her as her own daughter.'"[96] Brakke's illustration underscores the tension between life as a slave and life as a dedicated virgin. A slaveholding woman and not the slave herself made the decision for a slave to pursue an ascetic course. Moreover, entry into this life entailed separation of the slave from her former life. That some few slaves pursued ascetic ways is probable. However, the demands of ordinary slave lives were not compatible with the convictions and practices of ascetic Christians. Slaves, after all, knew the double bind of attempting to serve two masters.

In a world where householders treated their slaves as recalcitrant bodies to be restrained by corporal corrections, ascetic Christians emphasized the discipline and control of their own bodies. Just as householders regarded the control of unruly slave bodies to be a standard part of household management, ascetic Christians regarded the control of their own unruly bodies as a necessary dimension in the management of their spiritual houses. Just as the Pastor urged heads of household to keep the members of the house under tight control, ascetic Christians tightly reined in the members of their own bodies. We have the severe injunction of the ascetic desert mother Theodora, sounding much like a householder trying to maintain a semblance of order in the house: "Give the body discipline."[97]

Stoics like Marcus Aurelius also urged the pursuit of bodily regimens, but the practices they advocated were temperate and balanced.[98] In contrast, Christian ascetics like Melania the Younger learned to withstand physical miseries, which they characterized as torture, in antiquity strongly associated with the interrogation and punishment of slaves.[99] The biography of Melania includes a story that she is said to have recounted, which urges Christians to develop the virtues of submission and obedience, virtues characteristically advocated for slaves. A would-be disciple approached an aging holy man to beg him for instruction. The holy man advised the would-be disciple to obtain a scourge and to use it to whip a nearby statue. When the prospective disciple came back, the holy man asked whether the statue protested its physical abuse. Of course not, said the student. The holy man told him to return again to whip the statue, only this time he should also verbally insult and belittle the statue. The would-be disciple engaged in this routine and repeated it yet another time. Melania ended the story, "At last the old saint said to him, 'If you can become like that statue, insulted but not returning the insult, struck but not protesting, then you can also be saved and remain with us.'" She urged her hearers, "Thus let us, too, O children, imitate this statue and nobly submit to everything—to insult, reproach, contempt—in order that we may inherit the Kingdom of Heaven."[100] Melania thus urges ascetics to train their bodies to be ideal slaves, submitting without resistance to violent blows and standing silently, without honor, when verbally besieged by insults. The injunction to treat the body as a slave is even more explicit in the writings of other ascetic Christians. Paul drew on athletic metaphors to evoke his own struggles, saying that he had "punished and enslaved" his body.[101] Athanasius develops this metaphor when he urges virgins "to press the body all the more and make it a good servant for them."[102]

Christianity was born and grew up in a world in which slaveholders and slaves were part of the everyday landscape. In a context in which slaveholders treated slaves as bodies—available bodies, vulnerable bodies, compliant bodies, surrogate bodies—ascetic Christians learned to treat their own bodies as slaves. In one area, however, ascetic Christians recoiled from the treatment of bodies as slaves. Throughout this study, I have emphasized the sexual availability of slaves to their owners and others to whom their owners chose to give or lease access. I argue in chapter three that freeborn persons reacted with horror to the potential blurring of the sexual boundaries of free bodies. Patrick, for example, particularly protested the sexual bondage of free Christian women kidnapped and sold into slavery. Perhaps the most characteristic element of Christian ascetic discipline was the absolute rejection of even the near-occasion of sexual contact. The violent reaction of ascetic Christians against the sexual use of their bodies demarcated the voluntary character of the servility of the ascetic body. Ascetics, unlike slaves, could say "no" to the sexual use of their bodies. In fact, the utter refusal of ascetic Christians to participate in any sexual activities reinforces the horror of a central facet of slave life while it reinscribes the place of the slave outside the circle of honorable persons. Perhaps nowhere is this clearer than in the tale of Maximilla from the *Acts of Andrew*, which I discussed in the first chapter. Maximilla, a slaveholder drawn to the ascetic renunciation of sexual relations with her husband, thinks nothing of relying on her slave Euclia as an erotic body double: her humiliation purchases Maximilla's sexual purity. Maximilla relies on an enslaved body to secure the freedom of her own body.

The body-controlling practices of asceticism comprise one vector of early Christian life where we may seek the traces of a slaveholding culture. I expect, however, that the beliefs and practices of slaveholding had a far wider impact on the young churches as they grew up throughout the Empire. I have argued that the identification of slaves as bodies has historically interfered with the ability of scholars, more interested in the life of the soul, to acknowledge the impact of slavery on the structures and beliefs of early Christianity. Precisely that identification of slaves as bodies, then, should be a starting place for further investigation of the ideological and social impact of a slaveholding culture on the men and women who comprised the membership of the ancient Christian body.

Notes

Introduction

1. "In the Levant of the Principate, while commerce in slaves is amply attested along with large households of them in Palestine, there is otherwise nothing known, but for the period after 350 and especially in and around Antioch, the sources are exceptionally rich and the picture exceptionally clear: slaves are abundant in the city" (MacMullen, *Changes in the Roman Empire*, p. 238).

2. I refer rarely to sources before this time period. I do not rely on the classical Greek philosophers, for example. Aristotle's comments on slavery intersect in various ways with the concerns I raise in this study, but I think other sources bring us closer to the world views of the early Christians and their contemporaries.

3. Bradley, "Problem of Slavery in Classical Antiquity."

4. The ascendancy of Christian emperors was not a death blow to slavery, as is often asserted. See, for example, the discussion of Constantine's legislative support for slaveholders in Grubbs, *Law and Family in Late Antiquity*, p. 26.

5. White, *Tropics of Discourse*, p. 79.

6. *P.Tebt.* 2.407.

7. A Roman man who lost his estate to creditors could nonetheless retain ownership of his *filius naturalis*, the son born to him and one of his slave women. See Saller, "Hierarchical Household in Roman Society," pp. 116–117.

8. *P.Oxy.* 9.1209.

9. See, e.g., *P.Oxy.* 55.4058; *P.Turner* 22; *P.Kell.G.* 8; *P.Mich.* 5.278–279.

10. Rawson, "Family Life among the Lower Classes at Rome in the First Two Centuries of the Empire."

11. In his accessible account of the contributions that the Egyptian papyri make to reconstructing life in the Roman Empire, Bagnall writes, "How representative of the larger Greek and Roman world is the picture provided by the papyri? It has often been difficult to separate this question from the self-interest of those answering it, whether by papyrologists arguing in favor of typicality or by historians lacking expertise in the papyri (and, as papyrologists always suspect, adverse to the effort of acquiring it) against typicality" (*Reading Papyri, Writing Ancient History*, pp. 11–12).

12. As Harris concedes, "We no longer suppose that Egypt was an exception to every generalization that can be made about the economy and society of the Roman Empire" ("Demography, Geography and the Sources of Roman Slaves," p. 65). For documentary finds from Roman Britain, see Bowman, *Life and Letters on the Roman Frontier*.

13. Millar, "The World of the *Golden Ass*"; Hopkins, "Novel Evidence for Roman Slavery."

14. For related arguments, see Glancy, "Mistress-Slave Dialectic."

15. For these reasons and others, Harrill stresses the limits of the *Digest* as a reliable source for social history ("Using the Roman Jurists to Interpret Philemon").

16. Millar, "Greek East and Roman Law," p. 90.

17. Martin, "Slavery and the Ancient Jewish Family," p. 113. See also Flesher, *Oxen, Women, or Citizens?* who argues against reconstructing the behaviors of Jews in the Second Temple period on the basis of the Mishnah. Cf. Urbach, "Laws Regarding Slavery as a Source for Social History of the Period of the Second Temple, the Mishnah, and Talmud."

18. Cotton concludes that similarities between the marriage contracts that have been excavated and (later) Halakha derive from the influence of local customs on Halakha and not from the influence of Halakha on local customs ("Cancelled Marriage Contract from the Judaean Desert"). See also Cotton, "Guardianship of Jesus Son of Babatha: Roman and Local Law in the Province of Arabia," and the related fierce debate among Ilan, Schremer, and Brewer. Bibliography can be found in Brewer, "Jewish Women Divorcing Their Husbands in Early Judaism."

19. Reference to the remarks of Justin and Clement is standard in treatments of child exposure in the Roman Empire. Two sample references are Saller, "Slavery and the Roman Family," pp. 69–70, and Harris, "Child-Exposure in the Roman Empire," p. 10.

20. Clement of Alexandria, *Paedagogues* 3.3.21; Justin Martyr, *1 Apology* 27.

Chapter 1

1. Sotgiu, *Arch. Class.* 25/26 (1973–1974/1979) 688–97. Sotgiu argues that the use of a slave collar represents a merciful alternative to branding on the face. Cited in Reynolds, "Roman Inscriptions 1971–5," p. 196. Gustafson's discussion of late antique Christian attitudes toward tattooing should be taken into account in assessing this meliorist hypothesis ("*Inscripte in Fronte*").

2. Artemidorus, *Oneirocritica* 4.30.

3. Toni Morrison uses the expressions "surrogate (black) bodies" and "surrogate selves" to refer to the literary functions of "Africanist" (Morrison's term) characters in literature composed by Americans of European descent (*Playing in the Dark*).

4. Combes, *Metaphor of Slavery in the Writings of the Early Church*; Martin, *Slavery as Salvation*.

5. *Exegesis of the Soul* 128.5–12.

6. *P.Mich.* 5.323–325.

7. *P.Fam.Tebt.* 48.

8. *P.Mich.* 5.244; the constitution dates from 43 C.E.

9. *BGU* 4.1105.

10. One example among many is the quotation from the NRSV translation of Revelation 18:13, which follows.

11. Revelation 18:13. The NRSV translates the phrase as "slaves—and human lives."

12. For the insult to a free woman varying according to her garb, see *Dig.* 47.10.15.15; Plutarch, *Queast. Rom.* 101,288a; and the discussion in Walters, "Invading the Roman Body."

13. *Dig.* 47.10.1.2.

14. *P.Oxy.* 8.1120.

15. Gaius, *Inst.* 3.22.

16. *Dig.* 47.10.15.44.

17. See also Gaius, *Inst.* 3.22.

18. Jones, "*Stigma.*"

19. Petr., *Sat.* 103.

20. John 18:10; Matt. 26:51; Mark 14:47; Luke 22:50.

21. *Acts of Thomas* 6.

22. For a more general discussion of the methodological obstacles to using the papyrological record to draw conclusions about ancient violence, see Bagnall, "Official and Private Violence in Roman Egypt."

23. *P.Wisc.* 33.
24. Pliny, *Ep.* 3.14.6–8.
25. Artemidorus, *Oneirocritica* 1.76.
26. *Dig.* 47.10.7.2.
27. *Dig.* 47.10.11.7.
28. MacMullen, "Personal Power in the Roman Empire," p. 512.
29. *Dig.* 47.10.17.7.
30. *Dig.* 47.10.11.7.
31. Bagnall, "Slavery and Society in Late Roman Egypt," pp. 236–237.
32. See the discussion of the fictive strategies of petitioners in early modern France in Davis, *Fiction in the Archives.*
33. *P.Oxy.* 49.3480.
34. *P.Oxy.* 51.3620.
35. *Dig.* 47.10.173–4.
36. *BGU* 16.2604.
37. *Dig.* 25.2.21.2.
38. *Dig.* 44.7.20.
39. Apul., *Met.*, 10.2–12.
40. Acts of the Apostles 2:18.
41. Bagnall refers specifically to an article by Harris, "Child-Exposure in the Roman Empire." Bagnall writes, "Harris . . . remarks that 'an unbalanced sex ratio probably did prevail in the population of slaves, and one of the mechanisms by which this was brought about was perhaps the selective exposure of girls who were born to slave mothers.' He thus apparently supposes that the sex ratio among slaves was skewed toward masculinity, the reverse of what the data show" (Bagnall, "Missing Females in Roman Egypt," p. 127).
42. Harris, for example, expresses skepticism about Bagnall's conclusions. Harris nonetheless admits some weaknesses in his own method of reckoning the sex ratio in the slave population, based on epigraphic evidence ("Demography, Geography and the Sources of Roman Slaves," pp. 65–70).
43. "Described as *honeste nata*, Perpetua may have been of curial rank, although her father was beaten with *fustes* . . . a penalty from which *curiales* were exempt" (Grubbs, *Law and Family in Late Antiquity*, p. 10, n. 26).
44. *Passion of Perpetua* 7.
45. *Passion of Perpetua* 20.
46. Columella, *De Re Rustica* 1.8.19.
47. Petr., *Sat.*, 53.
48. Patterson, *Slavery and Social Death*, p. 13; Finley, *Ancient Slavery and Modern Ideology*, p. 143. In an issue of *Semeia* dedicated to studies of the New Testament and slavery, Callahan, Horsley, and Smith write, "Patterson was broadening the standard understanding of slavery. He insisted that the heinous human relation of slavery could not be reduced to the 'simple reality' of property, as in M. I. Finley's earlier . . . study of ancient Greek and Roman slavery" ("Introduction: The Slavery of New Testament Studies," pp. 1–2). For those unfamiliar with Finley's work, this summary does a profound disservice to his contributions to the study of slavery in classical antiquity. In his introduction to *Slavery and Social Death*, Patterson himself acknowledges Finley's influence: "All of us who work on the comparative study of slavery are in intellectual debt to Sir Moses Finley. . . . Above all, his theoretical writings constituted the intellectual springboard for my own reflections on the nature of slavery and slave societies. His personal encouragement of my work persuaded me that a nonspecialist could with benefit immerse himself in the . . . classical world" (p. xii).
49. Aulus Gellius, *Noctes Atticae* 12.1.6.

50. Aulus Gellius, *Noctes Atticae* 12.1.17.

51. Apul., *Met.* 8.10–14.

52. *Acts of Thomas* 119–121.

53. Joshel, "Nurturing the Master's Child."

54. Vogt, *Ancient Slavery and the Ideal of Man*, pp. 104–109.

55. Joshel, "Nurturing the Master's Child," p. 74.

56. Soranus, *Gynaecology* 2.18–20.

57. Jacobs, *Incidents in the Life of a Slave Girl*, p. 14.

58. Artemidorus, *Oneirocritica* 1.78.

59. Petr., *Sat.* 75.

60. *BGU* 4.1105.

61. "There was a considerable difference between the legitimate wife in an honorable marriage, who had the power to initiate divorce and walk away from an abusive husband, and the powerless slave, female or male" (Saller, "Symbols of Gender and Status Hierarchies in the Roman Household," pp. 85–91).

62. Jerome, *Ep.* 77.3.

63. Achilles Tatius, *Leukippe and Clitophon*, 6.20. For further discussion of this passage, see Shaw, "Body/Power/Identity."

64. Treggiari, *Roman Marriage*, p. 301.

65. *Acts of Andrew* 17.

66. *Acts of Andrew* 22=MacDonald, *Acts of Andrew and the Acts of Andrew and Matthias in the City of Cannibals*, p. 353. I have altered MacDonald's translation slightly by changing his translation of *syndoulous* from "fellow servants" to "fellow slaves" and his translation of *doulous* from "servants" to "slaves."

67. Grubbs, *Law and Family in Late Antiquity*, chap. 6.

68. Jacobs, "Family Affair," p. 129.

69. *Acts of Andrew* 17=MacDonald, *Acts of Andrew and the Acts of Andrew and Matthias in the City of Cannibals*, p. 347.

70. Bradley, *Slaves and Masters in the Roman Empire*, p. 118.

71. Xenophon of Ephesus, *An Ephesian Tale* 5.5.

72. Val. Max., *Memorable Deeds and Sayings* 6.7.1.

73. Plut., *Mor. Quaest. Rom.* 267D.

74. Kraemer, *Her Share of the Blessings*, p. 67.

75. Petr., *Sat.* 74.

76. Catullus 61.

77. Richlin, *Garden of Priapus*, p. 34.

78. Mart. 1.58.3.

79. Quint., *Inst.* 5.12.17–20.

80. Nonetheless, I think Montserrat goes too far in his reading of *P.Oxy.* 51.3617, which describes a runaway slave as a beardless man speaking in a shrill voice. According to Montserrat: "Naturally some of the bodily details are included here for entirely practical purposes, but there is a sub-text to their inclusion. Because he is a slave, he cannot be a 'real man,' and the adjectives applied to the body of this anonymous slave serve to set him physically apart and render him ridiculous. He is ugly and beardless and thus infantile . . . and like a child he goes around jabbering away as though he has delusions of grandeur" (Montserrat, *Sex and Society in Greco-Roman Egypt*, p. 55). I agree that we should be sensitive to rhetorical strategies in the papyri, but here I think Montserrat underplays the importance of describing a fugitive slave accurately.

81. Walters, "Invading the Roman Body," p. 31. See also L'Hoir, *Rhetoric of Gender Terms*.

82. For a discussion of the ambiguous category of the *pais* in classical Athenian literature, see Golden, "*Pais*: 'Child' and 'Slave.'"

83. Patterson, *Slavery and Social Death*, p. 96.

84. Even after manumission he would remain within the legal and social ambit of the former owner.

85. Matt. 8:5–13; Luke 7:1–10.

86. In the Matthean version, the centurion himself approaches Jesus for assistance. In the Lukan version, the centurion first sends Jewish elders, who vouch that the centurion has been supportive of the synagogue.

87. Matt. 9:18–26; Mark 5:21–43; Luke 8:40–56.

88. For parallel arguments, see Williams, *Roman Homsexuality*, pp. 30–34, which came to my attention after I had completed work on this section.

89. Moore and Anderson, "Taking It Like a Man," p. 250. Moore and Anderson build on the work of classicists who have explored ancient constructions of masculinity under the influence of Foucault. See, however, Richlin's feminist warning about the limits of a Foucaultian approach: "By adopting the point of view of his sources, Foucault ends by replicating their omissions. . . . Moreover, he meets his sources dressed in their Sunday best; it is hard to recognize in Foucault's contemplative, self-disciplined, married pederasts the men who made so many jokes about rape and ugly women" (Richlin, *Garden of Priapus*, p. xiv).

90. See Connolly, "Roman Oratory."

91. Harlow, "In the Name of the Father," p. 160.

92. Artemidorus, *Oneirocritica* 1.45.

93. See discussion of the symbolic dimensions of Roman fatherhood in Corbier, "Divorce and Adoption as Roman Familial Strategies."

94. "Servile relationships are what we might call 'anti-kinship'" (Bohannan, *Social Anthropology*, p. 180). Patterson emphasizes natal alienation as central to slave systems in *Slavery and Social Death*.

95. At the same time, Roman law implied an anxiety about widows who might attempt to pass off other babies as the progeny of their late husbands. The law specified that the husband's family could require repeated inspections by a midwife of the belly of the pregnant woman and even control the location and oversight of the delivery (*Dig.* 25.4.10).

96. Saller, "Hierarchical Household in Roman Society," p. 121.

97. Grubbs, *Law and Family in Late Antiquity*, chap. 6.

98. Scheidel argues that the "overall fertility of ex-slaves" would be low. He concludes, "As slave women were rarely manumitted during the period of prime fecundity, the population of freedwomen could not nearly reproduce itself. . . . For this reason, manumission as practiced by the Romans . . . limited the proportion of all citizens who were ultimately the descendants of slaves" ("Quantifying the Sources of Slaves in the Early Roman Empire," p. 167).

99. Patterson, *Slavery and Social Death*, p. 11.

100. Malina, *New Testament World*, p. 34. For a sense of the anthropological literature on which Malina relies, see Gilmore, ed., *Honor and Shame and the Unity of the Mediterranean*.

101. Malina, *New Testament World*, p. 49.

102. For the complexity of the issue, see Garnsey, *Social Status and Legal Privilege in the Roman Empire*.

103. "Slave women stood outside the value system of honor and chastity that regulated the lives of citizen women and also protected them. . . . There was a considerable difference between the legitimate wife in an honorable marriage, who had the power to initiate divorce and walk away from an abusive husband, and the powerless slave, female or male" (Saller, "Symbols of Gender and Status Hierarchies in the Roman Household," p. 89).

104. See discussion in Saller, "Hierarchical Household in Roman Society," pp. 123–124.

105. Grubbs, *Law and Family in Late Antiquity*, chap. 6. Grubbs outlines both continuities and discontinuities between imperial legislation before and after the fourth century.

106. Edwards, "Unspeakable Professions," p. 76.
107. Clement of Alexandria, *Paedagogues* 5.32.
108. *Acts of Thomas* 100.
109. Apul., *Met.* 8.22.
110. Patterson, *Slavery and Social Death*, p. 97.
111. Butler, "Notes on a *Membrum Disiectum*," pp. 248–249.
112. Skinner, "Introduction," p. 25.
113. *Acts of Thomas* 82–86.
114. Hershbell offers a worthwhile analysis of the *Discourses* as evidence for the opinions of a former slave ("Epictetus: A Freedman on Slavery").
115. Sen., *Ben.* 3.20.1–2.
116. Scarry, *The Body in Pain*.
117. Castelli, "Paul on Women and Gender," p. 231.
118. In this discussion of Galatians 3–4, I rely on the translation of Martyn, *Galatians*, p. 373.
119. Castelli, "Paul on Women and Gender," p. 231. See also Briggs, "Galatians," pp. 224–225.
120. Garnsey, "Sons, Slaves—and Christians."
121. Barrett, "Allegory of Abraham, Sarah, and Hagar in the Argument of Galatians."
122. *P.Oxy.* 9.1206. Admittedly, the late date of the contract mitigates its significance for understanding the first-century context of Galatians.
123. *BGU* 4.1058 (13 B.C.E.); *P.Ryl.* 2.178 (early first century C.E.).
124. *P.Oxy.* 1.37–38 (49 C.E.).
125. Corbier, "Divorce and Adoption," pp. 66 and 63.

Chapter 2

1. Apul., *Met.* 1.21–22.
2. Harrill argues that Rhoda exemplifies the *servus currens*, or running slave, a stock character in New Comedy ("Dramatic Function of the Running Slave Rhoda").
3. John 18:16.
4. *Acts of Paul* 18–19.
5. Sen., *Con.* 14.12.
6. Apul., *Met.* 1.21.
7. For an overview of comparative anthropological perspectives on slavery, see Lovejoy, *Transformations in Slavery*, pp. 1–18.
8. Bohannan, *Social Anthropology*, p. 181.
9. When Paul exorcises the Pythian spirit from the slave, her owners lose a ready source of income. Luke's treatment of the slave's oracular powers is ultimately more respectful than that of some other ancient authors, since he implies that the slave really had been possessed by a spirit of divination, albeit a spirit less powerful than the name of Jesus. In contrast, for example, Apuleius expresses cynicism toward the activities of oracles. When Lucius expresses confidence in the predictions of a Chaldean astrologer, who he encountered in Corinth, his host, Milo, debunks the tale by revealing how the same man had been revealed a fraud in Hypata. A mark of Apuleius's genius is that he leaves his ultimate attitude toward the oracle an open question; the astrologer's prediction that Apuleius will write a book about his journey ultimately proves true, as does his prediction that the book will not be taken as a serious work. Regarding the ambivalence of *The Golden Ass* toward all things supernatural, from fortune-telling and magic to the worship of Isis, see Winkler, *Auctor and Actor*.
10. Apul., *Met.* 2.12–14.

11. Acts of the Apostles 16:16-18.

12. Philo, *Leg. Spec.* 3.169. Quoted in Neyrey, "What's Wrong with This Picture?"

13. *Acts of Thomas* 89.

14. Corley also notes that the relegation of women to the private sphere is a phenomenon of the elite. Whether lower-status women considered their "freer" access to public spaces an advantage, as Corley implies, or whether they construed it as a lack of protection is a question that our sources do not permit us to answer (*Private Women, Public Meals*, pp. 15–16). Saller views the question from both perspectives: "The slave woman's lack of honor removed moral inhibitions to give her space for independent action, at the same time it denied her certain protections" ("Symbols of Gender and Status Hierarchies in the Roman Household," p. 89). For more sustained treatment of women in private and public spheres see Torjesen, *When Women Were Priests.*

15. *CIL* 6.9801, 9683; *IG* 11244.

16. Corley, *Private Women, Public Meals*, p. 128.

17. Luke 7:31-32a.

18. Joshel discusses the relation of work to identity among slaves, freedmen and freedwomen, and the freeborn poor (*Work, Identity, and Legal Status at Rome*).

19. E.g., *P.Oxy.* 7.1030, 41.2957; 49.3510.

20. Dyson, *Community and Society in Roman Italy*, pp. 115–116.

21. *P.Oxy.* 58.3921.

22. A bibliography accompanies a translation of an apprenticeship contract (*P.Mich.* inv. 5191a) in Pearl, "Apprentice Contract."

23. Biezunska-Malowist, *L'Esclavage dans l'Égypte Gréco-Romaine Seconde Partie*, pp. 99–101.

24. Matt. 24:45-51; Luke 12:41-48.

25. S. Casson, *Ancient Trade and Society*, pp. 104–110.

26. *P.Wisc.* 5 (186 C.E.).

27. Bradley, *Slavery and Society at Rome*, p. 58.

28. Luke 17:7-8b.

29. Clement of Alexandria, *Paedagogues* 4.26.

30. Joseph., *BJ* 1.488-489.

31. One basis for this assertion is the census returns preserved in Egypt: "Slaves in the returns are evidently for the most part domestic servants (only one slave has a declared occupation . . .)" (Bagnall and Frier, *Demography of Roman Egypt*, p. 49).

32. Hopkins, "Novel Evidence for Roman Slavery," p. 7.

33. Apul., *Met.* 10.13.

34. Petr., *Sat.* 27.

35. Matt. 26:51, 69, 71; Mark 14:47, 66, 69; Luke 22:50, 56; John 18:10, 16-18.

36. E.g., 1 Cor. 1:11, 16:15; Philem.; Acts of the Apostles 10, 16:13-14, 16:27-34, 18:8.

37. *P.Oxy.* 58.3916.

38. George, "Repopulating the Roman House."

39. George, "Repopulating the Roman House," p. 317.

40. Martin, *Slavery as Salvation*, pp. 2-7.

41. Martin, *Slavery as Salvation*, p. 7.

42. For example: "Incorporation into the Christian community as a consequence of social relationships rather than personal conviction is known to have been widespread in the early church. Household baptisms after the conversion of the *oikodespotēs* are reported in Acts . . . and alluded to by Paul" (Taylor, "Social Nature of Conversion in the Early Christian World," p. 132).

43. Dunn, *Acts of the Apostles*, pp. 220, 223, and 243.

44. The possibility is mentioned by Reimer, *Women in the Acts of the Apostles*, p. 108, and Witherington, *Acts of the Apostles*, p. 491.

45. Reimer, *Women in the Acts of the Apostles*, pp. 125–126. For discussion of the slaveholder Mary and the enslaved Rhoda, see Martin, "Acts of the Apostles," pp. 783–784.

46. *P.Mich.* inv. 5191a (271 C.E.), translated in Pearl, "Apprentice Contract."

47. I have argued elsewhere for the necessity of a hermeneutics of suspicion in interpreting ancient representations of relations between slaveholding and enslaved women. See Glancy, "The Mistress-Slave Dialectic" and "Family Plots."

48. Saller notes that the "institution of slavery may have increased the independence of elite women" ("*Pater Familias, Mater Familias*, and the Gendered Semantics of the Roman Household," p. 197). A female head of household would be known in Latin as a *domina* rather than as a *mater familias*, which connoted a chaste and respectable wife (Saller, "*Pater Familias, Mater Familias*, and the Gendered Semantics of the Roman Household," esp. p. 196).

49. Frilingos, "'For My Child, Onesimus.'"

50. Drawing on postcolonial theory, Jill Gorman has begun an investigation of such "household coercions" (private correspondence).

51. 1 Cor. 1:11.

52. Barclay, "Paul, Philemon, and the Dilemma of Christian Slave-Ownership."

53. 1 Cor. 12:13; Gal. 3:28; cf. Col. 3:11.

54. Bartchy notes that "neither the sexual risks for slaves nor the related temptations for their owners are mentioned specifically in NT documents" ("Slavery, Greco-Roman," p. 69).

55. Meeks, *First Urban Christians*, p. 73.

56. Finley, *Ancient Slavery and Modern Ideology*, pp. 95–96.

57. For attempts at reconstruction of *The Apostolic Tradition*, see Chadwick, *Treatise on the Apostolic Tradition of St. Hippolytus of Rome*; Botte, *La Tradition Apostolique de Saint Hippolyte*; and Hanssens, *La Liturgie D'Hippolyte*. Controversy surrounds the attribution of this text to Hippolytus in Rome in the early third century, especially since the document seems to have been more influential in the East than in the West. However, since I am only concerned to show that early Christians were more attuned to the complications of slavery than are modern scholars, the document's exact provenance is irrelevant to the present discussion.

58. Rousselle, *Porneia*, p. 104.

59. Finley, *Ancient Slavery and Modern Ideology*, pp. 94–96.

60. Saller, "Corporal Punishment, Authority, and Obedience in the Roman Household."

61. Plaut., *Persa* 1.1.42–43.

62. Finley, *Ancient Slavery and Modern Ideology*, pp. 95–96.

63. Sen., *Controv.* 4 praef. 10.

64. Treggiari, *Roman Marriage*, p. 301.

65. Saller, "Men's Age at Marriage and Its Consequences in the Roman Family."

66. Saller, "Slavery and the Roman Family," pp. 68–72.

67. Rei, "Villains, Wives, and Slaves in the Comedies of Plautus," p. 104.

68. Neusner, *Genesis Rabbah*, vol. 2, p. 152.

69. Galen cited in Hopkins, "Novel Evidence for Roman Slavery," p. 9; August., *Confessions* 9.9.20. See my discussion of Augustine's grandmother and her slaves (Glancy, "The Mistress-Slave Dialectic," pp. 1–2).

70. Clark, "Women, Slaves, and the Hierarchies of Domestic Violence."

71. Hock describes *Chaereas and Callirhoe* as "the most contemporary document we have for Paul's world in the Greek East of the first century" ("Support for His Old Age," p. 68).

72. Fantham, "*Stuprum*," p. 276.

73. Egger, "Women in the Greek Novel," p. 167.

74. See discussion in Saller, "Social Dynamics of Consent to Marriage and Sexual Relations."

75. Plaut., *Curc.* 32–37. Translation by Fantham in "*Stuprum*," p. 274.

76. Tucker, "Women in the Manumission Inscriptions at Delphi," p. 231.

77. Tucker, "Women in the Manumission Inscriptions at Delphi," p. 230.

78. Degradation and alienation typified the ancient Mediterranean slave trade. See Bradley, "'The Regular, Daily Traffic in Slaves.'"

79. *P.Oxy.* 42.3070, discussed in Montserrat, *Sex and Society in Greco-Roman Egypt*, pp. 136–138.

80. Grubbs, *Law and Family in Late Antiquity*, p. 28 and chap. 6.

81. Bradley, *Slaves and Masters in the Roman Empire*, p. 118.

82. MacDonald, *Early Christian Women and Pagan Opinion*, p. 55.

83. McGinn, *Prostitution, Sexuality, and the Law in Ancient Rome*, p. 310.

84. Rousselle, *Porneia*, p. 94.

85. McGinn, *Prostitution, Sexuality, and the Law in Ancient Rome*, p. 210.

86. McGinn, *Prostitution, Sexuality, and the Law in Ancient Rome*, chap. 8.

87. Dio Chrys., *Or.* 7.134.

88. McGinn, *Prostitution, Sexuality, and the Law in Ancient Rome*, p. 310.

89. Pomeroy, *Goddesses, Whores, Wives, and Slaves*, pp. 140, 192.

90. Justin Martyr, *1 Apology* 27; Clement of Alexandria, *Paedagogues* 3.3.21.

91. Based on records from Egypt in the third century B.C.E. See Pomeroy, *Women in Hellenistic Egypt from Alexander to Cleopatra*, p. 130.

92. Pomeroy, *Women in Hellenistic Egypt from Alexander to Cleopatra*, p. 130.

93. McGinn, *Prostitution, Sexuality, and the Law in Ancient Rome*, p. 254, n. 284.

94. Furthermore, "while the question of the extent to which Roman prostitutes found themselves in a condition of slavery or subservience cannot be addressed here, it is certainly true that many prostitutes, whether slave or free, would not have been able to decide how much to charge, how hard to work, or whether to remain a prostitute" (McGinn, "Taxation of Roman Prostitutes." p. 91).

95. McGinn, *Prostitution, Sexuality, and the Law in Ancient Rome*, p. 16, n. 80.

96. Montserrat, *Sex and Society in Greco-Roman Egypt*, p. 107.

97. Fleming, "*Quae Corpore Quaestum Facit*," p. 50.

98. Artemidorus, *Oneirocritica* 4.4.

99. Fleming, "*Quae Corpore Quaestum Facit*," p. 42.

100. Montserrat, *Sex and Society in Greco-Roman Egypt*, pp. 107–109.

101. McGinn, "Taxation of Roman Prostitutes." For qualifications to McGinn's argument, see Bagnall, "A Trick a Day to Keep the Tax Man at Bay?"

102. Fleming, "*Quae Corpore Quaestum Facit*," p. 56.

103. Fleming, "*Quae Corpore Quaestum Facit*," p. 43, n. 19.

104. Xenophon of Ephesus, *An Ephesian Tale* 5.7.

105. Rei, "Villains, Wives, and Slaves in the Comedies of Plautus," p. 95.

106. Treggiari, *Roman Marriage*, p. 224.

107. McGinn, *Prostitution, Sexuality, and the Law in Ancient Rome*, p. 17.

108. *Anth. Graec.* 7.403.

109. Dio Chrys., *Or.* 7.140.

110. For a survey of traditional Roman festivals, see Scullard, *Festivals and Ceremonies of the Roman Republic*.

111. Pomeroy, *Goddesses, Whores, Wives, and Slaves*, pp. 208–209.

112. Musonius Rufus, frag. 12. See discussion in Geytenbeck, *Musonius Rufus and Greek Diatribe*, pp. 71–77.

113. Grubbs, *Law and Family in Late Antiquity*, pp. 90–91, 233–249.

114. Jerome, *Ep.* 77.3.

115. For a review of scholarship, coupled with an argument for reading "vessel" as "sexual organ." see Elgvin, "'To Master His Own Vessel.'"

116. Best, *Commentary on the First and Second Epistles to the Thessalonians*, p. 165.

117. Williams, *1 and 2 Thessalonians*, p. 71.

118. Williams, *1 and 2 Thessalonians*, p. 71.

119. Yarbrough, *Not Like the Gentiles*, p. 77.

120. Carras, "Jewish Ethics and Gentile Converts."

121. Gaventa, *First and Second Thessalonians*, p. 53.

122. Gaventa, *First and Second Thessalonians*, p. 53.

123. Schrage, *Ethics of the New Testament*, p. 227.

124. Best, *Commentary on the First and Second Epistles to the Thessalonians*, p. 161.

125. Best, *Commentary on the First and Second Epistles to the Thessalonians*, p. 164.

126. Morris, *First and Second Epistles to the Thessalonians*, p. 121; Richard, *First and Second Thessalonians*, p. 198.

127. Fatum, "1 Thessalonians," p. 259; Perkins, "1 Thessalonians," p. 441; Gaventa, *First and Second Thessalonians*, p. 52.

128. Gaventa, *First and Second Thessalonians*, p. 52.

129. Weiss, *Der Erste Korintherbrief*; Barrett, *Commentary on the First Epistle to the Corinthians*; Fee, *First Epistle to the Corinthians*.

130. Allo, *Première Epître aux Corinthiens*; Conzelmann, *1 Corinthians*. Deming argues on other grounds for the structural unity of 1 Cor. 5–6, which would also suggest a break between chaps. 5 and 6 ("Unity of 1 Corinthians 5–6").

131. Wire, *Corinthian Women Prophets*, pp. 73–79.

132. 1 Cor. 5:1.

133. 1 Cor. 5:5.

134. 1 Cor. 5:9–12.

135. In his discussion of 5:1–13, Fee notes the divergence between first-century sexual mores and later Christian teaching, although he does not focus on the sexual vulnerability of slaves. He states that "the Judeo-Christian moral restrictions on human sexuality were not easily absorbed by pagan converts" (*First Epistle to the Corinthians*, pp. 196–197).

136. Conzelmann, *1 Corinthians*, p. 95; Senft, *Première Epître de Saint Paul aux Corinthiens*, p. 73.

137. This view is almost universally held in the commentaries and other secondary literature; see, for example, Robertson and Plummer, *Critical and Exegetical Commentary on the First Epistle of Paul to the Corinthians*, p. 95; Fee, *First Epistle to the Corinthians*, p. 195; Meeks, *First Urban Christians*, p. 130; Mitchell, *Paul and the Rhetoric of Reconciliation*, pp. 112–116; Campbell, "Flesh and Spirit in 1 Cor. 5:5"; and Hays, "Ecclesiology and Ethics in 1 Corinthians." An exception is Barrett, who holds that Paul's "first concern" is for the transgressor (*Commentary on the First Epistle to the Corinthians*, p. 127).

138. Conzelmann, *1 Corinthians*, p. 96.

139. Paul does not specify whether the man's father is alive or dead, whether the father has divorced the wife, or whether the man is living with his stepmother as wife or concubine. Most commentators think it unlikely that the father, if living, is still married to the woman in question because Paul does not refer to an adulterous relationship, but even this is unclear. For a discussion of relevant issues see Allo, *Première Epître aux Corinthiens*, pp. 117–120. Deming has suggested the possibility that the son might have an ongoing relationship with his stepmother as prostitute ("Unity of 1 Corinthians 5–6," p. 295). Paul had no reason to be more specific about these questions because the Corinthian congregation was already familiar with the details of the situation.

140. Robertson and Plummer, *Critical and Exegetical Commentary*, p. 96; Allo, *Première Epître aux Corinthiens*, p. 118; Conzelmann, *1 Corinthians*, p. 96, n. 24; Barrett, *Commentary on the First Epistle to the Corinthians*, p. 121; and Fee, *First Epistle to the Corinthians*, p. 197. Weiss

seems alone in his impression that Paul's silence on the woman stems from a belief that the responsibility for sexual transgression rests with the man (*Erste Korintherbrief*, p. 125).

141. Wire, *Corinthian Women Prophets*, p. 74. Deming refers to Wire's suggestion as "unlikely" without giving reasons for dismissing it ("Unity of 1 Corinthians 5-6," p. 298, n. 35).

142. Strab., *Geography* 8.6.20.

143. Engels, *Roman Corinth*, p. 52.

144. 1 Cor. 6:12.

145. 1 Cor. 6:13-20.

146. Bassler, "1 Corinthians," p. 332; also Conzelmann, *1 Corinthians*, p. 112; and Mitchell, *Paul and the Rhetoric of Reconciliation*, p. 120.

147. Fee, *First Epistle*, p. 260.

148. Martin, *Corinthian Body*, p. 176.

149. Wire, *Corinthian Women Prophets*, p. 76.

150. Fleming, "*Quae Corpore Quaestum Facit.*"

151. For a clear discussion of Paul's position on the theological ramifications of patronizing a prostitute, see Fisk, "ΠΟΡΝΕΥΕΙΝ as Body Violation," pp. 540-558.

152. Fee, *First Epistle to the Corinthians*, pp. 259-260.

153. Martin, *Corinthian Body*, p. 176.

154. In verse 19 Paul refers to "your" (plural) body as a temple, and in verse 20 he urges the Corinthians to glorify God in "your" (plural) body. I take the reference to be primarily to the body of the community, the collective body; the entire community should be vigilant about its purity, as in the discussion of 5:1-13. Others who interpret "your body" in 6:19-20 as an allusion to the community include Mitchell, *Paul and the Rhetoric of Reconciliation* (see index for references to 6:19-20), and Wire, *Corinthian Women Prophets*, p. 77. Most commentators, however, interpret "your body" primarily as an allusion to the individual Christian's body, despite the parallelism to 3:16. See, for example, Barrett, *Commentary on the First Epistle to the Corinthians*, p. 151; Fee, *First Epistle to the Corinthians*, p. 249, n. 5, and p. 260; and Senft, *Première Epître de Saint Paul aux Corinthiens*, p. 85. Conzelmann also takes this position in his discussion of verse 19, although elsewhere he seems to assume that verses 19-20 refer to the Christian community (*1 Corinthians*, p. 96, cf. p. 112).

155. Porter, "How Should κολλωμενος in 1 Cor. 6:16.17 Be Translated?" See also Harrill, "Indentured Labor of the Prodigal Son (Luke 15:15)."

156. Fee, *First Epistle to the Corinthians*, p. 264. Conzelmann suggests that the idea of redemption as "ransom" is traditional and says, "The metaphor is not developed. The point is merely that you belong to a new master. Beyond this the metaphor should not be pressed. There is, for example, no reflection as to who received the payment" (*1 Corinthians*, p. 113).

157. Martin, *Corinthian Body*, p. 178.

158. Bartchy, *First-Century Slavery*, p. 175.

159. Meeks, *First Urban Christians*, p. 161. See also Gnilka, *Der Kolosserbrief*, p. 190.

160. Harrill, *Manumission of Slaves in Early Christianity*, p. 123.

161. Wire, *Corinthian Women Prophets*, p. 91.

162. Deming, *Paul on Marriage and Celibacy*. The virgins of 7:25-28, 36-38 are a different case; Paul does not seem concerned about their willingness to marry.

163. Although commentators offer various divisions of the chapter, they agree that the advice to various groups provides structure to the discussion. For example, Conzelmann and Senft categorize verses 1-7 as general directions and verses 8-16 as advice to particular groups (Conzelmann, *1 Corinthians*, p. 114; Senft, *Première Epître de Saint Paul aux Corinthiens*, pp. 87-90), while Fee's taxonomy includes verses 1-7 in advice to the married, verses 8-9 in advice to the "unmarried" (who Fee posits are widowers) and widows, verses 10-11 in advice to believing couples, verses 12-16 in advice to couples with only one believing spouse, verses 25-

38 in advice about virgins, and verses 39–40 in advice to married women and widows (Fee, *First Epistle*, pp. 268, 287–288).

164. Robertson and Plummer, *Critical and Exegetical Commentary*, p. 141; Conzelmann, *1 Corinthians*, p. 121; Barrett, *Commentary on the First Epistle to the Corinthians*, p. 163; Fee, *First Epistle to the Corinthians*, p. 298; and Senft, *Première Epître de Saint Paul aux Corinthiens*, p. 165.

165. Harrill, *Manumission of Slaves in Early Christianity*, p. 123.

166. Harrill, *Manumission of Slaves in Early Christianity*, p. 122.

167. Harrill, *Manumission of Slaves in Early Christianity*, pp. 77–108.

168. Fee, *First Epistle to the Corinthians*, p. 319.

169. See also the discussion of syntax in Fee, *First Epistle to the Corinthians*, pp. 316–317.

170. Harrill, *Manumission of Slaves in Early Christianity*, pp. 108–121.

171. See also 7:15, 36, 39, and Harrill, *Manumission of Slaves in Early Christianity*, pp. 123–126; Fee, *First Epistle to the Corinthians*, pp. 268, 318; and Deming, "Diatribe Pattern in 1 Cor. 7:21–22."

172. Harrill, *Manumission of Slaves in Early Christianity*, p. 122. Robertson and Plummer write: "He [Paul] regarded marriage as a hindrance to the perfection of the Christian life (verses 32–35). Was not slavery, with its hideous temptations, a far greater hindrance?" (*Critical and Exegetical Commentary*, p. 148).

173. Robertson and Plummer, *Critical and Exegetical Commentary*, p. 144; Barrett, *Commentary on the First Epistle to the Corinthians*, p. 167; Conzelmann, *1 Corinthians*, p. 114; Fee, *First Epistle to the Corinthians*, p. 306; and Senft, *Première Epître de Saint Paul aux Corinthiens*, p. 95.

174. Bartchy, *First-Century Slavery*, p. 173. (Bartchy is referring specifically to 1 Cor. 7:17–24.)

175. Dunn, *Epistles to the Colossians and to Philemon*, p. 227.

176. Aletti, *Saint Paul Epître aux Colossiens*, p. 235.

177. Bruce, *Epistles to the Colossians*, p. 151.

178. Bruce, *Epistles to the Colossians*, p. 168.

179. Barclay, "Paul, Philemon, and the Dilemma of Christian Slave-Ownership."

Chapter 3

1. Aug., *Ep.* 10* and *Ep.* 24*.

2. Aug., *Ep.* 10*.5.

3. Aug., *Ep.* 10*.5.

4. Pliny, *Natural History* 7.56.

5. For an imaginative treatment of this theme, see Bradley, "Animalizing the Slave."

6. Tac., *Ann.* 14.44.

7. For a parallel argument, see Joshel, "Nurturing the Master's Child."

8. *P.Oxy.* 3.489, 3.494.

9. *P.Oxy.* 55.3784.

10. *P.Oxy.* 9.1209, 36.2777.

11. Some examples: *P.Mich.* 5.323; *P.Oxy.* 3.494, 3.496.

12. Scheidel, "Quantifying the Sources of Slaves in the Early Roman Empire"; Harris, "Demography, Geography and the Sources of Roman Slaves."

13. Dio Chrys., *Or.* 15.1.

14. Dio Chrys., *Or.* 15.26.

15. Dio Chrys., *Or.* 15.26.

16. *Shepherd of Hermas* Vision 1.1.1.

17. Not all scholars accept this etymology. For discussion and bibliography see Harris, "Child-Exposure in the Roman Empire," p. 8.

18. Pliny, *Ep.* 65–66.

19. Harris, "Towards a Study of the Roman Slave Trade"; Harris, "Demography, Geography and the Sources of Roman Slaves."

20. For the *Predictions of Astrampsychos*, see Rowlandson, ed., *Women and Society in Greek and Roman Egypt*, pp. 282–284.

21. *P.Oxy.* 4.744.

22. *P.Kell.* 1.8.

23. Bagnall advances this tentative proposal because one of the children of Tithoes has a typical Christian name ("Missing Females in Roman Egypt," p. 122).

24. *P.Abinn.* 36 = *P.Gen.* 53.

25. *Sibylline Oracles* 2:27–28.

26. *Did.* 2.2; *Ep. Barn.* 19.5.

27. Neiderwimmer, for example, asserts that the injunction of the *Didache* against infanticide "implicitly" forbids the exposure of children (*Didache*, p. 90). Neiderwimmer refers the reader to citations in Van der Horst's edition of *Sentences of Pseudo-Phocylides*; I do not find that the citations are relevant to his claim (*The Sentences of Pseudo-Phocylides*, pp. 232–234).

28. Bagnall has demonstrated that sufficient numbers of exposed infants (who were disproportionately female) survived to affect the sex ratio of the enslaved population ("Missing Females in Roman Egypt").

29. Clement of Alexandria, *Paedagogues* 3.3.21.

30. Justin Martyr, 1 Apology 27.

31. *P.Amh.* 2.144.

32. Ramin and Veyne argue that such transactions are likely to have been common among the indigent free poor in all periods of the Empire ("Droit romain et société," p. 483).

33. Joseph., *BJ* 7.379–386.

34. Neusner, *Lamentations Rabbah*, p. 171, cf. Lamentations 1:16.

35. *Dig.* 21.1.1.9.

36. Tac., *Ann.* 15.44.

37. Bradley proposes reading the metamorphosis of Lucius into an ass as a cautionary fable about the horrors of reduction to servitude ("Animalizing the Slave").

38. *P.Grenf.* 2.78.

39. Patrick, *Ep.* 10, 14.

40. Patrick, *Ep.* 15.

41. Patrick, *Ep.* 15.

42. Bartchy, *First-Century Slavery*, p. 47. Note that Ramin and Veyne, who have argued that self-sale should be taken seriously as a source of slaves, state: "It goes without saying that, in the great majority of cases, a freeborn man who sold himself into slavery remained a slave and had no hope to become a freedman; a freeborn man who sold himself did not recover his original status after an eventual manumission: he became a freedman and did not revert to his former status as a freeborn man" (author's translation) ("Droit romain et société," p. 495).

43. Bartchy, "Slavery, Greco-Roman," p. 70.

44. Harrill is one who has disassociated himself from Bartchy's position. The present discussion extends Harrill's critique (*Manumission of Slaves in Early Christianity*, pp. 30–31).

45. Along with self-sale, some New Testament scholars cite enslavement for debt as a source of slaves. Biezunska-Malowist notes that the papyri provide thicker documentation for imprisonment for debtors than for enslavement for debtors. Although some evidence suggests that there could be *temporary* reduction to bondage for debtors, such bondage terminated with the repayment of the debt and thus did not constitute a true source of chattel slaves (*L'Esclavage dans l'Egypte Gréco-Romaine Seconde Partie*, pp. 17–19).

46. Harris, "Demography, Geography and the Sources of Roman Slaves."

47. Harris, "Demography, Geography and the Sources of Roman Slaves," pp. 67–68.
48. Harris, "Demography, Geography and the Sources of Roman Slaves," p. 73.
49. *Dig.* 40.12.1.
50. *Dig.* 28.3.6.5. See also 1.5.5.1, 1.5.21, 40.12.7, 40.12.7.1, 40.12.40.
51. Ramin and Veyne, "Droit romain et société," p. 481.
52. Ramin and Veyne, "Droit romain et société," p. 472.
53. 1 Clem. 55.2.
54. 1 Clem. 55.1–3.
55. Petr., *Sat.* 57.
56. Dio Chrys., *Or.* 15.23.
57. Harrill, *Manumission of Slaves in Early Christianity*, p. 31.
58. Sen., *De Ben.* 4.13.3.
59. Crook, *Law and Life of Rome*, p. 60.
60. *Gospel of Philip* 79:13–15.
61. 1 Cor. 7:22–24.
62. Collins, *First Corinthians*, p. 278.
63. Hays, *First Corinthians*, p. 124. Classicists have been more critical than many New Testament scholars of Martin's thesis. Brent Shaw, for example, argues that Martin's "convoluted appeal" does not "agree . . . with the facts of slavery in the Roman empire" (see his introduction to the expanded edition of Finley, *Ancient Slavery and Modern Ideology*, pp. 70–71, n. 103).
64. Harris, "Demography, Geography and the Sources of Roman Slaves," pp. 67–70.
65. In the area of self-sale as in so many other areas of slave life, the family of Caesar represents an important exception. Reducing oneself to slavery in order to join the imperial family may not have had the same negative connotations. In one curious reference, a papyrus even refers to a man who has left Egypt in order to become a freedman of Caesar: "You should know, then, that Herminus went off to Rome and became a freedman of Caesar in order to take up official appointments" (*P.Oxy.* 46.3312). Could it be possible that a free person could bypass slave status and directly assume the status of an imperial freedman? I thank Roger Bagnall for this suggestion.
66. *Dig.* 48.19.14.
67. Richlin, "Cicero's Head," p. 194. Richlin quotes Paulus (*Dig.* 4.5.3.1).
68. *Dig.* 21.1.1.
69. *Dig.* 21.12.3, 21.12.4, 12.14.4.
70. *Dig.* 21.1.6.
71. Sen., *Ep.* 80.9.
72. Cited by Bradley in "'The Regular, Daily Traffic in Slaves,'" p. 128.
73. Sen., *Controv.* 1.2.3.
74. Bradley, "'The Regular, Daily Traffic in Slaves,'" p. 133.
75. Schiavone, *End of the Past*, p. 119.
76. *P.Oxy.* 42.3053.
77. *P.Oxy.* 60.4068.
78. Ath., *Deipnosophists* 1.27.
79. 1 Tim. 1:10.
80. Harrill, "Vice of Slave Dealers in Greco-Roman Society," p. 118.
81. Harrill may overemphasize the case for dishonest acquisition of merchandise, that is, kidnapping. As I discussed in the section on sources of slaves, kidnapping was a steady source of slaves during the centuries that marked the rise of Christianity but never supplied the majority of slaves. Transactions recorded in the documentary evidence from Egypt scrupulously document the origins of slaves. Of course, those are the sales that are officially recorded; perhaps less-honest slave dealers also avoided the process of documentation.

82. Harrill, "Vice of Slave Dealers in Greco-Roman Society," p. 105.

83. Pliny, *Ep.* 1.21.2.

84. Thurmond, "Some Roman Slave Collars in *CIL*," p. 493.

85. *P.Berl.Leihg.* 15.

86. Epic., *Discourses* 3.26.1–2.

87. Epic., *Discourses* 1.29.63.

88. *P.Turner* 41. For further discussion of papyri documenting fugitive slaves, see Bradley, *Slavery and Society at Rome*, pp. 118–119.

89. Daube, "Slave-Catching."

90. Deut. 23:15–16.

91. Cited by Mitchell, "John Chrysostom on Philemon," p. 145, n. 145.

92. *Synodical Letter of the Council of Gangra.*

93. Chrysostom, Homilies on the Epistle of St. Paul the Apostle to Philemon, the argument.

94. Callahan has provocatively argued that Philemon was not Onesimus's owner but his brother. I do not accept Callahan's conclusion. In Philem. 16, Paul urges Philemon to regard Onesimus no longer as a slave (*hōs doulon*) but as a brother. Callahan's argument runs thus. According to Patterson, slaves are not kin but, by definition, essentially aliens (*Slavery and Social Death*, pp. 38–45). Therefore, what Paul is really saying is that Philemon should no longer regard his estranged brother as an alien to Philemon's household of faith. However, identifying slaves as alien to kinship structures is not equivalent to calling all those alienated from kinship structures slaves (Callahan, "Paul's Epistle to Philemon"). For an incisive critique of Callahan's position see Mitchell, "John Chrysostom on Philemon," pp. 147–148, n. 47.

95. Winter, "Paul's Letter to Philemon."

96. Knox, *Philemon among the Letters of Paul*, pp. 17–18.

97. Osiek offers a typically clear overview of recent critical approaches to Philemon (*Philippians, Philemon*, pp. 126–131).

98. Callahan, "Paul's Epistle to Philemon," pp. 363–365. This is a case where "moral intuition" is at odds with biblical literalism, in Harrill's formulation ("Use of the New Testament in the American Slave Controversy").

99. *P.Kell.G.* 48.

100. Neusner, *Lamentations Rabbah*, p. 156.

101. Artemidorus, *Oneirocritica* 1.35.

102. Tac., *Ann.* 14.42.

103. Watson, "Slavery as an Institution," p. 6.

104. Watson, "Slavery as an Institution," p. 7.

105. Wiedemann, "Regularity of Manumission at Rome."

106. Bartchy, "Slavery, Greco-Roman," p. 70.

107. Weaver, "Children of Junian Latins," pp. 55–56.

108. Weaver, "Children of Junian Latins," p. 69.

109. Harrill, *Manumission of Slaves in Early Christianity*, p. 54.

110. Gardner elaborates on the legal barriers that freedmen and freedwomen would have encountered when they tried to pass on estates to their offspring. The law protected the inheritance rights of former owners (*Family and Familia in Roman Law and Life*, pp. 55–67).

111. Epic., *Discourses* 2.1.

112. Bradley, *Slavery and Society at Rome*, pp. 157–158.

113. Ign., *Pol.* 4:1–3.

114. For further discussion of Ignatius, see chap. 4 in Harrill, *Manumission of Slaves in Early Christianity*. Harrill tentatively cites several ambiguous references, which seem to encourage the manumission of slaves. None of them, I think, is sufficiently clear to draw conclusions about the practices of manumission among Christians (pp. 182–192).

115. Clark, *Life of Melania the Younger*, p. 100.
116. *Acts of Thomas* 1–3.
117. *Acts of Thomas* 108–113.
118. Castelli, "Romans," p. 294.
119. *Gospel of Philip* 80.23–81.13.
120. *Gospel of Philip* 69.1.
121. *Gospel of Philip* 35.12–14.
122. *Gospel of Philip* 54.30.
123. *Gospel of Philip* 83.25–29.
124. *Gospel of Philip* 52.2–3.
125. *Gospel of Philip* 52.29–53.5.
126. *Gospel of Philip* 85.28–29.
127. *Gospel of Philip* 84.10–11.
128. Gal. 5:1.
129. 1 Cor. 7:23; cf. 1 Cor. 6:20. These texts are discussed in a different context in chapter two.
130. Rom. 6:7.
131. Artemidorus, *Oneirocritica* 2.49.
132. Artemidorus, *Oneirocritica* 2.53, 54.
133. Phil. 2:6–11.
134. Briggs, "Can an Enslaved God Liberate?" p. 145.
135. Munro, *Jesus, Born of a Slave*, chap. 3, "In the Form of a Slave."
136. Martin, *Slavery as Salvation*, pp. xiv–xviii.
137. Apul., *Met.* 6.4, 9, 23.
138. Briggs, "Can an Enslaved God Liberate?" p. 143.
139. Here, I reiterate Castelli's formulation ("Romans").
140. Briggs, "Can an Enslaved God Liberate?" p. 143.

Chapter 4

1. Jacobs, *Incidents in the Life of a Slave Girl*, p. 108.
2. The inscription seems to date from either the period of the late Republic or the reign of Augustus. For further details, see Finley, *Ancient Slavery and Modern Ideology*, p. 95; and Bradley, *Slaves and Masters in the Roman Empire*; p. 122.
3. In the *Satyricon*, for example, Trimalchio has torturers on staff. Two men with whips stand by to punish the seemingly inept cook (Petr., *Sat.* 49).
4. Combes, *The Metaphor of Slavery in the Writings of the Early Church*, pp. 70-92.
5. Garnsey, *Ideas of Slavery from Aristotle to Augustine*.
6. Bradley notes this in his review of Garnsey ("Problem of Slavery in Classical Culture").
7. Garnsey notes this in another context. See Garnsey, "Philo Judaeus and Slave Theory," p. 33.
8. Christian literature is not unique in its reliance on slavery as metaphor. For example, Stoic literature often figures the individual as a slave to passions and emotions. The parallel between these metaphoric uses of slavery is noted by Garnsey, *Ideas of Slavery from Aristotle to Augustine*, p. 16.
9. See, however, Martin's study of the ideological function of the language of slavery in the Pauline epistles, *Slavery as Salvation*.
10. I discuss the exchange between Vogt and Finley concerning the laudability of the parabolic faithful slave below, in my treatment of the ideal of the faithful slave in Matthew's parables.

11. For a summary of these distinct approaches, see Tolbert, *Perspectives on the Parable*, pp. 18-23.

12. I rely here on the helpful formulation of an anonymous referee at the *Journal of Biblical Literature*.

13. Bradley, "Problem of Slavery in Classical Culture," p. 282.

14. *Shepherd of Hermas* Similitude 5.2.

15. See, e.g., Neusner, *Sifre to Deuteronomy*, pp. 35, 76, 156. These are merely a few instances of a common trope in rabbinic parables.

16. Sloan, "The Greatest and the Youngest," p. 66.

17. Dio Or. 1.34; Seeley, "Rulership and Service in Mark 10:41-45."

18. See discussion in Combes, *Metaphor of Slavery in the Writings of the Early Church*, pp. 72-74.

19. Dodd, *Parables of the Kingdom*, p. 5.

20. Ulpian, frag. i.18; quoted in notes to *P.Oxy.* 4.716.

21. *P.Oxy.* 4.716.

22. *P.Fam.Tebt.* 37, 38, and 40.

23. Beavis, "Ancient Slavery as an Interpretative Context."

24. I elaborate on my agreements and disagreements with Beavis in the section of this chapter entitled "Toward the Parables of Jesus."

25. This is pointed out by Landry and May in "Honor Restored."

26. *P.Wisc.* 5.

27. Beavis, "Ancient Slavery as an Interpretative Context," p. 41. Cf. Scott, *Hear Then the Parable*, p. 215.

28. G. M. Stroud, quoted in Finley, *Ancient Slavery and Modern Ideology*, p. 161.

29. Batten, "Dishonour, Gender, and the Parable of the Prodigal Son."

30. Weaver argues, however, that there were limits on the social mobility enjoyed by slaves and freedmen within the family of Caesar. For example, it was rare to cross from domestic to administrative service (*Familia Caesaris*).

31. Weaver, *Familia Caesaris*, p. 5.

32. Fitzmyer, *Gospel According to Luke*, p. 1235.

33. This is further developed in the discussion of slaves in managerial roles in the Matthean parables.

34. Jeremias, *Parables of Jesus*, pp. 210-212.

35. Derrett, *Law in the New Testament*, p. 33, n. 1.

36. Scott, *Hear Then the Parable*, p. 270.

37. Patterson, *Slavery and Social Death*, p. 299. Patterson relies on the standard treatment of Roman imperial slaves (Weaver, *Familia Caesaris*).

38. Patterson, *Slavery and Social Death*, p. 13.

39. Patterson, *Slavery and Social Death*, p. 303.

40. See, for example, Apuleius's description of slaves treated like animals in a mill (*Met.* 9.12) or Juvenal's casual reference to a slave's mundane task of scooping up dog refuse from a hallway (*Satires* 14.65-67). See also Hopkins's vivid description of domestic slaves as body slaves ("Novel Evidence for Roman Slavery").

41. As Bradley notes, "The impression is firm that physical punishments meted out to slaves by their owners were consistently brutal, showed little change over the course of time, and were not altered by any distinctions of status among the servile population as a whole" (*Slaves and Masters in the Roman Empire*, p. 137).

42. All of the slaves in the Matthean parables seem to be male, as do all of the owners.

43. Schweizer, *Good News According to Matthew*, p. 472.

44. Differing estimates of the slave's inaction are noted by Beare, *Gospel According to Matthew*, p. 490; Harrington, *Gospel of Matthew*, p. 353; and Hare, *Matthew*, p. 287.

45. Hare, *Matthew*, p. 287.

46. This is implied by Beare, *Gospel According to Matthew*, p. 486. In recognition of this problem, Fortna suggests reconstructing Jesus' parable so that it ends with a rebuke of the third slave to the master ("Reading Jesus' Parables of the Talents through Underclass Eyes").

47. Saller, "Corporal Punishment, Authority, and Obedience in the Roman Household," p. 160.

48. Vogt, *Ancient Slavery and the Ideal of Man*, p. 131.

49. Vogt, *Ancient Slavery and the Ideal of Man*, pp. 141–142.

50. Vogt, *Ancient Slavery and the Ideal of Man*, p. 145.

51. Finley, *Ancient Slavery and Modern Ideology*, p. 122.

52. Beavis, "Ancient Slavery as an Interpretative Context," p. 54.

53. Weaver, *Familia Caesaris*.

54. Parker, "Loyal Slaves and Loyal Wives," p. 51.

55. Sen., *Ben.* 3.17–28.

56. Sen., *Ben.* 3.27.

57. Val. Max. 6.8.1–7; App., *BCiv.* 4.26, 43–48.

58. Val. Max. 6.8.6.

59. See also the version of the tale in App., *BCiv.* 4.43.

60. Or perhaps the forehead of the slave was tattooed. See Jones, "*Stigma.*"

61. Val. Max. 6.8.7.

62. This construction recalls a speech of Phaniscus, an enslaved character in Plautus's play *Mostellaria*: "The master, I maintain, / Reacts in the way his servants most want him to: / If they're good, he behaves, / If they act wicked, he turns into a fiend" (ll. 1114–1117).

63. Segal, *Roman Laughter*, p. 140.

64. Fitzgerald, *Slavery and the Roman Literary Imagination*, pp. 34-35.

65. Apul., *Met.* 3.16.

66. Apul., *Met.* 9.17–21.

67. See book 47 of the *Digest of Justinian*, esp. Dig. 47.10.15.44. See also chapter one of this volume.

68. Although the Matthean parables do not depict slave owners killing (or even threatening to kill) their slaves, in many instances slave owners did exercise capital powers over their human chattel, often for the purpose of maintaining order in the household. See, for example, Tacitus, who remarks on the ways that German treatment of slaves differs from Roman treatment of slaves: "If they [slaves in German households] are killed, it is not usually to preserve strict discipline, but in a fit of fury, like an enemy" (*Germ.*, 25).

69. Segal, *Roman Laughter*, p. 138.

70. Wiseman, *Catullus and His World*, pp. 5–6; Saller, "Corporal Punishment."

71. Fitzgerald, *Slavery and the Roman Literary Imagination*, p. 32.

72. See Segal, *Roman Laughter*, and Parker, "Crucially Funny or Tranio on the Couch."

73. Others in the ancient world also inferred from contemporary disciplinary practices that after death a person might undergo a range of tortures for deeds committed in this life. Lucretius mocks this attitude as the speculation of fools: "But in this life there is fear of punishment for evil deeds, fear as notorious as the deeds are notorious, and atonement for crime, prison, and the horrible casting down from the Rock, stripes, torturers, condemned cell, pitch, red-hot plates, firebrands: and even if these are absent, yet the guilty conscience . . . applies the goad and scourges itself with whips, and meanwhile sees not where can be the end to its miseries or the final limit to its punishment, and fears at the same time that all this may become heavier after death" (Lucr. 3.1014–1022).

74. See pp. 97–99 of the present study and Castelli, "Romans," p. 294.

75. Livy 2.36.1; Suet., *Aug.* 45.4.

76. See Foucault's discussion of torture as a "liturgy of punishment." As he writes, "Public torture and execution must be spectacular" (*Discipline and Punish*, pp. 33–34). I am arguing that the Matthean parables enact such a spectacular liturgy.

77. Hunter concludes that in the Athenian context: "The slave . . . must know himself: he must recognize his status *as a slave.* Surely it is this recognition that corporal punishment aimed to instill, whether by the whip or through the stigmata of the tattooer" (*Policing Athens*, p. 182).

78. Foucault writes, "The public execution did not re-establish justice; it reactivated power" (*Discipline and Punish*, p. 49). Hunter writes that the purpose of flogging in Athens extended beyond retaliation and deterrence: " Where slaves are concerned, domination—the assertion of a master's total control—is also involved" (*Policing Athens*, p. 181).

79. Tac., *Germ.* 25.

80. Sen., *De Ira* 3.24.

81. Martial, *Epigrams* 3.94.

82. Juvenal, *Satires* 6.474–501.

83. Finley, *Ancient Slavery and Modern Ideology*, p. 93.

84. Saller, "Corporal Punishment," p. 151. Hunter makes a parallel argument with respect to Athenian slavery: "The whip, in particular, set the slave apart, being symbolic of his or her degradation. Nude and broken, the one who was whipped became a loathsome spectacle, all honor and integrity gone" (*Policing Athens*, p. 181).

85. Quint., *Inst.* 1.3.13–14.

86. Bruyn, "Flogging a Son," p. 249.

87. Munro, *Jesus, Born of a Slave*, p. 326. Munro's colleagues completed work on the manuscript after her death.

88. Crossan, "The Servant Parables of Jesus"; see also Crossan, *In Parables*, and Beavis, "Ancient Slavery as an Interpretative Context."

89. Crossan, "Servant Parables," p. 19.

90. Crossan, "Servant Parables," p. 25.

91. Crossan, *In Parables*, p. 119.

92. Crossan, *Historical Jesus.*

93. Scott, *Hear Then the Parable.*

94. Scott, *Hear Then the Parable*, p. 205.

95. Eisenstadt and Roniger, "Patron-Client Relations as a Mode of Structuring Social Exchange."

96. Beavis, "Ancient Slavery as an Interpretative Context," p. 40.

97. Saller, *Personal Patronage.*

98. Saller, *Personal Patronage*, pp. 17–18, 24.

99. Saller, *Personal Patronage*, p. vii. New Testament scholars who locate master-slave relations in the patron-client rubric regularly cite Saller without noting that he restricts his study to relations between free men.

100. I thank Professor Saller for responding to my query on this point (private correspondence, Dec. 10, 1997).

101. Wallace-Hadrill, "Introduction," p. 8.

102. I have already discussed the relevance of the patron-client rubric in the section titled: "Managerial Slaves."

103. Martin, *Slavery as Salvation*, pp. 25–26.

104. Martin, *Slavery as Salvation*, p. 29; D'Arms, review of *Personal Patronage*, p. 95.

105. Malina, *The Social World of Jesus and the Gospels*, p. 146. Malina goes even beyond this assimilation of the relations between slaveholders and slaves to the patron-client model to

present the patron-client model as a kind of kinship structure: "What patron-client relations essentially entail is endowing and outfitting economic, political or religious institutional arrangements with an overarching quality of kinship. Such relations 'kin-ify' and suffuse the persons involved with the aura of kinship, albeit fictive or pseudo-kinship. . . . Thus economic, political and religious interactions now take place between individuals bound together by mutual commitment, solidarity and loyalty in terms of generalized reciprocity, rather than the . . . negative reciprocity typical of superiors to their subordinates" (p. 104). Accepting this framework, in which slaves appear not only as clients of their exploiters but also as their fictive kin, contributes to a deceptively irenic representation of slavery. For further discussion, see Glancy, "Family Plots." As Claude Meillassoux writes of slave systems in Africa, "The presentation of slavery as an extension of kinship implies approval of the old paternalistic claim which has always been used as moral backing for slavery. It means falling into the trap of an apologist ideology in which the slave-owner tries to pass off those he exploits as his beloved children" (*Anthropology of Slavery*, p. 15).

106. Herzog, *Parables as Subversive Speech*, p. 7.

107. Herzog, *Parables as Subversive Speech*, p. 136. In a footnote, however, Herzog at least notes that the identification of a *doulos* as an official is disputed (p. 271 n. 3).

108. Herzog, *Parables as Subversive Speech*, p. 106.

109. Hester also offers a reading of the parable of the wicked tenants that stresses the political and economic implications of a dispute between a wealthy landowner and tenants who have presumably been dispossessed of their own land. Hester vacillates between references to the vineyard owner's servants and his slaves and never addresses the political or economic implications of violence against slaves ("Socio-Rhetorical Criticism and the Parable of the Tenants").

110. For example, Hester, "Socio-Rhetorical Criticism and the Parable of the Tenants," pp. 27–57; Hedrick, *Parables as Poetic Fictions*; Wohlegamut, "Entrusted Money"; and Horne, "Parable of the Tenants as Indictment."

111. Munro, *Jesus, Born of a Slave*, p. 352.

112. Munro, *Jesus, Born of a Slave*, pp. 355–356.

113. Munro, *Jesus, Born of a Slave*, p. 327.

114. Perkins highlights the anomaly of Christian identification with the suffering body (*The Suffering Self*).

115. As Moore writes in his haunting discussion of the physical agony of Jesus, "The central symbol of Christianity is the figure of a tortured man" (*God's Gym*, p. 4).

Chapter 5

1. Pliny, *Ep.* 10.96.

2. 1 Cor. 1:26–28.

3. Meeks, *First Urban Christians*, p. 73.

4. Meeks, *First Urban Christians*, p. 73.

5. Kidd, *Wealth and Beneficence in the Pastoral Epistles*, p. 74.

6. Justin Martyr, *Apology* 2.12.4; Athenagoras, *Plea for Christians* 35.3.

7. Nietzsche, *On the Genealogy of Morals*, p. 8.

8. Nietzsche, *Beyond Good and Evil*, p. 260.

9. David R. Andrews points out that, philosophically, a "slave" who is lazy, proud, and condescending may simply not qualify as a slave. Just as a "bad" artwork is, arguably, an oxymoron—a bad attempt at art is not art but something entirely else—a "bad" slave, a slave who is not subservient to a slaveholder, may not be a slave but something entirely else (which is entirely to the credit of the so-called slave). I am speaking here, however, of the moral frameworks of actual, historical slaves and slaveholders. Under Roman law, even slaves who behaved in a defiant

fashion toward their owners or refused to comply with their owners' mandates remained, legally, property (private correspondence, Feb. 14, 2001).

10. Artemidorus, *Oneirocritica* 2.25.
11. Artemidorus, *Oneirocritica* 2.68, 49.
12. *Dig.* 18.1.29. See also 21.2.3.
13. Neusner, *Genesis Rabbah*, p. 221.
14. Philem. 18–19a.
15. *Dig.* 47.2.17.3, 47.2.36.2.
16. Apul., *Met.* 8.15.
17. Bradley, "*Servus Onerosus.*"
18. Apul., *Met.* 8.31.
19. *Dig.* 11.3.1.4.
20. *Dig.* 11.3.1.5.
21. *The Sentences of the Syriac Menander* warns slaveholders to keep slaves away from cabarets, where they would become acquainted with the habit of stealing (2.49–51).
22. Ath., *Deipnosophists* 6.262.d.
23. Sen., *De Ira* 3.29, quoted in Fitzgerald, *Slavery and the Roman Literary Imagination*, p. 89.
24. *P.Oxy.* 18.2190.
25. Artemidorus, *Oneirocritica* 3.28.
26. See the excellent discussion in Schiavone, *End of the Past*, pp. 107–111.
27. Sen., *Ep.* 47.5.
28. Bradley, "Seneca and Slavery," p. 167.
29. Sen., *Ep.* 47.3–4.
30. Sen., *Ep.* 47.5.
31. Finley, *Ancient Slavery and Modern Ideology*, p. 184.
32. Bradley, *Slavery and Rebellion in the Roman World.*
33. Bradley, *Slavery and Rebellion in the Roman World*, p. 127.
34. Croix, "Early Christian Attitudes to Property and Slavery."
35. I have discussed elsewhere the problems that the New Testament household codes have posed and continue to pose in American political discourse (Glancy, "House Readings and Field Readings"). For a distinctive and complementary approach to the history of interpretation, see Martin, "The *Haustafeln* (Household Codes) in African American Biblical Interpretation."
36. See the broader discussion of patterns of institutionalization in post-Pauline churches in MacDonald, *Pauline Churches.*
37. MacDonald, *Pauline Churches*, pp. 104–105.
38. Col. 3:22–4:1.
39. Emphasized by Lincoln in "Household Code and Wisdom Mode of Colossians."
40. Pokorný, *Colossians*, p. 179.
41. MacDonald, *Colossians and Ephesians*, p. 165.
42. MacDonald, *Pauline Churches*, p. 105.
43. Crouch, *Origin and Intention of the Colossian Haustafel.* For an excellent discussion of the Christian women in Corinth, see Wire, *Corinthian Women Prophets.*
44. Crouch, *Origin and Intention of the Colossian Haustafel*, p. 150.
45. See, for example, Lincoln, "Household Code and Wisdom Mode of Colossians," p. 97, and MacDonald, *Colossians and Ephesians*, p. 163.
46. D'Angelo, "Colossians," p. 322.
47. D'Angelo, "Colossians," p. 315.
48. Osiek and Balch, *Families in the New Testament World*, p. 189.
49. For related ideas, see Kyrtatas, "Slavery as Progress." Throughout this section I refer extensively to MacDonald's commentary. Among full-length commentaries on Colossians, MacDonald

considers the situation of slaves and slaveholders more fully and seriously than other scholars. In some instances I agree and in other instances I disagree with her. However, even where I disagree with her, I find that she points the reader in the direction of critical questions.

50. MacDonald, *Colossians and Ephesians*, p. 165.

51. MacDonald, *Colossians and Ephesians*, p. 164.

52. Osiek and Balch, *Families in the New Testament World*, p. 189.

53. MacDonald, *Colossians and Ephesians*, p. 165.

54. Lincoln and Wedderburn, *Theology of the Later Pauline Letters*, p. 124.

55. Eph. 6:5–6.

56. 1 Tim. 3:4–5.

57. Throughout this work I emphasize that women as well as men were slaveholders. I assume this is true in the communities addressed in the Pastoral epistles. My concern here is with the image created by the Pastoral epistles of the male householder/slaveholder as the ideal church leader.

58. MacDonald, *Pauline Churches*, p. 200.

59. Saller, "Corporal Punishment."

60. Verner, *Household of God*, p. 141.

61. 1 Tim. 6:2.

62. 1 Tim. 6:1–2.

63. Towner, *Goal of Our Instruction*, p. 256.

64. Towner, *Goal of Our Instruction*, p. 179.

65. Horrell notes the tendency of scholars "to replicate and perpetuate the retrograde position of the [Pastoral] letter writer(s)." Horrell directs his criticism at those whose methodology is informed by the sociology of knowledge, in particular, Margaret MacDonald. I have found MacDonald more careful *not* to "replicate and perpetuate" the ideology of the Pastoral epistles than many others who write about these texts ("Converging Ideologies," p. 95).

66. Towner, *Goal of Our Instruction*, p. 178.

67. Even in their critique of greed, the Pastoral epistles ratify the status quo, since conservative elites frowned upon social climbing (Kidd, *Wealth and Beneficence in the Pastoral Epistles*).

68. Johnson, *Letters to Paul's Delegates*, p. 191.

69. Titus 2:9–10.

70. Verner, *Household of God*, p. 180.

71. Verner, *Household of God*, p. 141.

72. Johnson, *Letters to Paul's Delegates*, pp. 234–235.

73. Bradley, "*Servus Onerosus*," p. 144.

74. 1 Pet. 2:18–21.

75. 1 Pet. 2:23–24.

76. Osiek and Balch, *Families in the New Testament World*, p. 190.

77. Osiek and Balch, *Families in the New Testament World*, p. 190.

78. Stowe, *Uncle Tom's Cabin*, p. 382.

79. Stowe, *Uncle Tom's Cabin*, p. 382.

80. *Didache* 4:9–10.

81. Harrill, *Manumission of Slaves in Early Christianity*.

82. Ign., *Pol.* 4.3.

83. For this general theme in pagan (especially Stoic) and Christian authors, see Kyrtatas, "Slavery as Progress."

84. Schiavone inquires, what effect did the proximity of slaves have on "language, law, and the realms of affectivity and sexuality": "Let us attempt for a moment to consider what effect it must have had on the formation of character and worldview to be in daily contact with masses of men and women over whom was exercised total and absolute power, with no need to resort

to the most extreme of measures (the right to inflict death) to demonstrate its unprecedented coercive force; it was a violence built into the institution itself, entirely apart from the personal inclinations of individual masters" (*End of the Past*, p. 123).

85. Morrison, *Playing in the Dark*, p. 12.

86. Luke 7:8.

87. Bloomer, "Schooling in Persona," pp. 72 and 58. See also Dionisotti, "From Ausonius' Schooldays? A Schoolbook and Its Relatives"; and Bradley, *Slavery and Society at Rome*, p. 26.

88. Clement of Alexandria, *Paedagogues* 4.27.4.

89. For evidence regarding the presence of women at public baths, see Ward, "Women in Roman Baths."

90. Clement of Alexandria, *Paedagogues* 12.84.1.

91. Artemidorus, *Oneirocritica* 4.30.

92. Against the argument that ascetic renunciation often entailed a dimunition of status, Shaw concludes, "It seems to me, however, that in many of our sources the ascetic life enhanced or at least did not significantly diminish status" ("Practical, Theoretical, and Cultural Tracings in Late Ancient Asceticism," p. 79).

93. Clark, *Life of Melania the Younger*, prologue and section 7.

94. Clark, "Women and Asceticism in Late Antiquity," p. 36.

95. Athanasius, *First Letter to Virgins* 17 (in Brakke, *Athanasius and the Politics of Asceticism*, p. 279).

96. Brakke, *Athanasius and the Politics of Asceticism*, p. 24.

97. Text available in Kraemer, *Maenads, Martyrs, Matrons, Monastics*, pp. 123–124.

98. Foucault, *History of Sexuality*, p. 51.

99. Clark, *Life of Melania the Younger*, p. 54.

100. Clark, *Life of Melania the Younger*, p. 44.

101. 1 Cor. 9:27.

102. Athanasius, *First Letter to Virgins* 34 (in Brakke, *Athanasius and the Politics of Asceticism*, p. 285).

Bibliography

Note on ancient sources: Except where the notes indicate otherwise, quotations from the Bible are from the New Revised Standard Version (NRSV). I have generally relied on Loeb editions and translations of Greek and Roman sources. Exceptions are scattered throughout the bibliography. For early Christian sources, translations are available in the *Ante-Nicene Fathers* or the *Nicene and Post-Nicene Fathers*. Again, exceptions can be found in the bibliography. With all of these sources, I have at times modified the printed translations slightly, most often to help the reader sense consistency in the lexicon of slavery. In these cases I generally include the Greek or Latin vocabulary in brackets. I hope that readers who do not control those languages themselves will find these notations helpful.

Aletti, Jean Noel. *Saint Paul Epître aux Colossiens: Introduction, traduction et commentaire.* Vol. 20, *Ebib n.s.* Paris: Gabalda, 1993.

Allo, E. Bernard. *Première Epître aux Corinthiens.* Paris: Librarie Lecoffre, 1956.

Apuleius. *The Golden Ass.* Translated by P. G. Walsh. Oxford: Oxford University Press, 1995.

Artemidorus. *The Interpretation of Dreams (Oneirocritica).* Translated by Robert J. White. Park Ridge, NJ: Noyes Press, 1975.

Augustine. *Letters.* Vol. 6, *The Fathers of the Church.* Translated by Robert E. Eno. Washington, DC: Catholic University of America Press, 1989.

Bagnall, Roger S. "Missing Females in Roman Egypt." *Scripta Classica Israelica* 16 (1997): 121–138.

——. "Official and Private Violence in Roman Egypt." *Bulletin of the American Society of Papyrologists* 26 (1989): 201–216.

——. *Reading Papyri, Writing Ancient History, Approaching the Ancient World.* London: Routledge, 1995.

——. "Slavery and Society in Late Roman Egypt." In *Law, Politics and Society in the Ancient Mediterranean World,* edited by B. Halpern and D. Hobson, 220–240. Sheffield, England: Sheffield Academic Press, 1993.

——. "A Trick a Day to Keep the Tax Man at Bay? The Prostitute Tax in Roman Egypt." *Bulletin of the American Society of Papyrologists* 28 (1991): 5–12.

Bagnall, Roger S., and Bruce W. Frier. *The Demography of Roman Egypt.* Cambridge: Cambridge University Press, 1994.

Barclay, John M. G. "Paul, Philemon, and the Dilemma of Christian Slave-Ownership." *New Testament Studies* 37 (1991): 161–186.

Barrett, C. K. "The Allegory of Abraham, Sarah, and Hagar in the Argument of Galatians." In *Rechtfertigung: Festschrift fuer Ernst Kaesemann zum 70. Geburtstag,* edited by J. Friedrich et al., 1–16. Tuebingen, Germany: Mohr/Siebeck, 1976.

——. *A Commentary on the First Epistle to the Corinthians.* New York: Harper & Row, 1968.

Bartchy, S. Scott. *First-Century Slavery and 1 Corinthians 7:21.* Vol. 11, *Society of Biblical Litera-ture Dissertation Sereies.* Atlanta, GA: Scholars Press, 1973.

———. "Slavery, Greco-Roman." In *Anchor Bible Dictionary, Volume 6,* edited by David Noel Freedman, 65–73. Garden City, NY: Doubleday, 1992.

Bassler, Jouette M. "1 Corinthians." In *The Women's Bible Commentary,* edited by Carol A. Newsom and Sharon H. Ringe, 321–329. Louisville, KY: Westminster/John Knox Press, 1992.

Batten, Alicia. "Dishonour, Gender, and the Parable of the Prodigal Son." *Toronto Journal of Theology* 13 (1997): 187–200.

Beare, Francis Wright. *The Gospel According to Matthew: Translation, Introduction and Commen-tary.* San Francisco: Harper & Row, 1981.

Beavis, Mary Ann. "Ancient Slavery as an Interpretative Context for the New Testament Ser-vant Parables with Special Reference to the Unjust Steward (Luke 16:1–8)." *Journal of Bibli-cal Literature* 111 (1992): 37–54.

Best, Ernest. *A Commentary on the First and Second Epistles to the Thessalonians.* New York: Harper & Row, 1972.

Biezunska-Malowist, Iza. *L'Esclavage dans l'Égypte Gréco-Romaine Seconde Partie: Periode Romaine.* Warsaw, Poland: Polskiej Akademij Nauk, 1977.

Bloomer, W. Martin. "Schooling in Persona: Imagination and Subordination in Roman Educa-tion." *Classical Antiquity* 16 (1997): 57–78.

Bohannan, Paul. *Social Anthropology.* New York: Holt, Rinehart and Winston, 1963.

Botte, Bernard. *La Tradition Apostolique de Saint Hippolyte: Essai de Reconstitution.* Munster, Germany: Aschendorff, 1963.

Bowman, Alan K. *Life and Letters on the Roman Frontier: Vindolanda and Its People.* New York: Routledge, 1998.

Bradley, Keith R. "Animalizing the Slave: The Truth of Fiction." *Journal of Roman Studies* 90 (2000): 110–125.

———. "The Problem of Slavery in Classical Culture." *Classical Philology* 92 (1997): 273–282.

———. "'The Regular, Daily Traffic in Slaves': Roman History and Contemporary History." *Clas-sical Journal* 87 (1992): 125–138.

———. "Seneca and Slavery." *Classica et Medievalia* 37 (1986): 161–172.

———. "*Servus Onerosus:* Roman Law and the Troublesome Slave." *Slavery and Abolition* 11 (1990): 135–157.

———. *Slavery and Rebellion in the Roman World.* Bloomington: Indiana University Press, 1989.

———. *Slavery and Society at Rome.* Cambridge: Cambridge University Press, 1994.

———. *Slaves and Masters in the Roman Empire: A Study in Social Control.* Vol. 185, *Revue d'Etude Latines.* Brussels, Belgium: Latomus, 1984.

Brakke, David. *Athanasius and the Politics of Asceticism.* Oxford: Clarendon, 1995.

Brewer, David Instone. "Jewish Women Divorcing Their Husbands in Early Judaism." *Harvard Theological Review* 92 (1999): 349–357.

Briggs, Sheila. "Can an Enslaved God Liberate? Hermeneutical Reflections on Philippians 2:6–11." *Semeia* 47 (1989): 137–153.

———. "Galatians." In *Searching the Scriptures.* Vol. 2, *A Feminist Commentary,* edited by Elisabeth Schuessler Fiorenza, 218–237. New York: Crossroad, 1994.

Bruce, F. F. *The Epistles to the Colossians, to Philemon, and to the Ephesians.* Grand Rapids, MI: Eerdmans, 1984.

Bruyn, Theodore S. de. "Flogging a Son: The Emergence of the *Pater Flagellans* in Latin Chris-tian Discourse." *Journal of Early Christian Studies* 7 (1999): 249–290.

Butler, Shane. "Notes on a *Membrum Disiectum.*" In *Women and Slaves in Greco-Roman Culture: Differential Equations,* edited by Sandra R. Joshel and Sheila Murnaghan, 236–255. New York: Routledge, 1998.

Callahan, Allen Dwight. "Paul's Epistle to Philemon: Toward an Alternative *Argumentum*." *Harvard Theological Review* 86 (1994): 357–376.

Callahan, Allen Dwight, Richard A. Horsley, and Abraham Smith. "Introduction: The Slavery of New Testament Studies." *Semeia* 83–84 (1998): 1–15.

Campbell, B. "Flesh and Spirit in 1 Cor. 5:5: An Exercise in Rhetorical Criticism of the NT." *Journal of the Evangelical Theological Society* 36 (1993): 331–342.

Carras, G. P. "Jewish Ethics and Gentile Converts: Remarks on 1 Thes. 4:3–8." In *The Thessalonian Correspondence*, edited by Raymond F. Collins, 306–315. Leuven, Belgium: University Press, 1990.

Casson, Lionel. *Ancient Trade and Society*. Detroit: Wayne State University Press, 1984.

Castelli, Elizabeth. "Paul on Women and Gender." In *Women and Christian Origins*, edited by Ross Shepard Kraemer and Mary Rose D'Angelo, 221–235. New York: Oxford University Press, 1999.

———. "Romans." In *Searching the Scriptures*. Vol. 2, *A Feminist Commentary*, edited by Elisabeth Schuessler Fiorenza, 272–300. New York: Crossroad, 1994.

Chadwick, Henry, ed. *The Treatise on the Apostolic Tradition of St. Hippolytus of Rome*. London: SPCK, 1937/1968.

Charlesworth, James H., ed. *The Old Testament Pseudepigrapha*. 2 vols. Garden City, NY: Doubleday, 1983–1985.

Clark, Elizabeth A. *The Life of Melania the Younger*. Vol. 14, *Studies in Women and Religion*. Lewiston, NY: Edwin Mellen, 1984.

Clark, Gillian. "Women and Asceticism in Late Antiquity." In *Asceticism*, edited by Vincent L. Wimbush and Richard Valantasis, 33–48. New York: Oxford University Press, 1995.

Clark, Patricia. "Women, Slaves, and the Hierarchies of Domestic Violence: The Family of St. Augustine." In *Women and Slaves in Greco-Roman Culture: Differential Equations*, edited by Sandra R. Joshel and Sheila Murnaghan, 109–129. New York: Routledge, 1998.

Collins, Raymond F. *First Corinthians*. Vol. 7, *Sacra Pagina*. Collegeville, MN: Liturgical Press, 1999.

Combes, I. A. H. *The Metaphor of Slavery in the Writings of the Early Church: From the New Testament to the Beginning of the Fifth Century*. Vol. 156, *Journal for the Study of the New Testament Supplement Series*. Sheffield, England: Sheffield Academic Press, 1998.

Connolly, Joy. "Roman Oratory: Constructions of Identity in Roman Oratory." In *Women and Slaves in Greco-Roman Culture: Differential Equations*, edited by Sandra R. Joshel and Sheila Murnaghan, 130–151. New York: Routledge, 1998.

Conzelmann, Hans. *1 Corinthians: A Commentary on the First Epistle to the Corinthians*. Translated by J. W. Leitch. Philadelphia: Fortress, 1975.

Corbier, Mireille. "Divorce and Adoption as Roman Familial Strategies." In *Marriage, Divorce, and Children in Ancient Rome*, edited by Beryl Rawson, 47–78. Oxford: Oxford University Press, 1991.

Corley, Kathleen E. *Private Women, Public Meals: Social Conflict in the Synoptic Tradition*. Peabody, MA: Hendrickson, 1993.

Cotton, Hannah. "A Cancelled Marriage Contract from the Judaean Desert." *Journal of Roman Studies* 84 (1994): 64–86.

———. "The Guardianship of Jesus Son of Babatha: Roman and Local Law in the Province of Arabia." *Journal of Roman Studies* 83 (1993): 94–132.

Croix, G. E. M. Ste. "Early Christian Attitudes to Property and Slavery." In *Church, Society and Politics*, edited by Derek Baker, 1–38. Oxford: Basil Blackwell, 1975.

Crook, John. *Law and Life of Rome*. Ithaca, NY: Cornell University Press, 1967.

Crossan, John Dominic. *The Historical Jesus: The Life of a Mediterranean Jewish Peasant*. San Francisco: Harper & Row, 1992.

Crossan, John Dominic. *In Parables: The Challenge of the Historical Jesus.* New York: Harper & Row, 1973.

——. "The Servant Parables of Jesus." *Semeia* 1 (1974): 17–62.

Crouch, James E. *The Origin and Intention of the Colossian Haustafel.* Goettingen, Germany: Vandenhoeck & Ruprecht, 1972.

D'Angelo, Mary Rose. "Colossians." In *Searching the Scriptures.* Vol. 2, *A Feminist Commentary,* edited by Elisabeth Schuessler Fiorenza, 313–324. New York: Crossroad, 1994.

D'Arms, John. "*Personal Patronage under the Early Empire* by Richard P. Saller: Review." *Classical Philology* 81 (1986): 95–98.

Daube, David. "Slave-Catching." *Juridical Review* 64 (1952): 12–28.

Davis, Natalie Zemon. *Fiction in the Archives: Pardon Tales and Their Tellers in Sixteenth-Century France.* Stanford, CA: Stanford University Press, 1987.

Deming, Will. "A Diatribe Pattern in 1 Cor. 7:21–22: A New Perspective on Paul's Directions to Slaves." *Novum Testamentum* 37 (1995): 130–137.

——. *Paul on Marriage and Celibacy: The Hellenistic Background of 1 Corinthians 7.* Cambridge: Cambridge University Press, 1995.

——. "The Unity of 1 Corinthians 5–6." *Journal of Biblical Literature* 115 (1996): 289–312.

Derrett, J. M. D. *Law in the New Testament.* London: Darton, Longman, & Todd, 1970.

Dionisotti, A. C. "From Ausonius' Schooldays? A Schoolbook and Its Relatives." *Journal of Roman Studies* 72 (1982): 83–125.

Dodd, C. H. *The Parables of the Kingdom.* Rev. ed. New York: Scribner's, 1961.

Dunn, James D. G. *The Acts of the Apostles.* Valley Forge, PA: Trinity Press International, 1996.

——. *The Epistles to the Colossians and to Philemon: A Commentary on the Greek Text.* Grand Rapids, MI: Eerdmans, 1996.

Dyson, Stephen L. *Community and Society in Roman Italy.* Baltimore, MD: Johns Hopkins University Press, 1992.

Edwards, Catherine. "Unspeakable Professions: Public Performance and Prostitution in Ancient Rome." In *Roman Sexualities,* edited by Judith Hallett and Marilyn Skinner, 66–95. Princeton, NJ: Princeton University Press, 1997.

Egger, Brigitte M. "Women in the Greek Novel: Constructing the Feminine." Ph.D. diss., University of California at Irvine, 1990.

Eisenstadt, S. N., and L. Roniger. "Patron-Client Relations as a Mode of Structuring Social Exchange." *Comparative Studies in Society and History* 22 (1980): 47–72.

Elgvin, Torleif. "'To Master His Own Vessel': 1 Thess. 4:4 in Light of Qumran Evidence." *New Testament Studies* 43 (1997): 604–619.

Engels, Donald W. *Roman Corinth: An Alternative Model for the Classical City.* Chicago: University of Chicago Press, 1990.

Fantham, Elaine. "*Stuprum*: Public Attitudes and Penalties for Sexual Offenses in Republican Rome." *Echos du Monde Classique/Classical Views* 35, n.s., 10 (1991): 267–291.

Fatum, Lone. "1 Thessalonians." In *Searching the Scriptures.* Vol. 2, *A Feminist Commentary,* edited by Elisabeth Schuessler Fiorenza, 250–262. New York: Crossroad, 1994.

Fee, Gordon D. *The First Epistle to the Corinthians.* Grand Rapids, MI: Eerdmans, 1987.

Finley, Moses I. *Ancient Slavery and Modern Ideology.* Expanded ed. Princeton, NJ: Markus Wiener, 1998.

Fisk, B. N. "ΠΟΡΝΕΥΕΙΝ as Body Violation: The Unique Nature of Sexual Sin in 1 Corinthians 6:18." *New Testament Studies* 42 (1996): 540–558.

Fitzgerald, William. *Slavery and the Roman Literary Imagination.* Cambridge: Cambridge University Press, 2000.

Fitzmyer, Joseph A. *The Gospel According to Luke (X–XXIV), Anchor Bible.* Garden City, NY: Doubleday, 1983.

Fleming, Rebecca. "*Quae Corpore Quaestum Facit*: The Sexual Economy of Female Prostitution in the Roman Empire." *Journal of Roman Studies* 89 (1999): 38–61.

Flesher, Paul V. M. *Oxen, Women, or Citizens? Slaves in the System of Mishnah.* Atlanta, GA: Scholars Press, 1988.

Fortna, Robert T. "Reading Jesus' Parables of the Talents through Underclass Eyes." *Foundations and Facts Forum* 8, nos. 3–4 (Sept.–Dec.1992): 211–228.

Foucault, Michel. *Discipline and Punish: The Birth of the Prison.* Translated by A. Sheridan. New York: Vintage, 1979.

——. *The History of Sexuality 3: The Care of the Self.* Translated by Robert Hurley. New York: Pantheon, 1986.

Frilingos, Chris. "'For My Child, Onesimus': Paul and Domestic Power in Philemon." *Journal of Biblical Literature* 119 (2000): 91–104.

Gardner, Jane F. *Family and Familia in Roman Law and Life.* Oxford: Clarendon, 1998.

Garnsey, Peter. *Ideas of Slavery from Aristotle to Augustine.* Cambridge: Cambridge University Press, 1996.

——. "Philo Judaeus and Slave Theory." *Scripta Classica Israelica* 13 (1994): 30–45.

——. *Social Status and Legal Privilege in the Roman Empire.* Oxford: Clarendon, 1970.

——. "Sons, Slaves—and Christians." In *The Roman Family in Italy: Status, Sentiment, Space,* edited by Beryl Rawson and Paul Weaver, 101–121. Oxford: Clarendon, 1997.

Gaventa, Beverly Roberts. *First and Second Thessalonians.* Louisville, KY: John Knox Press, 1998.

George, Michele. "Repopulating the Roman House." In *The Roman Family in Italy: Status, Sentiment, Space,* edited by Beryl Rawson and Paul Weaver, 299–319. Oxford: Clarendon, 1997.

Geytenbeck, Anton Cornelius Van. *Musonius Rufus and Greek Diatribe.* Netherlands: Van Gorcum, 1962.

Gilmore, David G., ed. *Honor and Shame and the Unity of the Mediterranean.* Vol. 22, *American Anthropological Association Special Publication.* Washington, DC: American Anthropological Association, 1987.

Glancy, Jennifer A. "Family Plots: Burying Slaves Deep in Historical Ground." *Biblical Interpretation* 10, no. 1 (2002): forthcoming.

——. "House Readings and Field Readings: The Discourse of Slavery and Biblical/Cultural Studies." In *Biblical Studies/Cultural Studies: The Third Sheffield Colloquium,* edited by J. Cheryl Exum and Stepehn Moore, 465–482. Sheffield, England: Sheffield Academic Press, 1998.

——. "The Mistress-Slave Dialectic: Paradoxes of Slavery in Three LXX Narratives." *Journal for the Study of the Old Testament* 72 (1996): 71–87.

——. "Obstacles to Slaves' Participation in the Corinthian Church." *Journal of Biblical Literature* 117 (1998): 481–501.

——. "Slaves and Slavery in the Matthean Parables." *Journal of Biblical Literature* 119 (2000): 67–90.

Gnilka, Joachim. *Der Kolosserbrief.* Vol. 10.1, *Herders Theologischer Kommentar zum Neven Testament.* Freiburg, Germany: Herder, 1980.

Golden, Mark. "Pais, 'Child' and 'Slave.'" *L'Antiquité Classique* 54 (1985): 91–104.

Grubbs, Judith Evans. *Law and Family in Late Antiquity: The Emperor Constantine's Marriage Legislation.* Oxford: Clarendon, 1995.

Gustafson, W. Mark. "*Inscripte in Fronte*: Penal Tattooing in Late Antiquity." *Classical Antiquity* 16 (1997): 79–105.

Hanssens, Jean Michel. *La Liturgie D'Hippolyte.* 2 vols. Rome: Libreria Gregoriana, 1965–1970.

Hare, Douglas R. A. *Matthew.* Louisville, KY: John Knox Press, 1993.

Harlow, Mary. "In the Name of the Father: Procreation, Paternity and Patriarchy." In *Thinking Men: Masculinity and Its Self-Representation in the Classical Tradition,* edited by Lin Foxhall and John Salmon, 155–169. London: Routledge, 1998.

Harrill, J. Albert. "Dramatic Function of the Running Slave Rhoda (Acts 12:13–16)." *New Testament Studies* 46 (2000): 150–157.

——. "The Indentured Labor of the Prodigal Son (Luke 15:15)." *Journal of Biblical Literature* 115 (1996): 714–717.

——. *The Manumission of Slaves in Early Christianity.* Tuebingen, Germany: J. C. B. Mohr, 1995.

——. "The Use of the New Testament in the American Slave Controversy: A Case History in the Hermeneutical Tension between Biblical Criticism and Christian Moral Debate." *Religion and American Culture* 10 (2000): 149–186.

——. "Using the Roman Jurists to Interpret Philemon: A Response to Peter Lampe." *Zeitschrift fuer die Neutestamentliche Wissenschaft* 90 (1999): 135–138.

——. "The Vice of Slave Dealers in Greco-Roman Society: The Use of a Topos in 1 Timothy 1:10." *Journal of Biblical Literature* 118 (1999): 97–122.

Harrington, Daniel J. *The Gospel of Matthew.* Vol. 1, *Sacra Pagina.* Collegeville, MN: Liturgical Press, 1991.

Harris, William V. "Child-Exposure in the Roman Empire." *Journal of Roman Studies* 84 (1994): 1–22.

——. "Demography, Geography and the Sources of Roman Slaves." *Journal of Roman Studies* 89 (1999): 62–75.

——. "Towards a Study of the Roman Slave Trade." *Memoirs of the American Academy in Rome* 36 (1980): 117–140.

Hays, Richard B. "Ecclesiology and Ethics in 1 Corinthians." *Ex Auditu: An Annual of the Frederick Neumann Symposium on Theological Interpretation of Scripture, Princeton Theological Seminary* 10 (1994): 31–43.

——. *First Corinthians, Interpretation.* Louisville, KY: John Knox Press, 1997.

Hedrick, Charles W. *Parables as Poetic Fictions.* Peabody, MA: Hendrickson, 1994.

Hershbell, J. P. "Epictetus: A Freedman on Slavery." *Ancient Society* 26 (1995): 185–204.

Herzog, William R. *Parables as Subversive Speech: Jesus as Pedagogue of the Oppressed.* Louisville, KY: Westminster/John Knox Press, 1994.

Hester, J. D. "Socio-Rhetorical Criticism and the Parable of the Tenants." *Journal for the Study of the New Testament* 45 (1992): 27–57.

Hock, Ronald F. "A Support for His Old Age: Paul's Plea on Behalf of Onesimus." In *The Social World of the First Christians: Essays in Honor of Wayne A. Meeks*, edited by L. M. White and O. L. Yarbrough, 67–81. Minneapolis, MN: Fortress, 1995.

Hood, A. B. E., ed. *St. Patrick: His Writings and Muirchi's Life.* Totowa, NJ: Rowman & Littlefield, 1978.

Hopkins, Keith. "Novel Evidence for Roman Slavery." *Past and Present* 138 (1993): 3–27.

Horne, Edward H. "The Parable of the Tenants as Indictment." *Journal for the Study of the New Testament* 71 (1998): 11–16.

Horrell, David. "Converging Ideologies: Berger and Luckman and the Pastoral Epistles." *Journal for the Study of the New Testament* 50 (1993): 85–103.

Horst, P. W. Van der. *The Sentences of Pseudo-Phocylides, Studia in Veteris Testamenti Pseudopigrapha.* Leiden: Brill, 1978.

Hunter, Virginia. *Policing Athens: Social Control in the Attic Lawsuits, 420–320 B.C.* Princeton, NJ: Princeton University Press, 1994.

Ilan, Tal. "Notes and Observations on a Nelwy Published Divorce Bill from the Judean Desert." *Harvard Theological Review* 89 (1996): 195–202.

Jacobs, Andrew S. "A Family Affair: Marriage, Class, and Ethics in the Apocryphal Acts of the Apostles." *Journal of Early Christian Studies* 7 (1999): 105–138.

Jacobs, Harriet. *Incidents in the Life of a Slave Girl.* New York: Oxford University Press, 1988.

Jeremias, Joachim. *The Parables of Jesus.* New York: Scribner's, 1954.

Johnson, Luke Timothy. *Letters to Paul's Delegates: 1 Timothy, 2 Timothy, Titus.* Valley Forge, PA: Trinity Press International, 1996.

Jones, C. P. "*Stigma:* Tattooing and Branding in Graeco-Roman Antiquity." *Journal of Roman Studies* 77 (1987): 139-155.

Joshel, Sandra R. "Nurturing the Master's Child: Slavery and the Roman Child Nurse." *Signs: Journal of Women in Culture and Society* 12 (1986): 3-22.

——. *Work, Identity, and Legal Status at Rome: A Study of the Occupational Inscriptions.* Norman: University of Oklahoma Press, 1992.

Justin Martyr. *The First and Second Apologies.* Translated by Leslie William Barnard. Mahwah, NJ: Paulist Press, 1997.

Kidd, Reggie M. *Wealth and Beneficence in the Pastoral Epistles: A "Bourgeois" Form of Early Christianity?* Vol. 122, *Society of Biblical Literature Dissertation Series.* Atlanta, GA: Scholars Press, 1990.

Knox, John. *Philemon among the Letters of Paul: A New View of Its Place and Importance.* New York: Abingdon, 1935/1959.

Kraemer, Ross. *Her Share of the Blessings: Women's Religions among Pagans, Jews, and Christians in the Greco-Roman World.* New York: Oxford University Press, 1992.

Kraemer, Ross, ed. *Maenads, Martyrs, Matrons, Monastics.* Philadelphia: Fortress, 1988.

Kyrtatas, Dimitris J. "Slavery as Progress: Pagan and Christian Views of Slavery as Moral Training." *International Sociology* 10 (1998): 219-234.

Landry, David, and Ben May. "Honor Restored: New Light on the Parable of the Prudent Steward (Luke 16:1-8a)." *Journal of Biblical Literature* 119 (2000): 287-309.

L'Hoir, Francesca Santoro. *The Rhetoric of Gender Terms: 'Man,' 'Woman,' and the Portrayal of Character in Latin Prose, Mnemosyne.* Leiden: Brill, 1992.

Lincoln, Andrew T. "The Household Code and Wisdom Mode of Colossians." *Journal for the Study of the New Testament* 74 (1999): 93-112.

Lincoln, Andrew T., and A. J. M. Wedderburn. *The Theology of the Later Pauline Letters.* Cambridge: Cambridge University Press, 1993.

Lovejoy, Paul E. *Transformations in Slavery: A History of Slavery in Africa.* 2d ed. Cambridge: Cambridge University Press, 2000.

MacDonald, Dennis Ronald, ed. *The Acts of Andrew and the Acts of Andrew and Matthias in the City of Cannibals.* Atlanta, GA: Scholars Press, 1990.

MacDonald, Margaret Y. *Colossians and Ephesians.* Collegeville, MN: Liturgical Press, 2000.

——. *Early Christian Woman and Pagan Opinion: The Power of the Hysterical Woman.* Cambridge: Cambridge University Press, 1996.

——. *The Pauline Churches: A Socio-Historical Study of Institutionalization in the Pauline and Deutero-Pauline Writings.* Cambridge: Cambridge University Press, 1988.

MacMullen, Ramsay. *Changes in the Roman Empire: Essays in the Ordinary.* Princeton, NJ: Princeton University Press, 1990.

——. "Personal Power in the Roman Empire." *American Journal of Philology* 107 (1986): 512-524.

Malina, Bruce J. *The New Testament World: Insights from Cultural Anthropology.* Louisville, KY: Westminster/John Knox, 1993.

——. *The Social World of Jesus and the Gospels.* New York: Routledge, 1996.

Martin, Clarice. "Acts of the Apostles." In *Searching the Scriptures:* Vol. 2, *A Feminist Commentary,* edited by Elisabeth Schuessler Fiorenza, 763-799. New York: Crossroad, 1994.

——. "The *Haustafeln* (Household Codes) in African American Biblical Interpretation: 'Free Slaves' and 'Subordinate Women.'" In *Stony the Road We Trod: African American Biblical Interpretation,* edited by Cain Hope Felder, 206-231. Minneapolis, MN: Fortress, 1991.

Martin, Dale B. *The Corinthian Body.* New Haven, CT: Yale University Press, 1995.

Martin, Dale B. "Slavery and the Ancient Jewish Family." In *The Jewish Family in Antiquity*, edited by Shaye J. D. Cohen, 113–129. Atlanta, GA: Scholars Press, 1989.

——. *Slavery as Salvation: The Metaphor of Slavery in Pauline Christianity*. New Haven, CT: Yale University Press, 1990.

Martyn, J. Louis. *Galatians, Anchor Bible*. Garden City, NY: Doubleday, 1997.

McGinn, Thomas A. J. *Prostitution, Sexuality, and the Law in Ancient Rome*. Oxford: Oxford University Press, 1998.

——. "The Taxation of Roman Prostitutes." *Helios* 16 (1989): 79–100.

Meeks, Wayne A. *The First Urban Christians: The Social World of the Apostle Paul*. New Haven, CT: Yale University Press, 1983.

Meillassoux, Claude. *The Anthropology of Slavery: The Womb of Iron and Gold*. Translated by Alide Danois. Chicago: University of Chicago Press, 1991.

Millar, Fergus. "The Greek East and Roman Law: The Dossier of M. Cn. Licinius Rufinus." *Journal of Roman Studies* 89 (1999): 90–108.

——. "The World of the Golden Ass." *Journal of Roman Studies* 71 (1981): 63–75.

Mitchell, Margaret M. "John Chrysostom on Philemon: A Second Look." *Harvard Theological Review* 88 (1995): 135–148.

——. *Paul and the Rhetoric of Reconciliation: An Exegetical Investigation of the Language and Composition of 1 Corinthians*. Louisville, KY: Westminster/John Knox Press, 1991.

Mommsen, Theodor, Paul Krueger, and Alan Watson, eds. *Digest of Justinian*. 4 vols. Philadelphia: University of Pennsylvania Press, 1985.

Montserrat, Dominic. *Sex and Society in Greco-Roman Egypt*. New York: Kegan Paul International, 1996.

Moore, Stephen D. *God's Gym: Divine Male Bodies of the Bible*. New York: Routledge, 1996.

Moore, Stephen D., and Janice Capel Anderson. "Taking It Like a Man: Masculinity in 4 Maccabees." *Journal of Biblical Literature* 117 (1998): 249–273.

Morris, Leon. *The First and Second Epistles to the Thessalonians*. Rev. ed. Grand Rapids, MI: Eerdmans, 1991.

Morrison, Toni. *Playing in the Dark: Whiteness and the Literary Imagination*. New York: Vintage, 1993.

Munro, Winsome. *Jesus, Born of a Slave: The Social and Economic Origins of Jesus' Message*. Vol. 37, *Studies in the Bible and Early Christianity*. Lewiston, NY: Edwin Mellen, 1998.

Musurillo, H., ed. *Acts of the Christian Martyrs*. Oxford: Clarendon, 1972.

Neiderwimmer, Kurt. *The Didache*. Translated by Linda Maloney. Hermeneia. Minneapolis, MN: Augsburg Fortress, 1998.

Neusner, Jacob. *Genesis Rabbah: The Judaic Commentary on the Book of Genesis: A New American Translation, Volumes I–III*. Vols. 104–106, *Brown Judaic Studies*. Atlanta, GA: Scholars Press, 1985.

——. *Lamentations Rabbah: An Analytic Translation*. Vol. 193, *Brown Judaic Studies*. Atlanta, GA: Scholars Press, 1989.

——. *Sifre to Deuteronomy: An Analytic Translation, Volume I*. Vol. 98, *Brown Judaic Studies*. Atlanta, GA: Scholars Press, 1987.

Neyrey, Jerome H. "What's Wrong with This Picture? John 4, Cultural Stereotypes of Women, and Public and Private Space." *Biblical Theology Bulletin* 24, no. 2 (1994): 77–91.

Nietzsche, Friedrich. *Beyond Good and Evil: Prelude to a Philosophy of the Future*. Translated by Walter Kaufmann. New York: Vintage, 1966.

——. *On the Geneaology of Morals and Ecce Homo*. Translated by Walter Kaufman and R. J. Hollingdale. New York: Vintage, 1969.

Osiek, Carolyn. *Philippians, Philemon*. Nashville, TN: Abingdon, 2000.

Osiek, Carolyn, and David Balch. *Families in the New Testament World: Households and House Churches*. Louisville, KY: Westminster/John Knox Press, 1997.

Parker, Holt. "Crucially Funny or Tranio on the Couch: The *Servus Callidus* and Jokes about Torture." *Transactions of the American Philological Association* 119 (1989): 233–246.

——. "Loyal Slaves and Loyal Wives." In *Women and Slaves in Greco-Roman Culture: Differential Equations*, edited by Sandra R. Joshel and Sheila Murnaghan, 152–173. New York: Routledge, 1998.

Patterson, Orlando. *Slavery and Social Death: A Comparative Study*. Cambridge, MA: Harvard University Press, 1982.

Pearl, Orsamus. "Apprentice Contract." *Bulletin of the American Society of Papyrologists* 22 (1985): 255–259.

Perkins, Judith. *The Suffering Self: Pain and Narrative Representation in the Early Christian Era*. New York: Routledge, 1995.

Perkins, Pheme. "1 Thessalonians." In *Women's Bible Commentary*, edited by Carol A. Newsom and Sharon H. Ringe, 440–441. Louisville, KY: Westminster/John Knox Press, 1998.

Petronius. *Satyricon*. Translated by R. Bracht Branham and Daniel Kinney. Berkeley: University of California Press, 1996.

Pokorný, Petr. *Colossians: A Commentary*. Peabody, MA: Hendrickson, 1991.

Pomeroy, Sarah B. *Goddesses, Whores, Wives, and Slaves: Women in Classical Antiquity*. New York: Schocken, 1975.

——. *Women in Hellenistic Egypt from Alexander to Cleopatra*. New York: Schocken, 1984.

Porter, S. E. "How Should κολλώμενος in 1 Cor. 6:16–17 Be Translated?" *Ephemerides Theologicae Lovanienses* 67 (1991): 105–106.

Ramin, Jacques, and Paul Veyne. "Droit romaine et société: Les hommes libres que passent pour esclaves et l'esclavage volontaire." *Historia* 30 (1981): 472–497.

Rawson, Beryl. "Family Life among the Lower Classes at Rome in the First Two Centuries of the Empire." *Classical Philology* 61 (1966): 71–83.

Reardon, B. P., ed. *Collected Ancient Greek Novels*. Berkeley: University of California Press, 1989.

Rei, Annalisa. "Villains, Wives, and Slaves in the Comedies of Plautus." In *Women and Slaves in Greco-Roman Culture: Differential Equations*, edited by Sandra R. Joshel and Sheila Murnaghan, 92–108. New York: Routledge, 1998.

Reimer, Ivoni Richter. *Women in the Acts of the Apostles: A Feminist Liberation Perspective*. Minneapolis, MN: Fortress, 1995.

Reynolds, Joyce. "Roman Inscriptions 1971–5." *Journal of Roman Studies* 66 (1976): 174–199.

Richard, Earl J. *First and Second Thessalonians*. Vol. 11, *Sacra Pagina*. Collegeville, MN: Liturgical Press, 1995.

Richlin, Amy. "Cicero's Head." In *Constructions of the Classical Body*, edited by James I. Porter, 190–211. Ann Arbor: University of Michigan Press, 1999.

——. *The Garden of Priapus: Sexuality and Aggression in Roman Humor*. Rev. ed. New York: Oxford University Press, 1992.

Robertson, A., and A. Plummer. *A Critical and Exegetical Commentary on the First Epistle of Paul to the Corinthians, ICC*. Edinburgh: Clark, 1911/1967.

Robinson, James M., ed. *The Nag Hammadi Library in English*. 3d ed. New York: HarperSanFrancisco, 1990.

Rousselle, Aline. *Porneia: On Desire and the Body in Antiquity*. Translated by F. Pheasant. Oxford: Basil Blackwell, 1988.

Rowlandson, Jane, ed. *Women and Society in Greek and Roman Egypt*. Cambridge: Cambridge University Press, 1998.

Saller, Richard P. "Corporal Punishment, Authority, and Obedience in the Roman Household."

In *Marriage, Divorce, and Children in Ancient Rome*, edited by Beryl Rawson, 144–165. Oxford: Clarendon, 1991.

———. "The Hierarchical Household in Roman Society." In *Serfdom and Slavery: Studies in Legal Bondage*, edited by M. L. Bush, 112–129. London: Longman, 1996.

———. "Men's Age at Marriage and Its Consequences in the Roman Family." *Classical Philology* 82 (1987): 21–34.

———. "*Pater Familias, Mater Familias*, and the Gendered Semantics of the Roman Household." *Classical Philology* 94 (1999): 182–197.

———. *Personal Patronage under the Early Empire*. Cambridge: Cambridge University Press, 1982.

———. "Slavery and the Roman Family." In *Classical Slavery*, edited by Moses I. Finley, 65–87. London: Frank Cass, 1987.

———. "The Social Dynamics of Consent to Marriage and Sexual Relations: The Evidence of Roman Comedy." In *Consent and Coercion to Sex and Marriage in Ancient and Medieval Societies*, edited by Angeliki E. Laiou, 83–104. Washington, DC: Dumbarton Oaks, 1993.

———. "Symbols of Gender and Status Hierarchies in the Roman Household." In *Women and Slaves in Greco-Roman Culture: Differential Equations*, edited by Sandra R. Joshel and Sheila Murnaghan, 85–91. New York: Routledge, 1998.

Scarry, Elaine. *The Body in Pain: The Making and Unmaking of the World*. New York: Oxford University Press, 1985.

Scheidel, Walter. "Quantifying the Sources of Slaves in the Early Roman Empire." *Journal of Roman Studies* 87 (1997): 156–169.

Schiavone, Aldo. *The End of the Past: Ancient Rome and the Modern West*. Translated by Margery J. Schneider. Cambridge, MA: Harvard University Press, 2000.

Schneelmelcher, Wilhelm, and R. M. Wilson, eds. *New Testament Apocrypha*. 2 vols. Philadelphia: Westminster, 1965.

Schrage, Wolfgang. *The Ethics of the New Testament*. Translated by David E. Green. Philadelphia: Fortress, 1988.

Schremer, Adriel. "Divorce in Papyrus Se'elim 13 Once Again: A Reply to Tal Ilan." *Harvard Theological Review* 91 (1998): 193–202.

Schweizer, Eduard. *The Good News According to Matthew*. Translated by David E. Green. Atlanta, GA: John Knox Press, 1975.

Scott, Bernard Brandon. *Hear Then the Parable: A Commentary on the Parables of Jesus*. Minneapolis, MN: Fortress, 1989.

Scullard, H. H. *Festivals and Ceremonies of the Roman Republic*. Ithaca, NY: Cornell University Press, 1981.

Seeley, David. "Rulership and Service in Mark 10:41–45." *Novum Testamentum* 35 (1993): 234–250.

Segal, Erich. *Roman Laughter: The Comedy of Plautus*. Cambridge, MA: Harvard University Press, 1968.

Senft, Christophe. *La Première Epître de Saint Paul aux Corinthiens*. Geneve: Labor et Fides, 1979/1990.

Shaw, Brent. "Body/Power/Identity: Passions of the Martyrs." *Journal of Early Christian Studies* 4 (1996): 269–312.

Shaw, Teresa M. "Practical, Theoretical, and Cultural Tracings in Late Ancient Asceticism." In *Asceticism*, edited by Vincent L. Wimbush and Richard Valantasis, 75–79. New York: Oxford University Press, 1995.

Skinner, Marilyn. "Introduction." In *Roman Sexualities*, edited by Judith Hallett and Marilyn Skinner, 3–25. Princeton, NJ: Princeton University Press, 1997.

Slavitt, David R., and Palmer Bovie, eds. *Plautus: The Comedies*. 4 vols. Baltimore, MD: Johns Hopkins University Press, 1995.

Sloan, Ian. "The Greatest and the Youngest: Greco-Roman Reciprocity in the Farewell Address, Luke 22, 24–30." *Studies in Religion/Science Religieuses* 22 (1993): 63–73.

Stowe, Harriet Beecher. *Uncle Tom's Cabin.* New York: Airmont, 1967/1851.

Taylor, Nicholas H. "The Social Nature of Conversion in the Early Christian World." In *Modeling Early Christianity: Social-Scientific Studies of the New Testament in Its Context,* edited by Philip H. Esler, 128–136. London: Routledge, 1995.

Thurmond, D. L. "Some Roman Slave Collars in CIL." *Athenaeum* 82(72) (2) (1994): 459–493.

Tolbert, Mary Ann. *Perspectives on the Parables: An Approach to Multiple Interpretations.* Philadelphia: Fortress, 1979.

Torjesen, Karen Jo. *When Women Were Priests: Women's Leadership in the Early Church and the Scandal of their Subordination in the Rise of Christianity.* San Francisco: HarperSanFrancisco, 1993.

Towner, Philip H. *The Goal of Our Instruction: The Structure of Theology and Ethics in the Pastoral Epistles.* Vol. 34, *Journal for the Study of the New Testament Supplement Series.* Sheffield, England: Sheffield Academic Press, 1989.

Treggiari, Susan. *Roman Marriage: Iusti Coniuges from the Time of Cicero to the Time of Ulpian.* Oxford: Clarendon, 1991.

Tucker, C. W. "Women in the Manumission Inscriptions at Delphi." *Transactions of the American Philological Association* 112 (1982): 225–236.

Urbach, E. E. "The Laws Regarding Slavery as a Source for Social History of the Period of the Second Temple, the Mishnah, and Talmud." In *Papers of the Institute of Jewish Studies, London,* edited by J. G. Weiss, 1–94. Lanham, MD: University Press of America, 1964/1989.

Verner, David C. *The Household of God: The Social World of the Pastoral Epistles.* Vol. 71, *Society of Biblical Literature Dissertation Series.* Chico, CA: Scholars Press, 1983.

Vogt, Joseph. *Ancient Slavery and the Ideal of Man.* Translated by Thomas Wiedemann. Oxford: Oxford University Press, 1974.

Wallace-Hadrill, Andrew. "Introduction." In *Patronage in Ancient Society,* edited by Andrew Wallace-Hadrill, 1–13. London: Routledge, 1990.

Walters, Jonathon. "Invading the Roman Body: Manliness and Impenetrability in Roman Thought." In *Roman Sexualities,* edited by Judith P. Hallett and Marilyn B. Skinner, 29–43. Princeton, NJ: Princeton University Press, 1997.

Ward, Roy Bowen. "Women in Roman Baths." *Harvard Theological Review* 85 (1992): 125–147.

Watson, James L. "Slavery as an Institution, Open and Closed Systems." In *Asian and African Systems of Slavery,* edited by James L. Watson, 1–15. Berkeley: University of California Press, 1980.

Weaver, Paul. "Children of Junian Latins." In *The Roman Family in Italy: Status, Sentiment, Space,* edited by Beryl Rawson and Paul Weaver, 55–72. Oxford: Clarendon, 1997.

———. *Familia Caesaris: A Social Study of the Emperor's Freedmen and Slaves.* Cambridge: Cambridge University Press, 1972.

Weiss, Johannes. *Der Erste Korintherbrief.* Gottingen, Germany: Vandenhoeck & Ruprecht, 1910/1977.

White, Hayden. *Tropics of Discourse: Essays in Cultural Criticism.* Baltimore, MD: Johns Hopkins University Press, 1978.

Wiedemann, Thomas E. J. "The Regularity of Manumission at Rome." *Classical Quarterly* 35 (1985): 162–175.

Williams, Craig A. *Roman Homosexuality: Ideologies of Masculinity in Classical Antiquity.* New York: Oxford University Press, 1999.

Williams, David John. *1 and 2 Thessalonians, New International Biblical Commentary.* Peabody, MA: Hendrickson, 1992.

192   *Bibliography*

Winkler, John J. *Auctor and Actor: A Narratological Reading of Apuleius' "Golden Ass."* Berkeley: University of California Press, 1985.
Winter, Sara. "Paul's Letter to Philemon." *New Testament Studies* 33 (1987): 1–15.
Wire, Antoinette Clark. *The Corinthian Women Prophets: A Reconstruction through Paul's Rhetoric.* Minneapolis, MN: Fortress, 1990.
Wiseman, T. P. *Catullus and His World: A Reappraisal.* Cambridge: Cambridge University Press, 1985.
Witherington, Ben. *The Acts of the Apostles: A Socio-Rhetorical Commentary.* Grand Rapids, MI: Eerdmans, 1998.
Wohlegamut, Joel. "Entrusted Money (Matt. 25:14–28)." In *Jesus and His Parables: Interpreting the Parables of Jesus Today*, edited by V. George Shillington, 103–120. Edinburgh: Clark, 1997.
Yarbrough, O. Larry. *Not Like the Gentiles: Marriage Rules in the Letters of Paul.* Vol. 80, *Society of Biblical Literature Dissertation Series.* Atlanta, GA: Scholars Press, 1985.

Index